LIFE IN CHRIST

Register This New Book

Benefits of Registering*

- ✓ FREE **replacements** of lost or damaged books

- ✓ FREE **audiobook** – *Pilgrim's Progress,* audiobook edition

- ✓ FREE information about new titles and other **freebies**

www.anekopress.com/new-book-registration

*See our website for requirements and limitations.

LIFE IN CHRIST

Lessons from Our Lord's Miracles and Parables

The Miracles of Our Lord
Volume 2

Charles H. Spurgeon

We love hearing from our readers. Please contact us
at www.anekopress.com/questions-comments with
any questions, comments, or suggestions.

Life in Christ, Vol. 2 – Charles H. Spurgeon
Revisions Copyright © 2017

Please do not reproduce, store in a retrieval system, or transmit in any form
or by any means – electronic, mechanical, photocopying, recording, or
otherwise, without written permission from the publisher. Please contact us
via www.AnekoPress.com for reprint and translation permissions.

Scripture quotations are taken from the Jubilee Bible, copyright © 2000,
2001, 2010, 2013 by Life Sentence Publishing, Inc. Used by permission of
Life Sentence Publishing, Inc., Abbotsford, Wisconsin. All rights reserved.

Cover Design: Natalia Hawthorne, BookCoverLabs.com
Cover Painting: Matt Philleo
eBook Icon: Icons Vector/Shutterstock
Editors: Heather Thomas and Ruth Zetek

Printed in the United States of America
Aneko Press
www.anekopress.com
Aneko Press, Life Sentence Publishing, and our logos are trademarks of
Life Sentence Publishing, Inc.
203 E. Birch Street
P.O. Box 652
Abbotsford, WI 54405

RELIGION / Christian Life / Spiritual Growth
Paperback ISBN: 978-1-62245-468-6
eBook ISBN: 978-1-62245-469-3
10 9 8 7 6 5 4 3 2
Available where books are sold

Contents

Chapter 1

Jesus at Bethesda

After these things there was a feast of the Jews, and Jesus went up to Jerusalem. Now in Jerusalem there is a pool by the sheep gate, which in Hebrew is called, Bethesda, having five porches. In these lay a great multitude of those who were sick, blind, halt, withered, waiting for the moving of the water. For an angel went down at a certain time into the pool and troubled the water; whosoever then first after the troubling of the water stepped in was made whole of whatever disease he had. And a certain man was there who had an infirmity thirty-eight years. When Jesus saw him lying there and knew that he had been now a long time in that case, he said unto him, Dost thou desire to be made whole? The impotent man answered him, Sir, I have no man when the water is troubled to put me into the pool, but while I am coming, another steps down before me. Jesus said unto him, Rise, take up thy bed, and walk. And immediately the man was made whole and took up his bed and walked, and on that day was the sabbath. (John 5:1-9)

According to the evangelist, the scene of this miracle was Bethesda, a pool adjoining the sheep market or near the sheep gate. I suppose the cattle consumed by the inhabitants of Jerusalem would be driven through this gate. And the pool was likely where the sheep intended for sale to the sacrifice offerors in the temple were washed. Sickness was so common in the days of the Savior that the infirmities of men intruded on the place which had been allotted to cattle. And the place where sheep were washed became the spot where sick folk congregated in great multitudes, longing for a cure. We don't hear that anyone complained about the intrusion, or that anyone was shocked. The needs of mankind must override all considerations of appearance. The hospital must take precedence over the sheep market.

Today, we have another example of this same thing taking place. If the physical infirmities of Jerusalem were allowed to intrude into the sheep market, I wouldn't apologize if the spiritual sickness of London demands that this spacious place, which previously was a pasture, should be utilized for the preaching of the gospel, so the manifestation of the healing virtue of Christ Jesus has the opportunity to work among the spiritually sick. Just as the infirmed waited for a miracle by the sheep market pool, those who are spiritually sick gather here in exceedingly great multitudes.

We might never have heard of Bethesda if Jesus, the Son of God, had not honored it with his presence. It was the place where we should expect to meet him, for where should the physician be found if not in the place where the sick are gathered? Here was work for Jesus's healing hand and restoring word. It was only natural that the Son of Man, who came *to seek and to save that which was lost*, should make his way to the sick who waited by the side of the pool (Luke 19:10).

Jesus Christ's visit is Bethesda's historical significance. It lifted the name of that pool above the common rank of the springs and waters of the earth. If King Jesus comes into this place, it would be the glory of this hall, and it would be famous for it in eternity. If Jesus came here to heal, the remarkable size of the congregation would cease to be a wonder. The fame of Jesus and his saving love would eclipse all else, just as the sun obscures the light of the stars.

My brethren, Jesus will be here, because there are those who know him and have power with him, who have been asking for his presence. The Lord's favored people, by persistent cries and tears, have won from him his consent to be in our midst today. He walks among his people as ready to heal and as mighty to save as when he walked among men 2,000 years ago. *Behold, I am with you always even unto the end of the age* is an assurance which comforts the preacher's heart (Matthew 28:20).

A present Savior – present in the power of the Holy Spirit – will make this a day to remember for many who will be made whole.

The Patient

In order to observe the patient, I'll ask you to go with me to the pool with the five porches, around which the sick are lying. Walk tenderly among the groups of lame and blind. No, don't close your eyes. It will do you good to see firsthand the sorrowful sight of what sin has done and to what sorrows our father Adam has made us heirs.

Why are they all here? They're here because sometimes the waters bubble up with a healing power. Whether the waters are visibly stirred by an angel or not isn't necessary for us to discuss here. It was generally believed that an angel descended and touched the water. This attracted the sick from all quarters. As soon as the movement was seen in the waters, the whole mass probably leaped into the pool. Those who couldn't leap themselves were pushed in by their attendants. Sadly, many were disappointed, because only one was rewarded for the leap. Whoever stepped in *first* was healed, but only the first. For the very slim chance of winning this cure, the sick lingered in Bethesda's arches year after year. The sick man in this passage of Scripture had most likely spent the better part of his thirty-eight years waiting at this famous pool. His only hope rested fully on the chance that he might one day be the first of the multitude to enter the pool. On the Sabbath mentioned in the text, the angel had not come to stir the waters, but something better had come – Jesus Christ, the angel's Master, was there.

> It will do you good to see firsthand the sorrowful sight of what sin has done and to what sorrows our father Adam has made us heirs.

This man was fully aware of his sickness. He didn't dispute the failure of his health. He felt his sickness, and he owned it. He wasn't like some who are lost but don't know it or won't confess it. He was fully aware that he needed heavenly help, and his waiting at the pool showed it. There may be some people reading this who are equally convinced on this point. You have known for a long time that you are a sinner, and apart from grace, you can never be saved. You aren't an atheist and don't deny the gospel. On the contrary, you firmly believe the Bible and heartily wish that you had a saving part in Christ Jesus. Right now, you feel that you are sick, you desire to be healed, and you are willing to own that the cure must come from above. That's good, but it's not good to stop there.

The sick man waited by the pool expecting some sign or wonder. He hoped that an angel would suddenly burst open the golden gates and touch the waters which stood calm and stagnant, so that he could be healed. This is also the thought of many who feel their sins and desire salvation. They accept unbiblical and dangerous advice given to them by certain ministers. As they wait at the pool of Bethesda, they continue in the formal use of religious rituals and ordinances. They continue in unbelief and somehow expect some great thing to take place.

These same ones expect that they should experience some strange emotions, supernatural sensation, or a remarkable experience, even as they continue in their refusal to obey the gospel. They hope to see a vision, hear a supernatural voice, or be alarmed with hallucinations of horror. Dear friends, we won't deny that a few people have been saved by the direct intervention of God's hand in a manner completely outside the ordinary ways of divine procedure. We would be very foolish to dispute the truth of a conversion such as that of Colonel Gardiner. The very night when he planned to commit sin, he was arrested and converted by a vision of Christ upon the cross and by hearing the voice of the Savior tenderly pleading with him. It would be pointless to dispute that such cases have occurred, do occur, and may occur again.

However, I must beg unconverted people not to look for such direct intervention in their own cases. When the Lord commands you to believe in Jesus, what right do you have to demand signs and wonders instead? Jesus himself is the greatest of all wonders. For you to wait for a remarkable experience is as futile as it was for those to linger at Bethesda waiting for the long-expected angel, when he who could heal them already stood in their midst, neglected and despised by them. What a pitiful spectacle to see them gazing into the clouds when the physician who could heal them was in their presence, but they made no requests of him and sought no mercy at his hands.

When we encounter those who are waiting to see or feel some great thing, we explain that it is not the way God has commanded his servants to preach. I challenge the whole world to locate in the gospel of God where an unconverted man is told to abide in unbelief. Where is the sinner told to continue in his religious rituals, so he may be saved?

The gospel of our salvation is this: *Believe on the Lord Jesus Christ, and thou shalt be saved* (Acts 16:31). When our Lord gave his commission to his disciples, he said, *Go ye into all the world and preach the gospel to every creature* (Mark 16:15). And what was that gospel? Tell them to wait in their unbelief and in the use of rituals and ordinances until they see some great thing? Tell them to be diligent in prayer and read the Word of God until they feel better? Not an atom of it. The Lord said, *He that believes and is baptized shall be saved, but he that believes not shall be condemned* (Mark 16:16).

This was the gospel, and it's the only gospel which Jesus Christ ever commanded his ministers to preach. Those who say to wait for feelings or wonders preach another gospel. *I marvel that ye are so soon removed from him that called you into the grace of Christ unto another gospel, for there is not another; but there are some that trouble you and would pervert the gospel of the Christ* (Galatians 1:6-7). The lifting up of Christ on the cross is the saving work of the gospel ministry, and in the cross of Jesus lies the hope of men. *Look unto me, and be ye saved, all the ends of the earth* is God's gospel (Isaiah 45:22). "Wait at the pool" is man's gospel and it has destroyed thousands.

This ungospel-like gospel of waiting is immensely popular. I wouldn't be surprised if nearly half of you are satisfied with it. You don't hesitate to fill the seats in our places of worship and are seldom absent when the doors are open. But there you sit in confirmed unbelief, waiting for a mystical glimpse into heaven, but neglecting the gospel of your salvation. The great command of God, believe and live, receives no response from you but a deaf ear and a stony heart. Jesus said, *I AM the resurrection and the life; he that believes in me, though he is dead, yet shall he live* (John 11:25). All the while, you soothe your consciences with outward religious observances.

If God had said, "Sit in those seats and wait," I would be bold and urge you to do it with tears, but God has not said this. He said, *Let the wicked forsake his way, and the unrighteous man his thoughts: and let him return unto the LORD, and he will have mercy upon him* (Isaiah

55:7). He hasn't said, "Wait." But he has said, *Seek the LORD while he may be found; call upon him while he is near* (Isaiah 55:6). He also said, *Today if ye will hear his voice, harden not your hearts* (Hebrews 3:7-8).

Jesus says nothing to sinners about waiting, but very much about coming.

> *Come unto me, all ye that labour and are heavy laden, and I will give you rest.* (Matthew 11:28)

> *If any man thirsts, let him come unto me and drink.* (John 7:37)

> *And the Spirit and the bride say, Come. And let him that hears say, Come. And let him that is thirsty come; and whosoever will, let him take of the water of life freely.* (Revelation 22:17)

Why is waiting so very popular? It's because it dulls the conscience like a drug. When a minister preaches with power, and the hearer's heart is touched, the devil says, "Wait for a more convenient time." In this way, the archenemy pours this deadly drug into the soul. And instead of trusting Jesus on the spot and crying out for mercy, the sinner flatters himself and justifies his waiting, because he feels validated in his empty religious rituals. But these things are not a substitute for Christ crucified. When this is the case, religious busyness stands in the way of true salvation. A child should hear its parent's command, but what if the child puts hearing into the place of obeying? God forbid that I should glory in your listening to the gospel, if you are only hearing. My glory is in the cross. And unless you look to the cross, it would be better for you if you had never been born.

Why is waiting so very popular?

If you are one who has been waiting, I would like to mention one or two points. My dear friend, isn't this waiting a very hopeless business? Out of the multitude who waited at Bethesda, only a very few were ever healed. He who stepped down *first* into the pool was cured, but all the rest came up from the pool just as they went in. I tremble for some of you chapelgoers and churchgoers who have been waiting for years – how few of you get saved. Thousands of you die in your sins, as you wait in wicked unbelief. A few are snatched like brands from the burning coals, but those who are hardened waiters wait and wait, until they die in their sins.

I solemnly warn you that as pleasing to the flesh as waiting in unbelief may be, it's not something which any reasonable man would continue in for very long. You are a perfect example of its hopelessness. You've been waiting for years. You can't even remember when you first went to a place of worship. Your mother carried you there in her arms, and you've been nurtured under the shadow of the sanctuary like the swallows that build their nests under God's altars. What has your waiting in unbelief done for you? Has it made you a Christian? No, you are still without God, without Christ, and without hope.

I'll present it to you another way. Why do you think that if you wait another thirty years, you'll be any different than you are now? Isn't it probable that at sixty you will be as graceless as you are at thirty? Some of you have listened to the gospel preached to you with no mincing of words for years. I've been as plain with you as I know how to be, and I've never hesitated to declare the whole counsel of God. I've even dealt with individual cases as they've presented themselves. Short of actually mentioning people's names, I have attempted to present the gospel to the conscience of every man as in the sight of God.

Remember the warnings you've heard and the feelings you've experienced when the Word of God broke you down? Remember the invitations where you sat and waited? If all these have failed, what more can possibly be done in the way of hearing and waiting? Many of you have listened to many preachers whose words were earnest and tender. So if all these have had no effect on you, if waiting at the pool has done nothing for you, isn't it a waste of time to continue down that path? Isn't it time to try something better than merely waiting for the stirring of the water? Isn't it time to remember that Jesus Christ is ready to save you now, and that *if* you trust in him, you will have everlasting life this very day?

As we return to our text, there lies our poor friend still waiting at the water's edge. I don't blame *him* for waiting, because Jesus hadn't been there before, and it was right for him to pursue even the most slender chance of a cure. But it was sad that Jesus remained so unrecognized. He threaded his way among the blind and the lame and looked with gentleness upon them all, but none looked up to him. In other places, as soon as Jesus made his appearance, they brought the sick in their beds and laid them at his feet. As he went along, he healed them all and scattered mercy with both hands.

A blindness had come over the people at the pool. There they were, and there was Christ, who could heal them, but not a single one of them sought him. Their eyes were fixed on the water, expecting it to be troubled. They were so consumed with their own chosen way that the true way was neglected. No mercies were distributed, because none were sought. Will it be the same today? The living Christ is still among us in the power of his eternal Spirit. Will you look to your own good works? Will you trust in your regular church attendance?

Will you rely upon expected emotions, sensations, and fits of terror, and let Christ, who is able to save completely, see no glimmer of faith and hear no prayer of desire from any heart? If that's the way it will be, it's heartbreaking to think of it. Men, with an Almighty Physician in their house, dying while they are amused with the hopeless quackery of their own inventing. Will Bethesda be repeated today, and Jesus Christ, the present Savior, be neglected again?

If a king gave one of his subjects a ring and said to him, "When you are in distress or disgrace, simply send me that ring, and I will do all for you that is needed," and if that man willfully refused to send it, but purchased presents and performed acts of bravery to win his monarch's favor, you would say, "What a fool. Here is a simple way, but he will not allow himself to benefit from it. He wastes his energy by inventing new devices and toils his life away in following plans that only end in disappointment." Isn't this the case with all those who refuse to trust Christ? The Lord has assured them that if they trust Jesus, they shall be saved, but they chase after ten thousand imaginings, and let their God, their Savior, go.

Meanwhile, the sick man, so often disappointed, was growing into deep despair and becoming old. Thirty-eight years spent in illness is a long time out of a man's life. He felt that he would soon die. The brittle thread which connected him to this life was nearly snapped, and as the days and nights wearily wore on, though he waited, it became heavy work to wait.

My friend, is this the way it is with you? Is life wearing away at you? Are you starting to see gray hairs here and there? You've waited all this time in vain, and I warn you that you have sinfully waited. You've seen others saved. Your child is saved, your wife is converted, but you are not. You are waiting and will continue to wait, I fear, until the words "Earth to earth, dust to dust, ashes to ashes" rattle your coffin lid, and your soul finds itself in hell. Don't play with time any longer. Don't say, "There's enough time," for the wise man knows that time is never enough.

Don't be like the foolish drunkard who, staggering home one night, saw a candle lit for him. "Two candles!" he said, because his drunkenness made him see double. "I'll blow one out." As he blew it out, he found himself in the dark. Many a man sees double through the drunkenness of sin. He thinks that he has one life to sow his wild oats, and then the last part of life in which to turn to God. So, like a fool, he blows out the only candle that he has, and in the dark, he will have to lie down forever.

Hasten thee, traveler, thou hast but one sun, and when that sets, thou wilt never reach thy home. God help thee to make haste now!

The Physician

As we've already seen, on this occasion, our Lord walked, forgotten and neglected, through that throng of afflicted people. No one cried, *Jesus, thou Son of David, have mercy on me* (Luke 18:38). No struggling woman reached out to touch the hem of his garment, so she might be made whole. *And, behold, a woman who was diseased with an issue of blood twelve years came behind him and touched the hem of his garment; for she said within herself, If I may but touch his garment, I shall be free* (Matthew 9:20-21). All of those who lingered at the pool desired to be healed, but either no one knew or no one trusted Jesus. What a strange, soul-sickening sight it must have been, because Jesus was quite able and willing to heal, and to do it all without fee or reward. Yet, none sought him.

Is this same scene going to be repeated today? Jesus Christ is able to save you. There is no heart so hard that he can't soften it, and there is no man among you so lost that Jesus can't save him. Blessed be my dear Master, no case ever defeated him. His mighty power reaches beyond all the depths of human sin and foolishness. If there's a harlot,

Christ can cleanse her. If there's a drunkard or a thief, the blood of Jesus can make him white as snow. If you have any desire towards him, you haven't gone beyond the reach of his pierced hand. If you aren't saved, it's certainly not because of a lack of power in the Savior.

In addition to all these things, your poverty isn't a hindrance either, because the Master asks nothing from you – the poorer the wretch, the more he's welcome to Christ. My Master isn't a covetous priest who demands pay for what he does. He freely forgives us. He wants none of your merits, nothing at all from you. Come to him as you are, because he's willing to receive you just as you are. But here's my sorrow and complaint, that the blessed Lord Jesus, though present to heal, received no attention from most of the men. They looked another way and had no eyes for him.

Yet, Jesus was not angry. I don't find anywhere that he scolded a single one of those who lay in the porches of Bethesda or that he even thought harshly of them. But I'm sure he pitied them and said in his heart, "Poor souls, they don't even know when mercy is so near!" I'm only the Lord's poor servant, but I pity, from my inmost heart, those of you who live without Christ. I should weep for you who are trying other ways of salvation, because they will all end in disappointment, and if continued in, will prove to be your eternal destruction.

Observe very carefully what the Savior did. He looked around the whole multitude and made an election. He had a right to make whatever choice he pleased, and he exercised that sovereign prerogative. The Lord isn't bound to give his mercy to every single one or to any specific one. He has freely proclaimed it to you all, but as you reject it, he now has a double right to bless his chosen ones by making them willing in the day of his power. The Savior selected that man out of the great multitude. We don't know why, but certainly his reason was founded in grace.

If we ventured to give a reason for his choice, he may have selected him because his was the worst case, and he had waited the longest of all. Everyone spoke of this man's case. They said, "This man has been there for thirty-eight years."

Our Lord acted according to his own eternal purpose and did as he pleased with his own. He fixed the eye of his electing love on that one man, and, going up to him, he gazed upon him. He knew all his history. He knew that he had been a long time in that condition, and he pitied him. He thought of all the dreary months and years of painful disappointment which the man had suffered, and tears were in the Master's eyes. He looked and looked again at that man, and he yearned to heal him.

Now, I don't know whom Christ intends to save today by his powerful grace. I am bound to present a general appeal, which is all I can do. I shouldn't be surprised if he calls some of you who have been waiting long. I will bless his name if he does. I shouldn't be shocked if Jesus looks on some of you who never looked on him – until his look makes *you* look, and his pity makes you have pity on yourselves, and his irresistible grace makes you come to him so that you may be saved. Jesus performed an act of sovereign, distinguishing grace. I pray you don't kick against this doctrine. If you do, I can't help it, because it's true. I have proclaimed the

> If you seek him, he will be found by you.

gospel to every one of you as freely as man can do it. Surely, you who reject it shouldn't quarrel with God for bestowing on others that which you don't care to receive. If you desire his mercy, he will not deny it to you. If you seek him, he will be found by you. But if you refuse to seek mercy, don't criticize the Lord if he bestows it upon others.

Once Jesus singled out this man, he said to him, *Dost thou desire to be made whole?* I've already hinted that Christ didn't ask this because he wanted information. He wished to arouse the man's attention. It was the Sabbath, and the man wasn't thinking about being cured. To the Jew, it seemed a very unlikely thing that cures would take place on a Sabbath day. So Jesus brought his full attention back to the matter at hand, because the work of grace is a work upon a conscious mind, not upon senseless matter. Some pretend to regenerate unreasoning children by sprinkling their faces with water, but Jesus never attempted such a thing. Jesus saves men who have the use of their senses, and his salvation is a work upon motivated intellect and awakened affections.

Jesus brought back the man's wandering mind with the question, *Dost thou desire to be made whole?*

"Indeed," the man might have said, "I desire it above all things. I long for it. I pant for it."

Now, I will ask you the same question. *Dost thou desire to be made whole?* Do you desire to be saved? Do you know what being saved is?

"Oh," you say, "it's escaping from hell." No, no, no, that's the *result* of being saved, but *being* saved is a different thing. Do you want to be saved from the power of sin? Do you desire to be saved from being covetous, worldly minded, bad-tempered, unfair, ungodly, controlling, drunken, or profane? Are you willing to give up the sin that is dearest to you?

"No," says one, "I can't honestly say I desire all that." Then you aren't the man I'm talking to.

I'm talking to the one who says, "Yes, I long to be rid of sin, root and branch. I desire, by God's grace, this very day to become a Christian and to be saved from sin." Well, since you're already in a state of thoughtfulness, let's go a step further and observe what the Savior did. He gave the command, saying, *Rise, take up thy bed, and walk.* The power by which the man arose was not in himself, but in Jesus. It wasn't the mere sound of the word which made him rise, but it was the divine power which went with it.

I do believe that Jesus still speaks through his ministers. I trust that he speaks through *me* at this moment, when in his name I say to you who have been waiting at the pool, wait no longer, but believe in Jesus Christ this very moment! Trust him now. I know that my words won't make you do it, but if the Holy Spirit works through the words, you will believe. Trust Christ now, poor sinner. Believe that he is able to save you. Believe it now! Rely upon him to save you this moment. Rest in him now! If you are enabled to believe, the power will come from him, not from you. Your salvation will be accomplished, not by the sound of the word, but by the secret power of the Holy Spirit which goes with that word.

Although nothing is said about faith in the text, this man must have had faith. Suppose you had been unable to move your hands or feet for thirty-eight years, and someone said at your bedside, "Rise." You wouldn't even think of trying to rise, because you would know it to be impossible. You would have to have faith in the person who spoke the word, or you wouldn't make the attempt. I think I can picture the poor man. There he is, a heap, a writhing bundle of tortured nerves and powerless muscles, yet Jesus says, *Rise,* and up he rises in a moment.

Take up thy bed, says the Master, and the bed is carried. Here we see the man's faith. The man was a Jew, and he knew that, according to the Pharisees, it would be a very wicked thing for him to roll up his mattress and carry it on the Sabbath. But because Jesus told him to, he asked no questions. He bundled up his bed and walked. He did what he was told to do, because he believed in him who spoke.

Do you have this type of faith in Jesus, poor sinner? Do you believe that Christ can save you? If you do, then I say to you in his name, trust him now! If you trust Jesus, you will be saved – saved on the spot and saved forever. The cure which Christ worked was perfect. The man could carry his bed. The restoration was proven by a demonstration, and the cure was evident to all.

Also, the cure was immediate. He wasn't told to take a lump of figs, put it on the sore, and wait. He wasn't carried home by his friends, laid up for a month or two, and gradually nursed back to health. No, he was cured then and there. Half of our professing Christians think that regeneration can't take place in a moment. So they instruct poor sinners, "Go and lie at Bethesda's pool. Wait comfortably in your religious rituals. Humble yourself. Seek for deeper repentance."

Do away with such teaching! The cross, the cross, the cross – there hangs a sinner's hope! You must not rely on what *you* can do, nor on what angels can do, nor on visions and dreams, nor on feelings and strange emotions, or horrible hallucinations. You must rest in the blood of my Master and my God, slain for sinners. There is life when you look to the Crucified One, and there is life nowhere else. I come to the same point once again. The Lord says, *Look unto me, and be ye saved, all the ends of the earth.*

Application

I hope, believers, your hearts are going up in prayer. What a scene lies before us! If someone had told us that a mass of people would gather to listen to the gospel, hundreds would have doubted it. We have had no gorgeous ceremony to attract the multitudes. There's not even the sound of the organ. I declined its pealing notes, so we wouldn't seem to depend on it in the slightest degree for anything from a thread even to a shoe buckle. I didn't want anything to hinder the preaching of the gospel. The preaching of the cross is enough to draw the people and enough to save the people. If we include anything else, we lose our power and cut away the locks which make us strong.

The application of the text is just this: Why shouldn't we, on this very spot, have instantaneous cures of sick souls? Why shouldn't there be scores, hundreds, thousands, who hear the gracious words, *Rise, take up thy bed, and walk*? I believe it's possible, and I hope it will be done. Let me talk with you who doubt this matter. You still think that you must wait. You've waited long enough, and you're becoming weary, but still you stick to the old plan. Hopeless as it is, you still grab at it as drowning men do at straw.

I want to show you that this is all wrong. Regeneration is an instantaneous work, and justification is an instantaneous gift. Man fell in a moment. *And when the woman saw that the tree was good for food, and that it was desirable to the eyes, and a tree of covetousness to understand, she took of its fruit and ate and gave also unto her husband with her; and he ate* (Genesis 3:6). When Eve plucked the fruit, and Adam ate it, it didn't require six months to bring them into a state of condemnation. It didn't require several years of continued sin to cast them out of paradise. Their eyes were opened by the forbidden fruit. They saw that they were naked and hid themselves from God. Surely, Christ won't be longer about his work than the devil was about his. Is it reasonable to think that the devil destroyed us in a moment, and Jesus is unable to save us in a moment? Glory be to God, he has far more power to deliver than any which Satan uses for man's destruction.

> Regeneration is an instantaneous work, and justification is an instantaneous gift.

Look at the biblical illustrations of salvation. I will only mention three. Noah built an ark, and that was a type of salvation. Christ has built the ark for us, and we have nothing to do with building it. But when was Noah saved? Does anyone say, "He was saved after he had been in the ark a month, had put everything in order inside the ark, and then looked out on the deluge and felt his danger"? No! Noah was saved the moment he entered the ark, and the Lord shut him in. When he had been in the ark a second, he was as secure as when he had been there a month.

Take the cue of the Passover. When were the Jews safe from the destroying angel who went through the land of Egypt? Were they safe after the blood which was sprinkled on the door had been looked at and considered for a week or two? No! The moment the blood was sprinkled, the house was secured. And the moment a sinner believes and trusts in the crucified Son of God, he is pardoned at once. He receives salvation in full through Christ's blood.

One more instance: the brazen serpent. When the brazen serpent was lifted up, what were the wounded supposed to do? Were they told to wait until the brazen serpent was pushed into their faces or until the venom of the serpent showed certain symptoms in their flesh? No, they were commanded to look, and they did look. Were they healed in six months? No. They were healed as soon as their eyes met the serpent of brass, and the cure was complete. And as soon as your eye meets Christ, poor trembler, you are saved. Even though you were drunk and up to your neck in sin yesterday, if you look to my once-slain-but-now-exalted Master today, you will find eternal life.

Again, let's consider some biblical instances. Did the dying thief wait at the pool of religious rituals? You know how soon his believing prayer was heard. *And Jesus said unto him, Verily I say unto thee, Today shalt thou be with me in paradise* (Luke 23:43). Did the three thousand at Pentecost wait for some great thing? No, they believed and were baptized. *Now when they heard this, they were pricked in their heart and said unto Peter and to the rest of the apostles, Men and brethren, what shall we do? Then Peter said unto them, Repent and be baptized each one of you into the name of Jesus Christ for the remission of sins, and ye shall receive the gift of the Holy Spirit* (Acts 2:37-38).

Look at the jailer of Philippi. It was the dead of night, the prison was shaken, and the jailer was alarmed. After he realized everyone was accounted for, he said, "Sirs, what must I do to be saved?"

Did Paul say, "Well, you must use the means and look for a blessing upon the ordinances"? No! He said, "Believe in the Lord Jesus Christ, and thou shalt be saved, and thy house," and that very night he baptized him. *And the keeper of the prison, awaking out of his sleep and seeing the prison doors open, he drew out his sword and would have killed himself, supposing that the prisoners had fled. But Paul cried with a loud voice, saying, Do thyself no harm, for we are all here. Then he called for a light and came inside and fell down trembling before Paul and Silas and brought them out and said, Sirs, what must I do to be saved? And they said, Believe on the Lord Jesus Christ, and thou shalt be saved, and thy house* (Acts 16:27-31). Paul didn't take as much time as some think is so necessary. He believed as I do, that there is life in a look at Jesus. He asked men to look, and by looking, they lived.

You might see this even more clearly if I remind you that the work of salvation is all done. There is nothing for a sinner to *do* in order to be saved. It's all done for him. You want washing. The bath doesn't need filling. "There is a fountain filled with blood." You want clothing. You don't have to make the garment, because the robe is ready. The garment of Christ's righteousness is woven from the top to the bottom, and all you have to do is put it on. If some work remained for you to do, it might be a longer process, but all the doing is accomplished by Christ. Salvation is not of works, but of grace. To accept what Christ presents to you does not require a work of time.

I'll put it another way: salvation itself cannot take place over a long time, even where it seems to be most gradual. When we look at it closely, it turns out to be the work of a moment. We have a dead man. Now, if that man is raised from the dead, there must be an instant in which he was dead and another instant in which he was alive. The actual enlivening must be the work of a moment. At first, the life may be very feeble, but there must be a time when it begins. There must be a line between life and death. We can't always see it ourselves, but God sees it. A man can't be somewhere between dead and alive. He's either alive or dead. In the same way, you are either dead in sin or alive unto God, and the process can't involve a long period of time.

Finally, it doesn't take a century, or a year, for God to say, "I forgive you." The judge pronounces the sentence, and the criminal is acquitted. If God says to you this morning, "I absolve you," then you are absolved, and you may go in peace. I must share my own case. I never found mercy by waiting. I never obtained a gleam of hope by depending on religious rituals. *I found salvation by believing.* I heard a simple minister of the gospel say, "Look and live! Look to Jesus! He bleeds in the garden, and he dies on the tree! Trust him! Trust in what he suffered instead of you, and if you trust him, you will be saved."

The Lord knows I had *heard* that gospel many times before, but I had not obeyed it. That time, it came with power to my soul, and I did look. The moment I looked to Christ, I lost my burden.

"But," someone might say, "how do you know?"

"Did you ever carry a burden yourself?"

"Oh, yes," they say.

"Did you know when it was off? How did you know?"

"Oh," they say, "I felt so different. I knew when my burden was on, and, consequently, I knew when it was off."

It was the same in my case. I only wish some of you felt the burden of sin as I felt it, when I was waiting at the pool of Bethesda. I'm amazed that my waiting didn't land me in hell. But when I heard the word "Look," I looked, and my burden was gone. I wondered where it went, but I haven't seen it since, and I'll never see it again. It went into the Master's tomb, and it lies forever buried there. God has said it. *I have undone, as a cloud, thy rebellions, and thy sins, as a mist* (Isaiah 44:22).

You who are needy, come to my Master. Those of you who have been disappointed with rituals and ceremonies, feelings and impressions, and all the hopes of the flesh, come at my Master's command and look up to him! He's not here in the flesh, because he has risen. He has risen to plead for sinners, and *Therefore he is able also to save to the uttermost those that come unto God by him, seeing he ever lives to make intercession for them* (Hebrews 7:25). If there were some way I could know how to preach the gospel so that you would feel it, I would go to any school to learn! The Lord knows I would willingly consent to lose my eyes to get greater power in my ministry – and lose my arms, legs, and all my members. I would be willing to die if I could only be honored by the Holy Spirit to win your souls to God. I beg you, brothers and sisters, you who have power in prayer, pray for the Lord to bring sinners to Christ. Let me say, in all seriousness, to you who have heard the word today, I have told you the plan of salvation plainly. If you don't accept it, I am clear of your blood. I shake my skirts of the blood of your souls. If you don't come to my Lord and Master, I must bear swift witness against you at the day of judgment.

I have told you the way. I can't tell it to you more simply. I beg you to follow it! Look to Jesus! But if you refuse it, when you rise from the dead and stand before the great white throne, do me the justice to acknowledge that I begged you and attempted to persuade you to escape. I did my best to urge you to flee from the wrath to come. I pray for the Lord to save each one of you, and his shall be the praise forever. Amen.

Chapter 2

Impotence and Omnipotence

And a certain man was there who had an infirmity thirty-eight years. When Jesus saw him lying there and knew that he had been now a long time in that case, he said unto him, Dost thou desire to be made whole? The impotent man answered him, Sir, I have no man when the water is troubled to put me into the pool, but while I am coming, another steps down before me. Jesus said unto him, Rise, take up thy bed, and walk. And immediately the man was made whole and took up his bed and walked, and on that day was the sabbath. (John 5:5-9)

This man had been lying, with many others, around the pool hoping that it would be stirred by the angel, and that he might be put into the water first, so he might be healed. He waited there a long time, and waited in vain. Why did he wait? Because Jesus wasn't there. Where Jesus isn't, you must wait. If it's only an angel and a pool, you must wait. One may get a blessing, and many may get no blessing. But when Jesus came, there was no waiting. He walked in among the crowd of sick people, turned his attention to this man, commanded him to take up his mattress and walk home, and he was healed at once.

I commend this man for waiting. I admire him for his patience and his perseverance, but I beg you not to make his experience your own. He waited, because Jesus wasn't there. You don't have to wait, you must not wait, because Jesus is here. It was necessary for him to wait. As I've told you, there was an angel, a pool, and nothing more. But where Christ is, there should be no waiting. Any soul that believes in Christ tonight will be saved tonight. Any soul that looks to Christ tonight will be saved, even though he looks from the ends of the earth. Go ahead and look now, you are commanded to do so. *Behold, now is the acceptable time; behold, now is the day of saving health* (2 Corinthians 6:2). And *harden not your hearts, as in the provocation* (Hebrews 3:8). If you turn your eyes by faith to Jesus, the Living One on the throne of the Highest, you will obtain an immediate cure.

Waiting was fine at the pool of Bethesda, but waiting at the pool of religious ritual is not according to the Scriptures. I read nothing about waiting there, but I do read this: *Believe on the Lord Jesus Christ, and thou shalt be saved* (Acts 16:31).

However, to help some who have waited to the point of weariness, who have persevered in the use of other means until they have become despondent and disappointed, let's look at this case of the impotent man at Bethesda.

The Savior Knew the Case

Jesus knew the case. I only mention that to say that the Savior knows *your* case. Jesus saw him lying there. There were many objects for the Savior's eyes to rest upon, but he fixed his gaze upon this man who had been bedridden and afflicted for thirty-eight years. In the same way, Jesus knows all about your situation. He sees you just where you are right now – afflicted, without hope, without light, and without faith. He singles you out from among the multitude, wherever you are right now. His eye is scanning you from head to foot. He looks inside as well as outside and reads all that is in your heart.

Concerning the man at the pool, Jesus knew that he had been a long time in that condition, and he knows the years that you've been waiting. You remember being carried to the house of God by your mother. As a boy, you remember listening to sermons that seemed to startle you. You went home to your little bedroom and cried to God for mercy, but you forgot your conviction. It was like the morning mist that vanishes in the rising sun. You came to London and grew up to be a man. You became careless about divine things and shook off all your early convictions.

Still, you went to hear the Word preached and half-hoped that you might get a blessing. You heard the Word, but faith was not mixed with what you heard, so you missed the blessing. But you still always had a wish that the blessing would come to you. You could never despise godly people or the things of Christ. You thought you couldn't get those blessings for yourself, but you always had some lingering wish that you were numbered with the people of God. The Lord Jesus knows all about that and the many years in which you have been waiting as a hearer, but a hearer only, and not a doer of the Word. You were convicted at times, but you rejected those feelings and went back to a careless life.

He sees just who you are, where you are, and what you are.

My Lord knows all about you. I can't pick you out of a congregation, but as I preach, miracles will take place. The very nature of men will be changed, because Christ is being preached, and his gospel is being proclaimed. None of this is done in vain, and God will bless it. He is going to bless somebody. Who that somebody may be, or how many hundred somebodies there will be, we cannot guess. He will bless his own Word, and why wouldn't he bless you? He sees just who you are, where you are, and what you are.

In addition to this, our Lord knew all this poor man's disappointments. Many times, when he had attempted to get to the water's edge first and thought that he would be able to take the happy plunge, in went someone else before him, and his hopes were gone. Another came up out of the water healed, and then, with a heavy sigh, he fell back onto his couch and felt that it might be a long time before the angel stirred the water again. Even then, he might be disappointed again. He remembered the many times when he had lost all hope, and he lay there so close to despair.

Someone waiting by the pool of religious rituals today might say, "My brother found the Lord. My friend, who came to church with me, found the Lord. I have lived to see my mother die in sure and certain hope of glory. I have friends who have come to Christ, but I'm still living without him. When there were special services, I hoped that I might have been specially blessed. I have been to prayer meetings, have read my Bible in secret, and I have sometimes hoped that maybe, one of these days, I will be healed."

My Lord knows all about that, and he sympathizes in all the grief you feel. He hears those unspoken wishes of yours, and he knows you long to be healed.

The Savior Aroused the Man's Desires

He said to him, *Dost thou desire to be made whole?* There he lay. I'm not going to explain lying at the pool, except to apply it to you who are here in a similar condition. Beware of forgetting why you attend church. Beware of coming to the house of God and not knowing why you've come. Years ago, you went to places of worship in the hope of finding salvation. Well, you've kept on coming and haven't found it, but do you still look for it? Have you fallen into the habit of sitting and listening to sermons, and prayers, and so on, without feeling that you came for anything special for yourself? You come and you go, merely to attend a place of worship, and that's all.

The Savior wouldn't let the impotent man lie there satisfied by the pool. No. He said to him, "Why are you here? Don't you have any desire? Don't you want to be made whole?"

I wish that you were able to say "Yes" to this question. Did you come to listen to me so that your sin may be forgiven, that your soul may be renewed by divine grace, and that you may meet with Christ? If so, I want to keep you focused on that point, and not to let you come, get used to sitting here, and come, and come, and come, and be just like the door on its hinges which turns in and turns out again, and isn't a bit the better for it. Oh, don't get into mere religious habits! They will only be ritualistic habits to you. You come, you go, and you are satisfied. This will never do. Christ arouses your desire as he says, *Dost thou desire to be made whole?*

Also, avoid the despair that comes from indifference. I remember two brothers and a sister who heard me preach for a considerable time, and they were under great conviction, but, at the same time, they thought that they couldn't believe in Christ, and that they must wait. I hardly know what for, and they waited until they grew quite old. I didn't know better people morally or better hearers as far as interest in what they heard was concerned, but they never seemed to get any further. After a long time waiting, they seemed to feel that if it was to be, it would be. And if it wasn't to be, it wouldn't be. They felt that all they could do was just to sit still, be quiet, and be patient.

Patient under the fear of being lost forever? Why, I don't expect the man condemned to death to be happy and patient when he hears them putting up his gallows! He must be concerned and uneasy. I did my best to make these friends uneasy, but I confess that I'm afraid my efforts met with very small results. The Savior said to this man, *"Dost thou desire to be made whole?* You seem to be in such a state of indifference that you don't care whether you're made whole or not."* No worse condition than that can be found. It's so hard to deal with. I pray that God will save you from a gloomy indifference in which you leave yourselves to drift to destruction at the will of some unknown fate.

I pray for you to remember that it is yours to desire, for Christ said to this man, *Dost thou desire to be made whole?* You can't make yourself whole, but you can desire and wish to be made whole. God's Holy Spirit has given to many of you the desire to do according to his good pleasure. You will never be saved against your will. God drags nobody to heaven by the ears. There must be in you a desire and a consent to the work of his sovereign grace, and if it's there, I want you to exercise it right now, just as Christ wished this man to exercise it: *Dost thou desire to be made whole?* Do you have any wish, any desire, or longing for healing? If so, I want to stir this fire and make it burn. If there is only a spark of desire, I want to breathe upon it and pray for the Holy Spirit to breathe upon it and make it into a great flame. Paul said, *And I know that in me (that is, in my flesh) dwells no good thing; for I have the desire, but I am not able to perform that which is good* (Romans 7:18). I believe that there are some reading this who have the desire to be saved. Thank God for that!

Dost thou desire to be made whole? I think that the Savior asked this question for another reason, which I will turn into an exhortation: surrender all the ways that you think you are to be saved. The question isn't, "Do you desire to be put into that pool?" but, *Dost thou desire to be made whole?* The question isn't, "Are you willing to take this medicine? Or, do you desire that I do this or that to you?" but, *Dost thou desire to be made whole?* Have you come to the point that you are willing to be saved in God's way, in Christ's way?

One says, "I want to have a dream." Don't desire dreams, for they are only dreams.

Another says, "I want to see a vision." There is nothing in the plan of salvation about seeing visions.

"I want to hear a voice," says one. Then hear my voice, and may God the Holy Spirit make you to hear the voice of his Word through me!

"But I want . . . ." Oh yes, you want. You don't know what you want, like a silly child with its fads, fancies, whims, and wishes. Oh, if only all were willing to be saved by the simple plan of believe and live! If this is God's way, who are you that he should make a new way for you?

When I presented the way of salvation to a friend some time ago, she turned to me and said, "Oh, please pray for me!"

"No," I said, "I will not pray for you."

"Oh, but," she said, "how can you say that?"

I replied, "I set before you Christ crucified, and I beg you to believe in him. If you won't believe in him, you will be lost, and I won't pray for God to make a different way of salvation for you. You deserve to be lost if you won't believe in Christ."

Afterwards she said, "Oh, I see it now! I do look to Christ and trust him."

I replied, "*Now* I will pray for you. Now we can pray together and sing together if we need to."

Dear friends, don't set up your own ideas about how you ought to be converted. Can you find any two people who were converted in the same way? God doesn't make converts like men make steel pens, a whole lot of them in a box all the same. No. In each instance there is a living man created, and every living man, every living animal, every living plant, is somewhat different from every other of its kind. You must not look for uniformity in the work of regeneration. *Dost thou desire to be made whole?* Come, do you desire the pardon of sin? Do you long for a new heart and a right spirit? If so, stop disputing about how you are to get them, and do what Christ tells you to do.

Dost thou desire to be made whole? It's as if the Savior said, "Be more serious about it than ever before. I know that you desire to be made whole. Well, desire it more now than you've ever desired it before." Let your desire be exercised; act on your desire.

You are serious about being saved. Be more serious. You've come to an important crisis in your life. You may be at the point of death, who knows? We know that none of us are guaranteed tomorrow. If you want to be made whole, I desire that you would be made whole right now. I pray that you would feel something pressing you, something that makes you end your long delay, something that makes you feel, *I have no more time to waste. I can't afford to dawdle. I must be saved right now. I hear the distinct ticking of God's great clock, that stands in the hall of grace, and always says, "Now, now, now, now, now," and never utters any other sound.* Oh, may the Lord make it so by his own free grace!

Be more serious.

So the Savior aroused the desires of the man at the pool. First, he knew his case. Next, he aroused his desires.

The Savior Heard the Man's Complaint

Now, the Savior heard the man's complaint. *The impotent man answered him, Sir, I have no man when the water is troubled to put me into the pool, but while I am coming, another steps down before me.*

Some of the people who waited by the pool had kind friends who took turns watching day and night, and the moment the water was stirred, they lifted up their patient and plunged them in. This man had lost all his friends. Thirty-eight years of illness had worn them all out, and he said, "*I have no man when the water is troubled to put me into the pool.* How can I get into the water?" There are many in this position – they want help.

While I served at Menton, I had the joy of leading a number of friends to Christ. When I had to leave them and come back to London, more than one of them said to me, "What can we do without you? We won't have anybody to lead us down the right path now. We'll have no one to instruct us, no one to correct our objections, nobody to solve our doubts, and nobody we can talk to about the deepest cares of our hearts."

No doubt, some of you would talk the same way, and I must admit that the lack of a helper is serious. It's a great disadvantage to have no one to help you in these things. Sometimes, if a friend will come up after the sermon and just say a kind word, it will do more good than the sermon itself. Many troubled ones, who spent a long time in prison, might have been released sooner if only some kind friend had reminded the brother of a divine promise, which, like a key, would have opened the prison door. I agree with you that there is a great help in having a dedicated Christian friend to lift you over a difficulty, to carry you to the water's edge to which you cannot go by yourself, and to put you into the pool.

It's a great loss if you don't have this type of friend. I feel very sorry for you if you live in a village where there's nobody to speak to you about spiritual matters, you attend a ministry that doesn't feed you, and you have nobody to comfort you. There aren't many, after all, who can really help sinners come to Christ. Some who try to do so are a great deal too wise, and others are too hard-hearted. It requires special training in the school of grace for anyone to learn to sympathize with others so that they are really able to help them. I suppose one of you might be saying, "I have no mother to speak to. I have no Christian friend in the family. I have no one to go to for help, and that's why I'm stuck where I am."

Well, a helper is very valuable, but a helper may not be as valuable as you think. I've known some who have had plenty of Christian helpers as they sought the Lord, but none of them were really able to help them. If you trust in earthly helpers and think they're necessary, God won't bless their efforts, and they will be of no use to you. I am afraid that many seekers have had to say, even to good and devoted Christians, what Job said to his friends: *Miserable comforters are ye all* (Job 16:2). After all, how can a man be of much help in your soul's affairs?

No man can give you faith, or give you pardon. No man can give you spiritual life, or even spiritual light. Even though you have no man to help you, remember that it's possible to place too much importance on men, and you can trust too much in Christian helpers. I beg you to keep that in mind.

I'm afraid that there are some professors who have been helped a little too much. They heard a sermon and were really convicted by it. Then somebody was foolish enough to say to them, "That is conversion." It was never conversion at all. The friend then said, "Now, come forward and make a profession." So they came forward and made a profession of what they never had. Then the friend said, "Now, come to such-and-such a meeting and join the church." In this way, they were led, and led, and led, never having any real internal life or spiritual energy given to them from on high. They're just like children in go-carts, who are unable to walk alone. God save you from a religion that depends on other people!

There are some who have a kind of lean-to religion, resting on somebody else. When the support is taken away, what becomes of the lean-to? The good old lady who helped you for so many years dies. Where is your religion then? The minister used to keep you going. You were like a spinning top, and he kept you spinning. When he is gone, where are you? Don't settle for a religion of that kind. I beg you to examine yourself. Though a helper is very useful, under certain conditions, even a Christian helper may be a hinderer.

Now, this is the point I've come to: you have to deal with Jesus right now, and to deal with Jesus, you need no *man*. You don't have to deal with pools and angels – you have to deal with the Lord Jesus himself. Suppose that there is no man to help you. Do you even *want* a man when Jesus is here? You wanted the man to put you into the pool. He isn't necessary to introduce you to Christ. You may speak to him yourself. You may negotiate mercy for yourself, and you must confess your sin yourself. You don't want a priest. You want a mediator between your soul and God, but you don't want any mediator between your soul and Jesus. You can come to him where you are and as you are. Come to him now, tell him your case, and plead with him for mercy. He doesn't want my help, and he doesn't want the help of the archbishop of Canterbury. He doesn't want the help of anybody. He alone can meet your needs. Just put your entire life into his hand. Then, if you have no man to be your helper, you don't need to lie down and fret about it, because he is able to completely save those who come to God by him.

Now this is all very plain talk, but we want plain talk nowadays. I feel as if I have not shared anything worthwhile, unless I try to bring men to Christ. There are many high and sublime doctrines that I would like to speak of and many deep and rapturous experiences that I would like to describe, but I feel that I must often leave these things and keep to the much more commonplace. These seem much more useful in the matter of persuading men, as I work for Christ, that they should look away from man, and away from ordinances, and away from self, and deal with Jesus himself distinctly and directly. Then there will be no need of man, and certainly there will be no need of delay.

The Savior Satisfied the Man's Case Entirely

This is my closing point. The Savior satisfied the man's case entirely. This afflicted man has no other man to help him. Christ can help him without man's assistance. This man can't even move except with great pain. He has to crawl to the water's edge. But he doesn't need to crawl there or even move an inch. The power to heal that man was in the Christ who stood there – commissioned by God to save sinners and to help the helpless. Every bit of the power that saves isn't in the saved man, but in the Christ who saves. Ignore and reject those who say that salvation is an evolution. The only thing that can ever evolve out of the sinful heart of man is sin, and nothing else. Salvation is the free gift of God, by Jesus Christ, and its work is supernatural. It is performed by the Lord himself, and he has power to do it, however dead in sin the sinner may be. As a living child of God, I can say that:

> "Upon a Life
> I have not lived,
> Upon a Death
> I did not die,
> Another's Life;
> Another's Death,
> I stake my whole eternity."

You who desire to be saved must do the same. You must look right past yourself to him whom God has exalted to be a Prince and Savior to the sons of men. The Christ met that man's dire needs, and he was able to do anything for him that he required. He meets your needs, because he can do anything for you that is necessary. Between here and heaven's gate, there will never be anything required which he cannot provide,

He can do anything for you that is necessary.

or any help needed which he is not prepared to render, for he has all power in heaven and on earth.

Next, the Lord can do more for you than you ask of him. This poor man never asked anything of Christ, except by his looks and by his lying there at the pool. If you feel like you cannot pray, if you have needs that you cannot describe, if there's something you want, and you don't even know what it is, Christ can give it to you. You'll know what it is when you get it, but perhaps now, in his mercy, he doesn't let you know all your needs. But here's the point: he *is able to do exceeding abundantly above all that we ask or think* (Ephesians 3:20). May he do it in you now. Take comfort from the cure of the impotent man, cherish hope, and say, "Why shouldn't he also heal me?"

The way Christ worked was very unique. He worked by a command. It's not a way you and I would have selected, or a way which some nominal Christians even acknowledge. He said to the man, *Rise.* He couldn't rise. *Take up thy bed.* He couldn't take up his bed. He had been unable to get off his bed for thirty-eight years. *Take up thy bed, and walk.* Walk? He couldn't walk. I have heard some objectors say, "That preacher says to people, 'Believe.' They can't believe. He commands them to 'Repent.' They can't repent."

Well, our Lord is our example, and he said to this man, who could not rise and could not take up his bed and could not walk, *Rise, take up thy bed, and walk.* That was his way of exercising his divine power, and that's the way Christ still saves men today. He gives us faith enough to say, *O ye dry bones hear the word of the LORD* (Ezekiel 37:4). They can't hear. *Behold, I will cause spirit to enter into you, and ye shall live* (Ezekiel 37:5). They can't live, but they hear, and they do live. And while we're acting by faith, delivering a command which looks to be absurd and unreasonable, the work of Christ is accomplished by that command. In ancient times, didn't he say in the darkness, *Let there be light*? To what did the Lord speak that word of power? He spoke to darkness and to nothingness. *And there was light.*

Now, he speaks to the sinner and says, *Believe, and live.* He believes, and he lives. God wants his messengers to let the sinner know that he doesn't have the strength to obey, that he is morally lost and ruined, but in the name of the eternal God say, "The Lord commands you,

Rise, take up your bed, and walk. Believe, repent, be converted, and be baptized, every one of you, in the name of the Lord Jesus Christ." This is the way Christ's power is brought to the sons of men. He said to the man with the withered hand, *Stretch forth thine hand,* and he did so (Matthew 12:13). He says to the dead, *Come forth,* and they come forth (John 11:43). His commands are always given with the ability to obey. Where his commands are faithfully preached, his power goes with them, and men are saved.

I will close with this observation. In obedience, power was given. The man didn't stop and wrangle with Christ and say, "Rise? What do you mean? You look like a friend, but do you come here to make fun of me? Rise? I've been lying here for thirty-eight years, and you say, *Rise.* Do you think that there has ever been a minute in those thirty-eight years when I wouldn't have gladly risen if I could have done so? Yet you say, *Rise.* And you say, *Take up your bed.* How can I do so? It's been thirty-eight years since I could lift a pound, and you command me to shoulder this mat on which I lie. Are you joking?

> His commands are always given with the ability to obey.

"You say, *Walk.* Walk? Hear me, all you who lie sick around me, he tells me to walk! I can barely lift a finger, yet he commands me to walk!" In this way, he might have argued the matter out, and it would have been a very logical piece of argument. The Savior would have stood convicted of having spoken empty words.

Instead of saying these things, however, no sooner did Christ say to him, *Rise,* than he willed to rise. As he willed to rise, he moved to rise, and rise he did, to his own astonishment. He rose. Then he stooped down and rolled up his mattress, all the while filled with wonder. Every part of his body sang as he rolled it up and quickly put it on his shoulder. To his surprise, he found that the joints of his feet and legs could move, and he walked away with his mattress on his shoulder. The miracle was complete.

"Stop, man, stop! Come here! Did you have the strength to do this by yourself?"

"No, I lay there thirty-eight years. I had no strength until that word *Rise* came to me."

"But did you do it?"

"Oh yes, you can plainly see that I did it. I rose, folded up the mattress, and walked away."

"But you were under the influence of some unseen force that made you move your legs and your hands, right?"

"Oh no, I did it freely, cheerfully, gladly. My dear sir, I clap my hands for joy to think that I could do it. I don't ever want to go back to that old mat and lie there again."

"Then what did you do?"

"Well, I barely know what I did. I believed him and did what he told me, and a strange, mysterious power came over me. That's the whole story."

"Now explain it. Tell these people all about it."

"Oh no," says the man, "I know that it happened, but I can't explain it. One thing I know. I was a cripple, and now I can walk. I was impotent, and now I can carry my bed. I was lying there, and now I can stand upright."

I can't explain salvation to you or how it takes place, but I remember when I sat in the pew as despairing a sinner as ever lived. I heard the preacher say, "Look to Christ, and live." He seemed to say to me, "Look! Look! Look! Look!" I looked, and I lived. That moment, the burden of my sin was gone. Unbelief no longer crippled me. I went home a sinner saved by grace and to live to praise the Lord.

> "E'er since by faith I saw the stream
> Thy flowing wounds supply,
> Redeeming love has been my theme,
> And shall be till I die."

I'm thrilled that so many will obey this gospel command: "Believe, and live. Believe in the Lord Jesus Christ, and you will be saved." Oh, do it! Do it now! To God be the glory and peace and happiness to you forever! Amen and Amen.

Chapter 3

A Singular but Needful Question

Dost thou desire to be made whole? (John 5:6)

Jesus spoke to the man who had been afflicted for thirty-eight years and asked him, *Dost thou desire to be made whole?* It seems to be a very strange question to ask. Who wouldn't desire to be made whole? Would the poor man have been lying at the pool in the first place if he wasn't anxious to be healed? The answer to Jesus's question must have been written all over his face as he gazed up at the Savior. However, since our Lord didn't use confusing language, it could be reasoned that the paralysis of the man's body had to a certain degree numbed his mind and brought on a paralysis of his will. He had hoped until his heart was sick. He had waited until despair had dried up his spirit. It had almost come to the point that he barely cared whether he was made whole or not. The bow had been bent so long that all its elasticity was destroyed. He had hungered until his appetite itself was gone. He was now consumed by hopelessness for the future because of all of his many disappointments. The Savior touched a chord which needed to vibrate when he asked about his desire, his will. That question aroused something within the man which was essential to a cure. *Dost thou desire to be made whole?* This was the inquiry of a profound investigation, the scientific probe of a great physician, the resurrection from the grave of a great master-power of manhood.

Now, in the matter of preaching the gospel today, it may seem almost like a disrespectful question for me to ask those of you who are not saved, *"Dost thou desire to be made whole?"*

"Sure," you will reply, "everyone desires salvation." Believe me, I'm not quite as certain as you are about the truth of that statement.

"But our being here," says one, "our having been here so long and our attentive listening to the gospel prove that we are willing to be made whole if we could only discover where that health is found and what the balm of Gilead actually is." Yet, I'm not surprised that there are many who have waited so long that they are beginning to be paralyzed in the very desires that they once held so dear. Others, who have been here a long time without conviction, now occupy these pews as a mere matter of custom and have no desire for the wholeness of soul which the Great Physician is always prepared to give to those who seek his help.

I am persuaded that instead of the question being an unnecessary one, it should be one of the first presented to every hearer. To get a truthful answer to this question, from the innermost soul of every hearer, is my objective now. I believe it will be a very healthy thing for you even if you are honestly compelled to give a negative answer. It will at least expose the condition of your heart to itself, and that may lead to something better. As God helps me, I will do my best to lay before you this question: Unsaved man or woman, *Dost thou desire to be made whole?*

Dost thou desire to be made whole?

It's important to ask this question first, because it's a question that is not always understood. It's not the same as this question: "Do you desire to be saved from going to hell?"

Everyone answers, "Yes."

"Do you desire to be saved so you will go to heaven?"

At once, without even thinking, everyone says, "Yes."

We all have a strong desire for the harps of gold, for the songs of blessedness, and for the eternity of immortality, but that is not the question. Heaven and its joys come out of what is proposed in our question, as a result, as a consequence, but that's not the matter at hand right now. We aren't saying to the thief, "Will you have your imprisonment ended?" We are asking him an entirely different question. "Are you willing to be made an honest man?" We aren't asking the murderer, "Would you like to escape the gallows?" We know his reply. The question we are asking is, "Do you desire to be made righteous, upright, kind, forgiving, so that you give up all this evil of yours?" It's not, "Are you willing to sit at the festival of mercy and eat and drink like those who are in health?" but, "Are you yourself willing to be made spiritually healthy, and to pass through the divine process by which the foul disease of sin can be cast out, and the healthiness of sanctified manhood can be restored to you?"

To help you to understand what that question means, let me remind you that there were only ever two men who were whole, perfectly whole. They can be called the two Adams, the first and the second Adam. These both showed us what a man would be if he were whole. The first Adam dwelled in the garden. We should all be willing to be in paradise with him. We should all be delighted to walk beneath those never-withering boughs and gather ever-luscious fruits, without toil, without suffering, without disease, and without death. We all should be glad enough to welcome the return of the ancient gladness of Eden, but that is not the question. It is, are we willing to be made mentally and morally into what Adam was before his sin brought disease into mankind? And what was Adam? He was a man who knew his God. He also knew many other things, but mainly and chiefly he knew his God. His delight was to walk with God, to commune with him, and to speak with him as a man speaks with his friend. Until he fell, his will remained in submission to the will of his Creator. He desired to obey the Lord in all things. He was placed in the garden to till the ground, to keep and care for the garden, and he did it all with joy. He was a whole, flawless man. The entirety of his enjoyment consisted in his God. It was his one purpose as a living creature to do the will of him that made him.

He knew nothing of rioting and drunkenness. For him, there were no crude songs or extravagant deeds. The flash of immorality and the glitter of overindulgence was far from him. He was pure, upright, chaste, and obedient. How would you like to be made like him, sinner? You who are pursuing your own will, you who have sought out many fantasies, you who find happiness in sin and filthiness, would you be willing to come back and find your happiness in God, and from that moment serve him alone? Perhaps you say, blindly, "Yes." It's possible that you don't know what you're saying. If the truth were more clearly presented to you, you would stubbornly refuse to be made whole. Life, under those circumstances, would seem tame, joyless, and slavish to you. Without the fire of lust, the excitement of drink, the laughter of foolishness, and the fake face of pride, what would existence be to many? To them, our concept of flawless manhood is only another name for bondage and misery.

Take the other example of a man who was whole. It was Jesus, the second Adam. He dwelled here among the sons of men, not in a paradise, but in the midst of disgrace, temptation, and suffering. Yet he was a whole, flawless man. He took sicknesses upon himself as if they were his own. Our sins were placed on him as our substitute, but in him was no sin. The prince of this world searched him through and through, but could find no sin in him. The perfection of our Savior's existence in the form of a man was made clear in that he was holy, innocent, undefiled, and separate from sinners. *For it was expedient that we have such a high priest, who is holy, innocent, undefiled, separate from sinners, and made higher than the heavens* (Hebrews 7:26).

He was holy. That word is, in its root, the same thing as *whole*. He was a complete, perfect, uninjured, untainted man. He was whole towards his God. It was his meat and drink to do the will of God who sent him. Jesus in the form of man was man just as God desired man to be. He remained just as he came from the Maker's hand, without blot, without loss, without a hint of evil, and without the absence of any good thing. He was whole and holy. For that reason, he was innocent and never inflicted harm on others in word or deed. He remained undefiled, never affected by the influences that surrounded him in a way that caused him to become false to his God or unkind to man. Even though blasphemy passed by his ear, it never polluted his heart. He saw the lust and wickedness of man carried to its climax, but he himself shook off the viper into the fire and remained blameless.

He was also separate from sinners. He didn't align himself with the Pharisees and say, "Stay back, because I am holier than you." He ate with them and still stayed separate from them. He was never more separate than when his compassionate hand touched them, or when he entered most deeply into sympathy with them in their sorrows. He was separate by his own mental perfection, moral superiority, and spiritual grandeur. Do you wish to be like Jesus? There's the question. If you did, it would involve you in much of his experience. You would be laughed at, scoffed, persecuted, and, unless God restrained your enemies, you might also be put to death. Are you willing to be made like him, to have the evil which you now admire torn away from you, and to have implanted in you the good which you don't appreciate at the moment?

Now, would you be willing to be made whole? You might say, "I want to be like Jesus. I truly desire it." However, if you allow me to gently and affectionately whisper in your ear, that if you knew what I meant, if you knew what Jesus was, I'm not so sure that you would be so inclined. I'm afraid that struggles and rebellion would rise up in your heart if you proceeded in the direction of making yourself whole as Jesus Christ was whole.

Allow me to further illustrate the meaning of the question, *Dost thou desire to be made whole?* When a man is whole, complete, and what a man should be, there are certain evil inclinations which are done away with and certain moral qualities which he is sure to possess. For instance, if a man is made whole before God, he is also made honest before men. No man can be whole while he is still guilty of wrongdoing in his business, in his thinking, in his conversation, or in his actions towards his neighbors. Sinner, many of your business practices would not stand the tests of God's all-searching eye. You often say in your dealings things that aren't true. You dismiss them with the excuse that others do the same. I'm not here to listen to your excuses, but I'm about to ask you in all seriousness, *Dost thou desire to be made whole?* Do you desire to be made, from this point forward, a devoted and honest man? No more lying, exaggerations, overreaching, and taking advantage. So, what do you think? There are some who could no longer carry on their business. The trade is rotten, and if you don't fall into its practices, you can't make a living. The district is a rough place, and no one can thrive in it but cheats. We would have to shut up the shop if we were perfectly honest. "Why," cries one, "I would be eaten alive by the competition. I can't believe that we must be so extremely honest." I see how it is; you don't want to be made whole.

He who is completely whole becomes restrained in all matters. *Not that which goes into the mouth defiles the man; but that which comes out of the mouth, this defiles the man* (Matthew 15:11). And, *for the kingdom of God is not food and drink,* yet men still frequently sin in both food and drink, and especially in the sin of drunkenness (Romans 14:17). Now I suppose it would be difficult to find a drunkard who, when he is sober, doesn't desire to be saved. But drunkard, understand the question. It is not, do you desire to go to heaven? It is this: Would you give up your drunkenness and no longer delight yourself in those cups of excess? *Now* what do you say? From this moment, are you willing to be done with all your disorder and immorality and throw them all away? Perhaps in the morning, some might say, "Yes," when their eyes are red, and they're experiencing the consequences of excess. But how about in the evening, when the throng of immoral behavior surrounds the man, and the wine sparkles in the cup, would he be made whole then and renounce those things which ruin his body and soul? No. Many say, "I would be made whole," but they don't mean it. *But it has happened unto them according to the true proverb, The dog returns unto his own vomit, and the sow that was washed to her wallowing in the mire* (2 Peter 2:22).

> A man who is made whole can forgive even to seventy times seven.

To be made whole produces universal truthfulness in the man. Now, there are people who can't stand to speak the truth. To them, two must always be twenty. In their eyes, the faults of any neighbor are crimes, and the noble virtues of any, except their favorites, are always tinged with vice. Naturally, they stir up malicious judgment towards others, and they are envious of anything honorable in their fellow man.

Now, what do you say, sir? Are you willing to be made whole, and from this hour speak nothing but the truth towards God and man? I am afraid many who don't lack for words now would have very little to say if they spoke nothing but the truth. And many men would, if they were honest enough to say it, refuse the blessing of being made perfectly truthful.

When it comes to the matter of forgiveness, a man who is made whole can forgive even to seventy times seven. When you can't forgive a wrong suffered, it's because your soul is sick. When a wrong is resented strongly, you are ill for the moment. When it's resented constantly, you suffer from a chronic disease. Some people are so far from wishing to know how to forgive that they would almost pray that they might live and die to fulfill their passion for revenge. They would follow the man who has done them a wrong through this world and the other too. They would be damned with him if they could only have the satisfaction of seeing him surrounded by the flames. Revenge is sweet to many men, and it's useless for a man to say, "I would be made whole," while he still cultivates hate and carries resentment towards his fellow man.

In this same way, I could present each of the virtues and vices and show that my text isn't quite as simple a question as some people think. Some men are afflicted with a miserly, grasping disposition. If they were whole, they would be generous, kind to the poor, and they would be ready to give from their abundance to the Lord's work. But would they choose to be made whole? No. They think generosity is weakness, and compassion is foolishness. What's the good of having money and giving it away? They say, "What's the good of getting it if you're not going to keep it? Truly, it's a wise man who can hold the most and part with as little of it as possible." This man doesn't want to be made whole. He considers his paralyzed hand and ossified heart to be the very evidence of health. He considers himself to be the only mentally healthy man around, even though his narrow-mindedness and withering soul are visible to all. He is a skeleton and the picture of sickness, and yet he believes himself to be the outstanding example of health. Those who admire their failings clearly have no desire to be free from them.

"What a beautiful cataract I have in my eye," says one.

"What a precious oozing sore decorates my arm," says another.

"What a delightful bow this is in my leg," says a third.

"What an attractive hump adorns my back," says another.

Men don't speak this way concerning their bodily diseases, or we would think they were crazy. But they often glory in their shame and rejoice in their iniquities. Whenever you meet a man who has a fault which he mentally elevates into a virtue, you have a man who would not wish to be made whole, and who would ignore a physician's visit if he waited at his door. These people are more common than we would think.

If a man is made whole, not only moral virtues will abound in him, but also spiritual graces. A man who is whole is fit in spirit as well as in outward character. So what would happen to a man if he were made whole in his spirit? *Two men went up into the temple to pray, the one a Pharisee, and the other a publican. The Pharisee stood and prayed thus with himself, God, I thank thee that I am not as other men are: extortioners, unjust, adulterers, or even as this publican. I fast two meals every sabbath; I give tithes of all that I possess. And the publican, standing afar off, would not lift up so much as his eyes unto heaven, but smote upon his breast, saying, God, reconcile me, a sinner. I tell you, this man went down to his house justified rather than the other; for anyone that exalts himself shall be humbled, and he that humbles himself shall be exalted* (Luke 18:10-14). You see, that Pharisee there is thanking God that he is as good as he should be and a great deal better than most people. Now, if that man is ever made whole, he will say, "God be merciful to me a sinner."

But if I were to ask him if he would like to change places with the publican, he would reply, "Why should I? He is a vulgar and wicked wretch. The language he uses is very appropriate to him, and I'm glad he uses it. It would be wrong for me to make the same confession as he does, and I don't intend to do it." That man doesn't want to be made whole, because he thinks he's whole already.

He who is made whole becomes a self-renouncing man. Paul was whole when he said, *And doubtless I even count all things as loss for the excellency of the knowledge of Christ Jesus my Lord, for whom I have suffered the loss of all things and do count them but dung, that I may win Christ and be found in him, not having my own righteousness, which is of the law, but that which is through the faith of Christ, the righteousness which is of God by faith* (Philippians 3:8-9). He counted his own righteousness to be dung, so he might win Christ and be found in him. He was a whole man. Sickly men think their own righteousness is good enough, wrap themselves in it, decorate it with the outward appearance of ceremony, and then conclude that they are right enough for heaven. They are so consumed by pride that they rave about their imagined goodness while they call real goodness hypocrisy.

He who is whole spiritually is a man of habitual prayer. He feels constant gratitude and exhibits continual praise. He is a man of abiding devotion. Whatever he does, he does it unto God and seeks only God's glory in it. His mind is fixed on things unseen and eternal. His heart isn't enslaved by the things that are seen, because he knows that they are unfruitful. Now, if we appealed to many, and they fully understood what we meant by it, and said, "Would you be made whole? Would you from this hour become a prayerful man, a man full of praise, a holy man, a God-serving man?" I believe that the majority, even of our congregations, if they spoke honestly, would say, "No. We don't want to be made whole. We would like to go to heaven, but we don't want this. We desire to escape from hell, but we don't have any desire to practice all this Puritanical precision which you call holiness. No. We would like to enjoy ourselves with sinners first, and go to heaven with the saints last. The poison is too sweet to give up right now, but we will take the antidote in the end. We will take breakfast with the devil and supper with Christ. We're in no hurry to be made pure. Our tastes are leading us in another direction for now."

Many Replies

Now that I've explained the question, I'll point out that this question can produce many different replies. Because of this, it's even more necessary for it to be asked and answered.

First, there are some whose reply to this question can be called *no answer at all.* They don't want to hear or consider anything of the sort. *Dost thou desire to be made whole?* "Well, we don't know what to say. We don't even want to be bothered with it. We are young, and there's plenty of time for us to think about these things later. We're business people, and we have more important things to do besides worry our minds about religion. We have money, we can't possibly be expected to look at these things the same way as poor and ignorant people are required to." Or, "We have a lot of health issues, and just taking care of ourselves takes up too much time to allow us to be concerned about theological difficulties." People will come up with any excuse to put from their mind the one thing that is necessary. The unencumbered soul is most precious and least valued.

Oh, how some of you play games with your souls and toy with your immortal interests! For a time, I did the same thing. If tears of blood could express my regret, I would attempt to weep them. The time wasted through a long carelessness about our soul's interests is something very serious. It's a loss of time which even mercy can't restore to us and even the grace of God can't give back. Young people, I wish that these were the things on your minds.

I can't even express to you how much I desire for these questions to be important, even pressingly, overwhelmingly important to you, so that you can't ignore the pressure on your spirit from the Holy Spirit who wants to awaken you. I desire for God to make you wise enough to desire the magnificent development of spiritual life, and the destruction of everything detrimental to your best welfare. Consider carefully this first and most important question. Don't give it the go-by. Your dying hour may be much nearer than you think. The tomorrow in which you plan to consider these things may never arrive. Let me put it another way. If you're going to put off anything, let it be something that can safely wait. If anything is to be postponed, don't let it be an eternal thing, a spiritual thing, *but seek ye first the kingdom of God and his righteousness* (Matthew 6:33).

There are some people who have invested a great deal of energy in religious activity, and still their answer to this question isn't a very sincere one. Years ago, they were aroused. When they heard a sermon, they treasured every word. They persisted in prayer, and their desires were full of enthusiasm, but they have never obeyed the command which says, "Believe in Christ and live." Misery and unbelief has become a habit to them. They have become accustomed to continuing under the burden of sin, which they will persist in carrying, when there's a dear Savior waiting to relieve them of the burden. And their answer to the question is neither one thing nor the other. They groan out feebly, "I wish that I wished, I want to desire, but my heart is hard."

> "'If aught is felt 'tis only pain
>   To find I cannot feel.'"

See to what a state you've brought yourself? May God help you to make a desperate effort with that will of yours. May the moving of his Spirit bless this word, so full of love, to your heart. I pray that you may say, "Yes! Out of my deep despair, out of the pit where there is no water, I still cry to you, my God. I desire deliverance out of the belly of hell. I will, I will, I desire to be saved. Oh, give me grace, so I may be made whole." May none of you continue to be numbered with those who virtually give no answer to the question.

Secondly, there are too many who give very evasive replies to the question. I must ask them the same question. *Dost thou desire to be made whole?* I'm anxious to present this question to every unconverted one, but I'm sure that from several I'll get no distinct reply. I'll hear one say, "How am I supposed to know if I'm God's elect or not?" That is not the question. That question can't be answered at this stage, but it will be answered.

So why do you need to bring up that subject, except to distract yourself from the serious question the text raises? Will you, or will you not, be made whole? Come on, don't shirk the question. Face it like a man. Are you willing to be reconciled to God and be obedient to him, or not? Say yes or no, and speak up. If you desire to be God's enemy and to love sin and unrighteousness, just say so. Be honest with yourself and see yourself in the light of truth.

But if you desire to be purified from sin and be made holy, say so. It's not something to boast in. "Well," says another, "I don't have the power to stop sinning." Again, I say, that is not the question. A distinction must be drawn between the will and the power. God will give the power, rest assured, in the same proportion as he gives the will. It's because our will is not there that the power is not there. When

> Are you willing to be reconciled to God and be obedient to him, or not?

a weak will comes, a small amount of power comes. But when the will becomes intense, then the power becomes intense too. They rise and fall together. But that isn't the question. I don't say, "What can you do?" but, "What do you desire to be?" Do you desire to be holy? Are you honestly anxious to be set free from the power of sin? There's the question, and I pray, for your soul's sake, that you look into your heart and answer this question like you're standing before God.

"But I've been so guilty in the past," says one, "that my former sins alarm me." Even though I'm glad you have a sense of your sin, I'll remind you that this is not the question. It's not how sick you are, but are you willing to be made whole? I know you're a sinner, and a much worse one than you think yourself to be. However black your sin is to your own eye, it's ten times blacker to God's eye, and you are an utterly condemned and lost sinner by nature. But the question now is, *Dost thou desire to be made whole?* It's not, "Do you desire to have your past forgiven and be delivered from the penalty of it?" Of course you do. But do you desire to be set free from the lusts that have been your delight, from the sins that have been your treasure? Do you desire to be delivered from the wants of your flesh and of your mind, the things your heart hungers after? Do you desire to be made like the saints are and like God is, holy and set free from sin? Is that the yearning of your spirit, or isn't it?

Now, I'll move on to the many people who say "No" to this. They don't evade the question, but they honestly say, "No." Actually, I must retract that statement. I question whether they honestly say "No." However, they say "No" by their actions. "I desire to be made whole," says one. But when the church service is over, he goes back to his sin. A man says he desires to be cured of his disease, but he continues to indulge in the very thing which gave him the disease. Is he untruthful or insane?

The eating of a certain meat may be the cause of the disease, the doctor tells the patient. The patients says he desires to be healed, but then immediately eats the very dish that caused his sickness. He is a liar, is he not? And he who says he desires to be made whole, and yet lingers in his old sin, doesn't he lie to himself and to his God? When a man desires to be made whole, he frequents the places where healing is given.

There are some who barely ever visit the house of God, who go once in a while on Sunday to hear the gospel, or who attend places because they are called places of worship. Here the gospel isn't preached, the conscience is never broken, and the demands of God's law and the promises of God's gospel are never fully insisted on. Still, they're quite content to go there and think they've done well, like a sick man who doesn't go to the physician who understands the case, but visits a quack's shop where there's a profession of curing, even though no one was ever cured. Such a person doesn't desire to be made whole. He wouldn't act like this if he did.

Again, how many hear the gospel but don't really listen? A bit of news on the Exchange, and they read it with both of their eyes – will there be a rise or fall of stocks? An article from which they can judge the general current of trade, they devour it with their minds, suck in the meaning, and then go and practice what they've gathered from it.

They hear a sermon, and the minister is judged on how he preached it. They are as critical as a man reading a book who says the capital letter wasn't well inked on the press, or the dot to the "i" had dropped off the letter. Like a man reading a business article who criticizes the style of the article, instead of trying to get at its meaning and act upon its advice. Men will think it to be the height of perfection to say they liked or disapproved of a sermon. As if the God-sent preacher cared one bit whether you did or did not like his sermon. His business is not to please your tastes, but to save your souls. It's not to win your admiration, but to win your hearts for Jesus and bring you to be reconciled to God.

Whether a sermon is liked should hardly be considered in the question. Similarly, a surgeon's scalpel is seldom admired by his patient. The surgeon who conscientiously removes the proud flesh, or prevents a wound from healing too rapidly, cannot expect admiration for his use of the knife while the sufferer still feels it. Nor does the preacher, when he faithfully declares the truth, expect the praise of men. If their actions endorse his words, it is enough.

My hearers, you give us lukewarm and critical hearing, anything but practical hearing. All this goes to prove that after all, even though you crowd our houses of prayer, you do not want to be made whole. Too many pick up the gospel like a man who likes to read might pick up a surgical manual to amuse himself with the pictures, but not to find out what will remove his own sickness. You do the same thing with the Bible. You read it as a sacred volume, but see no application to your own life. How little you understand of the deep heart, longing to find Jesus, to be reconciled to God, and to be delivered from the wrath to come! There are men who both by their non-hearing and their hearing, say, "We do not want to be made whole."

There are also many who don't desire to be made whole, because being made whole would involve their losing their present position in society. They don't want to part with their ungodly gains or wicked companions. Religion would involve them in some degree of persecution. They wouldn't like to be sneered at as a Methodist or Presbyterian.

They couldn't afford to go to heaven if the road was a little rough. Instead, they would prefer to go to hell, as long as the road which leads there is smooth and pleasant. They would rather be praised by fools, than be saved and suffer the disrespect of the wicked. They think it's inconvenient to be kind, annoying to be godly, shameful to be devoted, and foolish to believe in right and wrong. They would prefer to have the crown without the fight and the reward without the service. They would enjoy the benefits of a healthy soul, but don't want to lose the advantages of associating with the leprous and defiled. Poor fools.

Thank God, there are some who say, "Yes, I desire to be made whole." Whenever a positive answer is given to this question, we can be sure that a work of grace has begun in the soul. If anyone can earnestly say, "Yes, the desire of my heart is to be set free from sin," then my dear friend, I am happy and feel privileged to speak to you. If you say, "My motivation isn't fear of punishment, sin is punishment enough for me. If I could be in heaven and remain the sinner I am, it wouldn't be heaven to me. I want to be freed from every fault of thought, word, and deed. And if I could be perfect, I would be perfectly happy even if I were sick and poor."

If the Lord has made you long after holiness, there is in your heart already the embryo of grace, the seed of everlasting life. Before long, you will rejoice that you are born again, and are passed from death unto life. "Oh," you say, "I wish I could see that, I wish I could feel it!" I don't believe that any person devoid of grace could ever have hearty, earnest, intense longings after holiness, for its own sake. Now if you desire to get the joy and peace that comes from that grace, I have to say to you the same thing Jesus said to the poor man at Bethesda. He said, "Take up thy bed, and walk." Hear the word of the Lord and trust, right now, in the finished work of Jesus Christ, who was punished as a substitute for your guilt. Rely on him, and you will be a saved soul.

"Do I have the power to believe in Christ?" says one.

I answer, "Yes, you have the power. I wouldn't say to every man, 'You have the power to exercise faith,' because the desire of the will is the death of moral power. But if you are willing, you have the right, you have the privilege, and you have the power, to believe that Jesus died for you. You have the power to believe that God, who has made you to long after holiness, has prepared holiness for you. And the instrument that will work it in you is your faith. *For it is God who works in you both to will and to do of his good pleasure* (Philippians 2:13). Look to Christ and be saved." I pray that some of you may come to perfect peace, right now, by looking to Christ.

"I want holiness," you say. Yes, and it may seem a strange thing, but it's true, that while you seek holiness in yourself, you will never have it. But if you look away from yourself to Christ, then holiness will come to you. Even that very desire of yours has come to you from him. It's the beginning of the new birth in your soul. Look away from even your best desires to Christ on the cross, and this day shall be the day of your salvation.

It may seem a very little thing to have a desire, but the type of desire I have described is no little thing. It is more than human nature ever produced by itself, and only God the Eternal Spirit can implant it. I am convinced that a living, saving faith always goes with it. Sooner or later, it comes to the surface and brings joy and peace with it.

Finally, when this question is answered in the negative, it involves a most fearful sin. I wish I didn't have to teach on this last point, but I must, as painful as it is. There are some who are not willing to be made whole. You, my unconverted brethren, are unwilling. Face that now, because you will have to face it soon. It's just this: you prefer yourself to God. You prefer to please yourself before pleasing him, and you prefer sin to holiness.

Sin is your own deliberate choice.

Look at it closely and fairly. Sin is your own deliberate choice. You're making it now. You've made it before, and, I fear, will continue to make it if God's grace doesn't prevent you. Look it in the face, because soon, on your deathbed, you will see the whole matter in the light of eternity. Then you'll discover that you preferred the pleasures of this life to heaven. You preferred the parties, amusement, self-righteousness, pride, and self-will of a few fleeting years, over the glory and bliss of perfectly obeying Christ and being in his presence forever. When it's time to die – and certainly when you live in another state – you will curse yourself for having made such a choice as this. When you lie dying and unsaved, you will remember, *I am not here an unsaved man unwillingly. I refused to be made whole. I chose not to be a believer. I chose to be unrepentant. I heard the gospel. It was presented clearly to me, and I deliberately chose to ignore it and remain what I am. Now I'm dying unforgiven and unholy, and that was my choice.*

No spiritually unsound man can enter heaven. He must be made whole, or be shut out of glory. We can't stand in the most holy place until we are made perfect. So you, unhealed soul, remaining as you are, will never stand in God's presence. You choose, you deliberately choose, never to be admitted to the courts of paradise.

Furthermore, and this will strike you in a short time (how short I don't know, nor do you), there will be no entrance into heaven for you, because you elected not to enter heaven. There will remain only one other thing. You will be driven from his presence into the eternal burnings of his wrath. It will surely be one of the stings of hell, that you perish of your own free will. How you will cry, "I chose this, I chose this? I was a fool. I chose this." For what is hell? It is sin full-blown. Sin is evil in the conception, hell is sin fully developed. What will you think about in hell? *I chose misery from which there never can be any escape and a death out of which there can be no deliverance. I must die to God, to holiness, to happiness, and exist forever in everlasting death and eternal punishment, and all as the result of my own free will.*

Please look that in the face, I beg you. It seems to me to be the most dreadful element about the entire case of the lost sinner. When cast into hell, if they could say, "I'm here because of God's decree, and for no other reason," then they could find something with which to harden their spirit and endure the misery of their lost condition. But if they are forced to feel that their ruin is their own doing, and that they perish for their own sin and their personal rejection of Christ, then it is hell indeed. *Those flames, are they of my own kindling? This prison house, is it my own building? That door locked so tightly to never open, is it my own barring?* With this, the last remnant of consolation is taken away from their soul forever.

I hope you say, "I do desire to be made whole." Let me remind you again, that the place to find the fulfillment of that desire is at the foot of the cross. Stand there and hope in the great Redeemer. There is some life in you already, and the dying Savior will increase it. Stand at the foot of the cross where the precious drops of blood fall. See the flowing of his soul-redeeming blood, believe that he shed that blood for you, and you are saved. To those who desire to be made whole, Jesus says, *I will; be thou clean* (Matthew 8:3).

Chapter 4

The Hospital of Waiters
Visited with the Gospel

Jesus said unto him, Rise, take up thy bed, and walk.
(John 5:8)

It was the Sabbath day. Where would Jesus spend that day, and how? He would not spend it, we're quite sure, in any unholy manner or in any insignificant way. *What* would he do? He would do good, because it is lawful to do good on the Sabbath day. *Where* would he do good? He knew that there was a sight in Jerusalem which was particularly painful. The sight of a number of poor people – blind, lame, and afflicted – who were lying around a pool of water and waiting for a blessing which seldom came. He thought he would go and do good there, because good was most wanted there.

I pray to God that all Christ's servants would feel that the most urgent need had the greatest claim upon them, and that they ought to exercise the most kindness where there is the most need. I ask that he would impress upon his servants that no way of spending the Sabbath could be better than carrying the gospel of salvation to those who are most in need of it.

But it was a feast day as well. It was a great festival of the Jews, and Jesus had come up to Jerusalem to keep the feast. Where will he feast? Had someone asked him to their house? There were Mary and Martha and Lazarus down at Bethany. Would they ask him? Sometimes even

Pharisees and publicans would open their houses and make a banquet for him, but he wouldn't want the superficial praise of men. Where would he go?

Was it an unusual choice for him to say to himself, *My feast shall be kept among the blind, the afflicted, and the lame*? No, it was not unusual, because he had said to one who had invited him to his house, *But when thou makest a banquet, call the poor, the maimed, the lame, the blind, and thou shalt be blessed, for they cannot recompense thee; for thou shalt be recompensed at the resurrection of the just* (Luke 14:13-14). What he urged others to do, he would be sure to do himself.

It was just like him to say, "I will spend my feast in a hospital. I will use this day, sacred to joy and rest, by going where the sick multitudes lie thickly clustered together. It makes me happy to show mercy. To bless men is to find rest for my heart." Christ never feasts more joyfully than when he is doing good to others. The greater the act of his liberality, the more his blessed nature is filled with rest and joy.

So we see the Savior going down to the pool of Bethesda. He determined that he would exercise his mercy and overcome evil in the spot where sorrow and disease reigned supreme. I'll ask you to go with me, and with the Savior, down to Bethesda's pool. While we're there, we'll notice that Jesus Christ fixes his eyes upon the most helpless person among that waiting company. Then we'll see how our Lord dealt with the man in a gospel fashion.

First, we'll go down to the pool of Bethesda with its five porches. I call it the hospital of the waiters, because all the people who were there were doing one thing: they were waiting for the moving of the waters. There was nothing else they could do. They were lying sick with anxious eyes gazing upon the little pool, hoping to see it bubble up, hoping to see a widening circle forming upon its calm surface. They were waiting to plunge in immediately, because whoever plunged in first would receive a cure – one and no more. Wasn't I truthful when I said that it was a hospital of waiters?

Too easily, we could find a large company of waiters nowadays. I wish it wasn't so, but large numbers are always waiting. I think I personally know enough to fill all five porches.

Some are waiting for a more convenient time. Perhaps they believe that this more convenient time will come to them on a sick bed, or possibly even upon their deathbed. It's a great mistake. They've heard the gospel, and they believe it to be true, but they haven't accepted it. They attend a place of worship continually, and they say to themselves, "We hope that one of these days we'll be able to grab ahold of Christ and be healed of the disease of sin, but not now."

How many years have you been waiting for the convenient time? Some of you have been waiting five, six, eight, ten, or twenty years. I even know some who have been waiting more than twenty years. I remember speaking to them about their souls, and they said then that they didn't intend to neglect the matter. They were waiting, and the time had not quite come. They didn't exactly explain what stood in the way, but it was something that was to be resolved in a few months or maybe even weeks. But it hasn't been resolved, and they are still waiting.

I fear that they will wait until the judgment day comes and finds them unsaved. They always imagine a good tomorrow, but tomorrow is a day which you won't find in the almanac. It's found nowhere but in the fool's calendar. The wise man lives today. What his hand finds to do, he does at once with all his might. Today is God's time. And when we are saved, it will be our time too. But, sadly, many lie waiting until their joints stiffen, their eyes fail, their ears are heavy, and their hearts are more and more indifferent. Will it be this way forever? Will you wait until you are cast into hell?

In our second porch, a crowd of waiters waits for dreams and visions. You might think these are very few, but they are not as few as you imagine. They have an idea that perhaps one of these nights they'll have such a vivid dream of judgment that they will wake up alarmed, or such a bright vision of heaven that they will wake up fascinated by it. They've read in somebody's biography that he saw something in the air, or heard a voice, or had a text of Scripture "laid home to him" (as it's called). They are waiting until similar signs and wonders happen to them. I recognize that they are very anxious for this to happen, but their mistake is that they want it, or expect it, to happen at all.

They lie there by the pool of Bethesda waiting, and waiting, and waiting, as though they couldn't believe God, but they could believe in a dream. They couldn't place their confidence in the teaching of Holy

Scripture, but they could believe in a voice which they imagined to be sounding in their ears, even though it might be the chirp of a bird, or might be nothing at all. They could trust their imagination, but they can't trust the Word of God as it is written in the inspired volume. They want something over and above the sure word of testimony. The witness of God is not enough for them. They demand the witness of their desire, or the witness of feeling, and they are waiting in the porch by the pool until that comes. What is this but an insulting unbelief? Is the Lord not to be believed until a sign or a wonder corroborates his testimony? Such waiting provokes the Most High.

A third porch full of people will be found waiting for a sort of compulsion. They've heard that those who come to Christ are drawn by the Spirit of God. They believe the doctrines of grace, and I'm glad, because they are true, but they misinterpret those doctrines. They think the Spirit of God makes men do this or that against their wills, by exercising force. Their belief seems to be that men are taken to heaven by their ears or dragged by force. And, because we speak of cords of love and bands of a man, they pick out the imagery and mistranslate it.

Believe me, the Spirit of God never treats the human heart in the same way as you and I might treat a box to which we've lost the key. He doesn't wrench it and break it open. According to the laws of our nature, he acts with men *as men*. He draws with cords, but they are cords of love, and with bands, but they are bands of a man. It is by shining light on the judgment that he influences the will of man. He leads us to see things in a different light by the instruction which he gives to us. By that clearer light, he influences the understanding and the heart. The things we formerly loved, we see to be evil, and we hate them. And the things we once hated, we see to be good and choose them.

These people like to think that they will be made to repent whether they desire it or not. Somehow, they will be made to believe in Jesus Christ whether they want to or not. But that is not the way the Holy Spirit acts. Let me warn you about the great sin of putting the Holy Spirit into contrast or rivalry with Jesus Christ. The gospel is, *Believe on the Lord Jesus Christ, and thou shalt be saved.* So for you to say, "I am waiting for the Holy Spirit," is to place Jesus in a kind of opposition to the Holy

Spirit. When in reality, the Father, Son, and Holy Spirit all agree. They *are* one, and the testimony of Jesus is the testimony of the Holy Spirit.

So when the Holy Spirit works in men, he works with the things of Christ, not with any new things. He takes of the things of Christ, and reveals them to us. If a man rejects the gospel which says, *Believe and live*, he rejects the Holy Spirit. He will not bring any other gospel, but will leave him to believe in Jesus, or to die in his sins.

> When the Holy Spirit works in men, he works with the things of Christ, not with any new things.

You must have Christ, or perish. If you refuse to obey his gospel word, neither will God the Father nor God the Spirit intervene to deliver you. Jesus Christ has the Spirit to bear witness of him. When the Holy Spirit comes, he convinces men of sin, because they don't believe on Christ. He doesn't lead them to trust in some work over and above the work of Jesus, but to rest simply and alone on the atonement which Christ has provided. Woe to those who linger anywhere short of this!

The fourth porch is attractive to many people, especially at this peculiar time in history. They are waiting for a revival. We've heard happy news, in which we rejoice, of great revivals in different parts of England, Scotland, and Ireland.

There are some who say, "Oh, if a revival came here, I would be converted."

Another might proclaim, "If the two honored servants of God would come here and hold services, then, surely, we would be converted."

They look to men for their motivation. I thank God for every genuine revival. Whenever he works, I rejoice in it, but for any man to suppose that the gospel command is suspended for a time until a revival comes, is to suppose a lie. The gospel says, *Repent and be baptized each one of you* (Acts 2:38). So said Peter on the day of Pentecost. Or in other words, *Believe on the Lord Jesus Christ, and thou shalt be saved.*

The gospel call is, *Today if ye will hear his voice, harden not your hearts* (Hebrews 3:7-8). It doesn't say, "Wait, wait, wait for times of refreshing. Wait for a revival." I am inclined to think that even if a revival did come, people who are currently using it as an excuse for delay would be very unlikely to get a blessing from it. Or if they thought they got a blessing, it would in all probability be a mistake altogether, because they would be depending upon men, or upon fleshly excitement. They wouldn't be looking to Jesus Christ, who is just as able to save them now as he would be in a revival. He's just as able to save them by my voice now, or by no voice at all, as he would be by any other man, however useful that man may be. I fear there are many waiting in that porch.

Many are waiting in the porch of strong emotional experience. They want an experience, so they want the minister to preach a very alarming sermon. They want him to be very warmhearted and passionate, as he ought to be, but they also want him to fix them, to shoot the arrow into their flesh, so they will be pierced in the heart. It is for this that they wait. They come here every Sunday, and they have been touched a great deal and made to feel very uneasy. They've felt as if they could hardly sit through the sermon, but they somehow managed to do it. They have managed to wait and wait.

When will I reach you? How am I to preach? Surely, if I knew how I could bring you to Jesus Christ, it would be my delight to do it. But I can't preach any other gospel than the one I preach, and I can't do it more plainly. Neither do I think I can do it with more passion, because I desire the salvation of sinners with my whole soul. Many may preach it better, but none more from the heart than I do. If you're looking for me to do something more, you will look in vain, because I have nothing better to bring. I have pointed you to a Savior's flowing wounds and begged you look to him and live. If you won't accept his salvation, then I have no other hope to set before you. If you won't trust my Lord, not even an angel from heaven could give you any other hope. If men won't hear the gospel I've preached, neither will they be converted even if one rises from the dead. *And he said unto him, If they do not hear Moses and the prophets, neither will they be persuaded, even though one rose from the dead* (Luke 16:31).

I've shown you five porches of waiting. Now, I'll tell you why I'm sure they are wrong to wait. I will set before you their theory. The people around the pool waited, because an angel would come and stir the water, and whoever stepped in first would be healed. That was their idea. They weren't looking to Jesus, any of them.

Hadn't they heard that Jesus was healing the sick? Had they never heard about the woman who came behind him in the crowd, touched his garment, and was healed from her issue of blood? Had they never heard of a nobleman's son who was at the point of death and was made to live? Had they never heard of any of this? I don't know, but it's clear that they never tried to get to Jesus, nor did they cry out to him. They trusted wholly in the pool, the angel, and the stirring of the water.

If they had been wise, they would have said, "This is uncertain and only happens occasionally, but Jesus says, *he that comes to me I will in no wise cast out* (John 6:37). He is able to save completely those who come to God by him. It would make the most sense to crawl as best we can to those dear feet and look up into his face and say, *Jesus, thou Son of David, have mercy on me* (Luke 18:38)."

Here we have the opposition theory to the gospel, and I want to knock it to pieces if the Holy Spirit will help me. It's the theory of waiting and of looking for something, instead of looking to Christ alone. These people attach great importance to *the place*. They remained at the pool of Bethesda. There was the place. If they would ever get anything good, they would get it there. In the same way, I find that waiters often attach great importance to the place of worship. They expect to find salvation there only. Don't you know that Jesus can save your souls tomorrow morning while you're at work, just as well as next Sunday in the tabernacle? Don't you know that Jesus is just as much a Savior on Saturday as on Sunday? Don't you know that when you are walking in the streets, in Cheapside or in the Borough, if you breathe a prayer to him, he is just as mighty to save you as he would be if you were on your knees, or at home, or sitting here and listening to the gospel? He is wherever there is a heart that wants him. Wherever there is an eye that desires to look to him with the glance of faith, there Jesus is. There are no pools of Bethesda now. Those would only be places set apart to monopolize the dispensation of divine mercy.

> "Wherever we seek him, he is found,
> And every place is hallowed ground."

So get to him in these pews, because this is a place where he is. If you were lying on your sickbed, I would tell you he was there. If you were hard at work at a carpenter's bench or out in the fields driving the plough, I would have nothing more to say to you than this: *The word is near thee, even in thy mouth and in thy heart: that is, the word of faith, which we preach, that if thou shalt confess with thy mouth the Lord Jesus and shalt believe in thine heart that God has raised him from the dead, thou shalt be saved* (Romans 10:8-9). The theory that we are to wait at the pool of rules is antichrist's gospel. Christ's gospel is *Believe on the Lord Jesus Christ, and thou shalt be saved.*

Then they say that they are waiting for signs and wonders. Those who waited at Bethesda waited for an angel. I don't know whether they ever saw an angel or if the water was stirred mysteriously by an invisible wing, but they waited for an angel – a mystery. People like a mystery, but the craving is evil, because even though the gospel is in one respect the mystery of godliness, as far as sinners are concerned, it's the plainest thing in all the world. It is this: *Believe on the Lord Jesus Christ, and thou shalt be saved.* God has presented Him to be a payment for sin.

> Whoever trusts Christ to stand in his place, and so accepts Christ to be his substitute, is a saved man.

The blood of Jesus is a substitutionary offering to God's justice instead of our death. Whoever trusts Christ to stand in his place, and so accepts Christ to be his substitute, is a saved man. Priests try to make a mystery out of everything nowadays, and this is that word which is written upon the forehead of the whore of Babylon, according to the book of Revelation. *Upon her forehead was a name written, MYSTERY, BABYLON THE GREAT, THE MOTHER OF THE HARLOTS AND OF THE ABOMINATIONS OF THE EARTH* (Revelation 17:5). Her mass is a mystery, and her ceremonies are all mysteries. The Latin language is used to make the service a mystery. The priest himself is a mystery. Baptism is a mystery.

However, in the gospel of Jesus Christ, the essential truth is as plain as the nose on your face. In his poem "Truth," William Cowper writes, "Legible only by the light they give, stand the soul-quickening words – believe, and live." A man who is almost an idiot can even understand this. Trust Christ. Accept Christ to be your substitute before God, and you are saved on the spot, saved in an instant. No, they wait and pine for a mystery. They even believe that the Holy Spirit himself has come upon them to confuse the gospel, when in reality, what he does is make the gospel even more clear to us. When he comes, he tears the mystery away, removes the scales from our eyes, and makes us see that it's a simple matter to receive Jesus and become the sons of God.

Again, these waiters, who attach so much importance to place and are waiting for mysteries, appear to be waiting also for an influence which is intermittent. It was only at a certain season that the angel stirred the pool. So they seem to think that there are only certain times and seasons when Christ is willing to receive sinners, and occasional intervals when they can hope to find salvation.

However, the mercy of my God isn't like the pool of Bethesda, stirred only now and then. It's a well of water always springing up, and whoever believes in Jesus, whether it's morning, noon, or night, will find that Christ is ready to receive sinners. The words *Come, for all things are now ready* are one of the gospel proclamations (Luke 14:17). Things are ready, and ready now. They're not ready sometimes, but at all times. It's not now and then, occasionally, on Sundays, high days, and revival days. He says, *Today if ye will hear his voice* (Hebrews 3:15). Also, *now is the acceptable time; behold, now is the day of saving health* (2 Corinthians 6:2).

Therefore, because these people think that there's a certain intermittent influence, they believe that all they have to do is wait, but they wait in a very strange way. If I was scheduled to be hanged tomorrow morning, and I knew that an application had been made for pardon, I would wait for the result. But how do you think I would wait? Suppose I had no hope of heaven, and knew I would be hanged tomorrow, and I had a slim chance a pardon might come, I would wait for it. But how would I wait? Would I go to sleep tonight? Would I make a feast and get drunk?

No, my life, my very life is in jeopardy. I can't take it lightly. How do sailors on a wrecked vessel wait for the lifeboat? Do you think they are idle? No, they strain their eyes as they watch for help and busy themselves with signals of distress, begging for help. Do they go to sleep on the wreck and say, "If we are to be saved, we will be saved. Let's go to sleep"? No, they are waiting, and if a vessel appeared with a rope, they would grab ahold of it without hesitation and wait no more.

It's a lie, nine times out of ten, when men say they are waiting for Christ, because they don't have intense anxiety or the painful uneasiness of mind which goes with true waiting. It's really only a make-believe waiting, a mere excuse. Whatever sort of waiting it is, it is the direct opposite to the gospel, which never says a word about waiting, but commands men to believe and live.

Besides, these people are waiting for a very limited influence. Only one person was healed at a time at Bethesda, and he was the first who plunged in. So when the waiters hear of anyone being saved, they think that he was in more favorable circumstances than themselves, that he was placed in a better position for obtaining salvation. They seem to be in the rear of the ranks, and unable to get to this wonderful pool of theirs.

It's all a mistake. Jesus Christ is as near to one seeker as another. If a man has been moral, the gospel says to him, *believe*. If a man has been immoral, the gospel cries to him, *believe*. If a man is a king, the gospel commands him to *believe*. If he is a beggar, it begs him also to *believe*. If a man is full of self-righteousness, the gospel points him to Christ and tells him to give up his righteousness. If a man is full of depravity and rotten with sin, it points him to Christ and begs him to give up his sin and look to Jesus.

So the basis upon which the gospel addresses sinners is the same at all times. It doesn't say less or more to the child of the harlot than to the child of the Christian woman. It presents the same pardon to the great sinner and the little sinner (if there is such a thing), and presents the same rich blessing to the chief of sinners as it does to the children of godly parents. Don't get false notions in your head. The same Lord over all is generous to all who call upon him. Like-faith obtains a like-blessing. There is a limit, because *The Lord knows those that are his* (2 Timothy 2:19). But in the preaching of the gospel, we are not bound by a decree which is secret, but by our marching orders. *And he said unto them, Go ye into all the world and preach the gospel to every creature. He that believes and is baptized shall be saved, but he that believes not shall be condemned* (Mark 16:15-16). He who commanded me to preach to every creature didn't exempt one soul from my message.

There you have it. I have tried to show why so many wait, and I will add only one thing more on this point. Some of these people who are waiting rely heavily on other people. Even this poor man said, *I have no man when the water is troubled to put me into the pool.* I receive letters every week from people in distress who ask me to pray for them, which I cheerfully do, but as a general rule I say to them, "Dear friends, I beg you not to try quieting your mind by asking me to pray for you. That's not your hope. *Believe on the Lord Jesus Christ, and thou shalt be saved,* whether you are prayed for or not."

I try to get them away from their reliance on anybody's prayers, to look to Jesus alone. Don't say, "I'll ask my friends to pray for me and then be at ease." You may say it if you like, but don't rest in that, I beg you. Jesus Christ is to be looked to, not other people's prayers. If you look to Jesus you will have immediate salvation. But even if the whole church of God went down on its knees at one time and stayed there for the next fifty years praying for you, you would certainly be damned if you didn't believe in Jesus. If you pray for yourself and look to Jesus alone, you shall most assuredly be saved. Isn't that enough about the dreary hospital full of waiters?

Now let's look at this from another angle. When Jesus Christ entered the hospital, he looked around and picked out the most helpless man in the whole world. I noticed on the theater billboard a line which said, "The poorest people are the most welcome." That's a gospel sentence, and that's how it is with Christ. He always loves to give his mercy to those who want it most. There lay that man, and he didn't think of Christ, but Christ stood and looked at him. He didn't know Jesus Christ, but Jesus Christ knew him, and he knew that he had been a long time in that condition. He knew that he had been sick for thirty-eight years. He knew all that, and he knew, before the man told him, that he must have been disappointed quite often, and, indeed, he *had* been. He had often tried, as well as his paralyzed body would enable him, to get into the water, but somebody, even some blind man who had managed to get nearer the edge and had the use of his limbs, plunged in first and came up with his eyes open while this poor, nervous creature couldn't get into the water in time.

He had seen many others cured, and that had made his disease even more painful to him. Their cures had not encouraged him, but rather made him sadder. He was the most indecisive, wavering kind of man you've ever met. In comparison, read the story of the man whose eyes were opened by Christ. He said, *one thing I know, that having been blind, now I see* (John 9:25). There's a fine, hardheaded fellow. He might have been a Scotsman! But *this* man was indecisive, wavering, and weak in mind.

You even know some such people. Perhaps you have them in your family. You can't help them. If you set them up in business, they are sure to fail. Whatever they do, it never succeeds. They are a poor, weak, childish sort of people, who need to be put in a basket and carried on somebody else's back all through life. There are people of this sort when it comes to religion, and this man was the type of them.

He desperately longed to be healed, but he didn't say that. Jesus asked him, *Dost thou desire to be made whole?* He didn't say, "Oh Lord, I desire it with all my heart." Instead, he went on with a rambling story, saying, *I have no man when the water is troubled to put me into the pool,* and so on. When our Lord *did* heal him, he didn't ask Christ his name. When he found that out afterwards, he went like an idiot to the Pharisees and told them directly who his benefactor was, and so got the Lord into trouble.

The wonders of grace belong to God.

There are still these kinds of people. They barely know their own mind. They know they want to be saved, but they seldom say as much. They are convicted easily enough, but they get convicted the other way almost as easily. They are indecisive and unstable. However, our Lord and Master picked out this very man to be the subject of his healing energy.

The wonders of grace belong to God. He said himself, *I thank thee, O Father, Lord of heaven and earth, that thou hast hid these things from the wise and prudent and hast revealed them unto babes; even so, Father; for so it seemed good in thy sight* (Luke 10:21). For *God has chosen that which is the foolishness of the world to confound the wise, and God has chosen that which is the weakness of the world to put to shame the things which are mighty; and that which is vile of the world and that which is despised God has chosen, and things which are not, to bring to nought the things that are* (1 Corinthians 1:27-28).

This poor, hapless, helpless, paralyzed man, almost as paralyzed in his brain as he was in his body, was pitied by our gracious Lord. So who is the most helpless man or woman in this place today? I know some of you are saying, "I'm afraid that's me." I have good news for you. You're just the sort our Lord loves to begin with. Don't be offended by the description, but be willing to embrace it. You're probably looking back on your past life and are compelled to say, "Well, that's really what I've been. I have plenty of wits about me in business, and I'm sharp enough there. But when it comes to religion, I'm afraid that I'm just that kind of fool. I have no resolution. I have no fixed determination. I'm always being led around by temptation or drawn the wrong way by evil companions." My poor friend, lie down at the feet of Jesus Christ in all your helplessness, in all your stupidity, and pray for the Lord to look upon you.

A brother once said to me, "I wish you would never speak to any-body but *sensible* sinners."

I said, "Well, I'm happy to preach to sensible sinners when they come to hear me, but so many stupid sinners come along with them that I'm bound to preach to them as well." And I do. I present the gospel to those who feel like they're oblivious and stupid in everything, and who consider themselves among the foolish. Jesus has come to seek and save poor, lost, ruined, dead sinners, and I pray for him to look on you at this time.

My third point is how Jesus Christ dealt with the man. If Jesus Christ had belonged to a certain class of ministers, he would have said, "Well done, man, you're lying at the pool of religious rules, and there you had better lie." He didn't belong to that way of thinking, so he didn't say anything of the sort. Neither did he say, as some brethren do, "My dear friend, you should pray." Very proper advice in some respects, but Jesus didn't give it. He knew better. He didn't say, "Now, you must begin to pray and wait before the Lord." That's a very good thing to say to some people, but it's not the gospel for sinners.

Jesus Christ didn't say to his disciples, "Go into all the world and tell people to pray." No. He said, *Go ye into all the world and preach the gospel to every creature. He that believes and is baptized shall be saved.*

So what did Jesus Christ do to him? He gave him a command. *Rise, take up thy bed, and walk.* The words sound like three thunderclaps. "But he can't, he can't. He is paralyzed!" Yes, but the gospel is a command,

and we read about some who disobey the gospel. A man can't disobey what isn't a command. He can't be disobedient unless there is a command to begin with. Jesus Christ brought the gospel blessing of healing to him as a command. He said, *Rise, take up thy bed, and walk.* It was a command which implied faith, because the man could not rise, and could not take up his bed, and could not walk of himself. However, if he believed in Jesus Christ, he could rise, and take up his bed, and walk. So it was really a command to exercise faith in Jesus and to prove it by practical works. But the man couldn't do it. That has nothing to do with it. The power isn't in the sinner, but in the one giving the command. He couldn't rise on his own, but Jesus Christ could make him do so. And when I, or any other minister of the Lord Jesus, in the power of the Holy Spirit, address you, chosen sinner, and say to you, "Trust Jesus Christ," we don't do so because we believe there is any strength in you, any more than there was in the paralyzed man. We speak in the power of the name of Jesus of Nazareth, who has sent us to say to you, "Rise up and walk." I trust the Lord to send his power with the gospel. I know very well that I have no power of my own, but he who sent me will bless his own message as he pleases.

If you are to get salvation, you will get it by believing in Jesus and rising at once out of the state you are now in. By his power, through the simple act of believing in him, you will be made whole. The man believed in Jesus. That was all he did. The wavering fool that he was, indecisive and all that, he had enough sense, and God gave him enough grace, to simply believe in Jesus. He made up his mind to try his legs, and to his surprise – oh, how astonished he must have been – those poor legs would bear him! He stood and found he could stoop, and he rolled up his mattress, picked it up, and walked away with it. What joy went through his body.

You've been ill, but the Lord has restored you. You got up and found yourself able to walk. Wasn't it a delight to you? I know the sensation well. What must it be like to be paralyzed for thirty-eight years, and then to be able to stoop, roll up a bed, put it on your back, and walk away? It must have been a delight to feel new life leaping through his nerves and muscles and veins. Now, if a sinner says, "Well, I never tried it before, but by the grace of God, I will trust my soul in the hands of Jesus.

> "I do believe, I will believe,
>   That Jesus died for me,
> And on the cross he shed his blood
>   From sin to set me free."

Then, sinner, you will rise up and walk. You will be surprised yourself to find the mighty change which God is working in you by his blessed Spirit through that simple act of faith. You will descend those tabernacle steps hardly knowing where you are, singing for joy, because the Lord has taken you out of the hospital of waiters, and placed you among the believers. He has said, *Then the lame one shall leap as a hart, and the tongue of the dumb shall praise; for waters shall be dug in the wilderness, and streams in the desert* (Isaiah 35:6).

> **Then, sinner, you will rise up and walk.**

Jesus Christ treated this man in a gospel way, for the way in which faith came into that man is very remarkable. He didn't know Jesus Christ, so why did he believe in him? It was this. He didn't know who he was, but he knew he was somebody very wonderful. There was a look about him, a majestic gleam in his eye, a wonderful force in the tone of that voice, a power very different from what the man had ever seen before. He didn't know who he was and didn't know his name, but somehow confidence was born in his soul.

How much more, then, may faith come to you who know that Jesus Christ is the Son of God. You know that he died and made a full atonement for sin, that he has risen from the dead, and that he sits at the right hand of God the Father. You know that all power is given to him in heaven and on earth, and that *he is able also to save to the uttermost those that come unto God by him, seeing he ever lives to make intercession for them* (Hebrews 7:25). Don't say, "I'll try and get faith." That's not the way. If I want to believe a statement, how do I accomplish that? Why, I hear it, and *faith comes by hearing* (Romans 10:17). If I have any doubt about it, I hear it again and ask to have it repeated to me more fully. And, when I've heard it again, conviction flashes upon me. So Jesus in the gospel says, *Incline your ear, and come unto me: hear, and your soul shall live; and I will make an eternal covenant with you, even the sure mercies of David* (Isaiah 55:3). *Hear me; believe me* – this is, in its briefest form, the gospel which Jesus preaches to men's hearts. God gives his witness concerning Christ that he is his Son, for out of heaven he spoke and said, *This is my beloved Son, in whom I am well pleased* (Matthew 3:17). Won't you believe him? *And there are three that bear witness on earth, the Spirit and the water and the blood; and these three agree in one* (1 John 5:8). Believe Jesus Christ. The evidence is strong. Yield up your soul to it, and you will find joy, peace, and eternal life.

The man's belief in Jesus, actively proved by his rising, settled the matter. That's a very different scenario than lying and waiting. I think that this man, if he had thought about it, would go back and say to others lying and waiting, "Why are you waiting and lying still? I was lying and waiting for thirty-eight years, and I got nothing at all by lying and waiting. Neither will you." Simple as he was, he would have said, "I'll tell you what is better than lying and waiting. There's a man among us, Jesus Christ, the Son of God. If we trust him, he will heal us, because he heals all kinds of diseases. If you can't go to him, send a messenger to him, because he even healed a nobleman's son from many miles away. Believe him, and blessing will go out of him, for it's not possible for any to trust him and not be healed." I would have liked to have been that man, simpleton as I might have been, to have the opportunity to tell those poor souls who were lying and waiting, the difference between lying and waiting, and immediately believing. I would put it in the simplest way I could, because I waited myself when I was a child. I heard a lot of preaching that led me to wait. I think I would have kept on waiting if I hadn't heard a poor Primitive Methodist brother cry, "Look, young man, look now!" I looked then and there, and I found salvation on the spot, and I've never lost it.

I have nothing else to say to you, but there is light in a look at the Crucified One, and every man who looks will have it *here, now,* and *at once.* Oh, that many would look! Don't you understand? Christ took upon himself the wrath of God, instead of those who trust him. Jesus Christ took the sins of all who trust him. He was punished instead of every believer, so that God will not punish a believer, because he has punished Christ in his place. Christ died for the man who believes in him, so that it would be injustice on the part of God to punish that man, because how will he punish twice for the same offence? Faith is the seal and evidence that you were redeemed nineteen hundred years ago upon the bloody tree of Calvary. You are justified, and who will bring any charges against you? *Who is he that condemns them? Christ, Jesus, is he who died and, even more, he that also rose again, who furthermore is at the right hand of God, who also makes entreaty for us* (Romans 8:34). This is the gospel of your salvation.

"Oh, but I don't feel." Did I say anything about feeling? You will have feeling after you have faith.

"But I'm not right." I don't care what you are or aren't. Jesus says, *Verily, verily, I say unto you, He that believes in me has eternal life* (John 6:47).

"Oh, but . . . ." Away with your "buts." Here's the gospel: *And the Spirit and the bride say, Come. And let him that hears say, Come. And let him that is thirsty come; and whosoever will, let him take of the water of life freely* (Revelation 22:17). What the Spirit and the bride of Christ say, surely I may say, and *do* say. May God bless the saying of it, and may you accept it, you waiting ones. May you look, believe, and live, for Jesus's sake! Amen.

Chapter 5

The Work of Grace

He answered them, He that made me whole, the same said unto me, Take up thy bed and walk. (John 5:11)

Just a few observations on the narrative itself. It was a feast day, and Jesus Christ came up to Jerusalem to find opportunities for doing good among the crowds of his countrymen. I can picture the whole city glad and the voice of rejoicing in every house as they kept the high festival and ate the fat and drank the sweet wine. *Then he said unto them, Go, eat the fat, and drink sweet wine, and send portions unto those who have nothing prepared; for this day is holy unto our Lord, and not sad; for the joy of the LORD is your strength* (Nehemiah 8:10).

But where does Jesus keep the feast? How does he spend his holiday? He walks among the poor, whom he loves so well. We see him in the hospital. There was one notable Bethesda, or house of mercy, in Jerusalem. It wasn't enough for the city's abounding sickness, but such as it was it was greatly prized. There was a pool which every now and then was stirred by an angel's wing and worked an occasional cure. Around it, charitable people had built five porches, and there on the cold stone steps a number of blind, lame, and withered folk were lying, each one upon his own wretched pallet, waiting for the moving of the waters.

There were the weary children of pain, suffering while others were feasting, racked with pain in the midst of general rejoicing, sighing in the presence of universal singing. Our Lord was at home among this misery, because there was room for his tender heart and powerful hand. His soul feasted by doing good. Let us learn this lesson: in the times of our brightest joys, we should remember the sorrowful and find a still higher joy in doing them good. If we are privileged to experience joy in our day, let us in the same proportion make it joyful to the sick and poor around us. Let us keep the feast by sending portions to those for whom nothing is prepared, so their hunger doesn't bring a curse upon our feasting. When we prosper in business, let us set aside a portion for the poor. When we are full of health and strength, let us remember those to whom these privileges are denied and aid those who minister to them. Those who visit the sick and care for them like the Lord Jesus will be blessed.

As he entered the hospital, our Lord noticed a certain man whose situation was a very sad one. There were many painful cases there, but he singled out this man. It would seem that the reason for his choice was that the poor creature was in the worst condition of all. If misery has a claim on pity, then the greater the sufferer, the more mercy is attracted to him. This poor victim of rheumatism or paralysis had been bound by his infirmity for thirty-eight years. Let's hope there was no worse case in all of Bethesda's porches! Thirty-eight years is more than half the appointed period of human life. One year of pain or paralysis is a wearying length of torture, but think of thirty-eight! We should pity the man who endures the pain of rheumatism even for an hour, but how can we sufficiently pity him who hasn't been free from it for close to forty years?

Even if his condition wasn't one of pain, but of paralysis, the inability to work and the consequent poverty of so many years were by no means a small evil. So our Lord selects the worst case to be dealt with by his curing hand, as a type of what he often does in the kingdom of grace, and as a lesson instructing us to give our first aid to those who are most in need.

The man whom Jesus healed was by no means an attractive character. Our Savior said to him when he was healed, *Sin no more, lest a worse thing come unto thee.* From that statement, it's not a stretch to think that his first infirmity had come upon him by his sinful lifestyle or some habit of excess. In some way or other, he had done something which brought upon his body the suffering which he was enduring.

It's generally considered to be a point beyond all dispute that we should help the worthy, but when a man brings calamity upon himself by wrongdoing, we are justified in letting him suffer, so he may reap what he has sown. This cold, pharisaic idea is very palatable to minds which are focused on saving their coins. It springs up in many hearts, or rather in places where hearts ought to be, and it is generally regarded as if it were a rule of wisdom which it would be sinful to dispute, an infallible and universal principle.

I will venture to say that our Savior never taught us to confine our giving to the deserving. He would never have bestowed grace on any one of us if he had carried out that rule. If you and I had only received what we deserved from the hand of God, we would have never been in this house of prayer. We cannot afford to mold our charity into a sort of petty justice, and spoil our giving by man-made rules. When a man is suffering, let us pity him, however the suffering has come. When a man had been in misery for as long as thirty-eight years, it was time to consider his infirmity more than his iniquity and to think about his present sorrow more than his former folly. That's how Jesus thought.

> When a man is suffering, let us pity him, however the suffering has come.

So he came to the sinner, not with reproach, but with restoration. He saw his disease rather than his depravity and gave him pity instead of punishment. Our God is kind to the unthankful and to the evil. *Be ye therefore merciful, as your Father also is merciful* (Luke 6:36). Our Lord said, *But I say unto you, Love your enemies, bless those that curse you, do good to those that hate you, and pray for those who speak evil about you, and persecute you; that ye may be sons of your Father who is in the heavens, for he makes his sun to rise on the evil and on the good and sends rain on the just and on the unjust* (Matthew 5:44-45). Let us imitate him in this, and wherever there is pain and sorrow, let it be our joy to relieve it.

In addition to the assumption that this man had at some time been grossly guilty, it seems pretty clear from the text that he was a poor, lazy, discouraged, lifeless, stupid sort of being. He had never managed to get into the pool, even though others had done so who were just as afflicted as him. He had never been able to win a friend or secure a helper. Considering the extreme length of his infirmity, one would have thought that at some point or another he might have found a man to place him in the pool when the angel gave it the mystic stir. Our Savior asked him, *Dost thou desire to be made whole?* This leads us to think that he had fallen into such a listless, despairing, heartsick condition, that even though he came daily to the edge of the pool as a matter of habit, he hadn't only ceased to hope, but had also almost ceased to desire.

Our Lord touched the chord which was most likely to respond – his will and desire to be made whole. But the response was a very feeble one. His answer shows what a poor creature he was, because there's not a glimmer of hope in it, or even of desire. It's a wail, a hopeless dirge, a grievous complaint. *I have no man when the water is troubled to put me into the pool, but while I am coming, another steps down before me.*

However, the utter imbecility and lack of a brain of the poor creature is most seen in the fact that like a simpleton he went to Christ's enemies and told them that it was Jesus who had made him whole. I am sure there was no malice in his informing our Lord's enemies. If there had been, he would have said, "It was Jesus who commanded me take up my bed." Instead, he said that it was Jesus who had made him whole.

I hardly dare to hope, as some do, that there was much gratitude about this testimony, though I have no doubt that the poor soul was grateful. I believe that his long endurance of pain, acting upon a weak mind, had brought him to an almost imbecilic state of mind, so that he spoke without thought. Therefore, our Lord didn't require much of him. He didn't even ask for a distinct declaration of faith from him, but only for that small measure of it which might be implied in his answering the question, *Dost thou desire to be made whole?*

This poor man displayed none of the shrewdness of the man born blind, who answered the Pharisees so intelligently. He was of quite another type and could do no more than state his own case to Jesus. Thank God, even that was enough for our Lord to work with. The Lord Jesus saves people of all sorts. He has among his disciples men of quick and ready wit, who can baffle their opponents, but just as often:

"He takes the fool and makes him know
   The wonders of his dying love:
To bring aspiring wisdom low,
   And all its pride reprove."

Here, he chose this poor simpleton of a creature and performed a great marvel upon him, to the praise of his heavenly grace.

We must also note that this man's mind, though there wasn't much of it, was engrossed and filled up with the fact that he had been made whole. He knew next to nothing about the person of Jesus. He had only seen him for an instant, and he didn't know that it was Jesus. His one idea of Jesus was: *He that made me whole.*

Now, beloved brethren, this was natural in his case, and it will be equally natural in our own. Even when the saved ones are more intelligent than this poor paralytic, they must still first think of the Son of God as their Savior, as he that made them whole. They may not know much about the Lord, but they do know that he has saved them. They were burdened with guilt and full of misery. They couldn't rest day or night until he gave them peace. They may not be able to tell another much concerning the glory of his person, his attributes, his relationships, his offices, or his work, but they can say, "One thing I know. I was blinded by error, but now I see. I was paralyzed by sin, but now I'm able to stand upright and walk in his ways."

This poor soul knew the Lord through experience, and that's the best way of knowing him. Actual contact with him yields a surer knowledge and a truer knowledge than all the reading in the world. In the kingdom of Christ, wonderful things happen, such as conversion and finding peace with God. Happy are those to whom these things are personal experiences. Great deeds are done by the Lord Jesus when men are turned from the error of their ways and their hearts find rest and peace in Christ. If you are acquainted with these two things, even though you might be ignorant of a great deal else, don't be afraid to emphasize their importance, but set your mind on them, and call Jesus by that name – *He that made me whole.* Think of him that way, and you will have a very valuable and influential idea of him. You will see greater things than these, but for the present, let these happy and sure facts fill your mind, even as his being made whole filled this man's mind.

As for the faultfinding Pharisees, they took no notice of the glorious fact of the man's cure. They willfully ignored what Christ had done, but they pounced on that little, insignificant fact that it had been done on the Sabbath day. Then they invested all their thoughts and emotions on that side issue. They make no mention of the man being restored, but they rage, because he carried his bed on the Sabbath day.

It is much the same with the men of the world today. They habitually ignore the fact of conversion. If they don't deny it, they look at it as being a matter not worth caring about. Even though they see the harlot made pure, the thief made honest, the profane made devout, the despairing made joyful, and other moral and spiritual changes of the utmost-practical value, they forget all this and attack some peculiar point of doctrine, mode of speech, or different practice, and raise a storm concerning these.

Is it because the facts themselves, if looked at fairly, would establish what they don't want to believe? They persistently forget the fact that Christianity is doing marvels in the world, such as nothing else ever did, but that fact is just what you and I must as persistently remember. We must dwell on what Christ has, by his Holy Spirit, worked within our nature by renewing us in the spirit of our minds. We must make this work of grace our focus, which will establish our faith and justify our conduct. This poor man did so. He didn't know much else, but he knew that he had been made whole, and from that fact he justified himself in what he had done. *He that made me whole, the same said unto me, Take up thy bed and walk.*

This is the truth I want to expand on. First, by saying that the work of Christ furnishes us with a justification for our obedience to his command – *He that made me whole, the same said unto me, Take up thy bed and walk* – that is our complete justification for what we do. In the second place, the work of Jesus Christ places an obligation on us to do what he asks of us. If he that made me whole says to me, *Take up thy bed and walk,* I am bound to do it, and I should feel the obligation of his goodness pressing upon me. Thirdly, it's not only a justification and an obligation, but the deed of grace also becomes a pressure to obedience.

"He that said unto me, *rise,* and so made me whole, by that same word of power he made me take up my bed and walk." The power which saves us also moves us to obey our Savior. We don't fulfill the will of our Lord with our own might, but with power which the Healer gives us in that very moment. Therefore, you see the drift of our discourse. May the Holy Spirit lead us into the power of this truth, because I am persuaded that a sense of the Lord's work within us is a great force, and should be stimulated and applied to the highest ends.

Justification

This poor man could not defend the action of taking up his bed and walking, because his enemies were educated in the law, and he was not. You and I could defend it very easily, because it seems to us a very proper thing to do under the circumstances.

The weight of his bed wasn't much more than a heavy coat; it was a simple rug or mat upon which he was lying. There really was no violation of God's law of the Sabbath, so there was really nothing to excuse. But the rabbis laid down rules of which I will give you but one example: *It is unlawful to carry a handkerchief loose in the pocket, but if you pin it to your pocket or tie it round your waist as a girdle you may carry it anywhere, because it becomes a part of your dress.* To my unsophisticated mind, it would have seemed that the pin increased the cumbersome burden and added the weight of the pin which was more than was necessary!

> The power which saves us also moves us to obey our Savior.

This was quite serious business according to rabbinical estimates. Most of the rabbinical regulations with regard to the Sabbath were absolutely ludicrous, but this poor man was not in a position to say so or even to think so, because, like the rest of his countrymen, he stood in awe of the scribes and doctors. These learned Pharisees and priests were too highly regarded for this poor creature to answer them in their own manner. So he did what you and I must always do when we are at all puzzled – he hid behind the Lord Jesus and pleaded, *"He that made me whole, the same said unto me, Take up thy bed."* That was quite enough for him, and he quoted it as if he felt that it should be enough for those who questioned him. Truly, it should have been. I may not be able to find in my own knowledge and ability an authority equal to the authority of learned unbelievers, but my personal experience of the power of grace will stand me in as good a position as this man's cure was to him. He argued that there must be enough authority in the man who made him whole to match the greatest rabbi who ever lived. Even his poor, feeble mind could grasp that, and surely you and I have the ability to do the same. We can defend ourselves behind the protection of our Savior's gracious work and the undeniable authority which belongs to him.

There are certain ordinances which a Christian man is bound to pay attention to, about which the world raises a storm of questions. The world does not take notice that a man was once a drunkard and has through divine grace become sober, and because of this has become a good father, a good husband, and a good citizen. It lets that miracle pass by unnoticed, but when he is going to be baptized, they immediately object to the ordinance. Or when he plans to join a Christian church, they jeer at him as a Presbyterian or a Methodist. It doesn't really matter what sort of label they give him as long as he is a better man than them, and is redeemed from sin, and taught to be upright and pure in the sight of God.

The work of grace counts for nothing with them, but they treat the peculiarities of sect or religious rite as a matter of life or death. They are blind creatures to despise the medicine which heals because of the bottle which contains it, or the name on the label. However, our answer is, "He that made us whole." He gave us a command, and we will stand by that command. We seek no justification but this: that he who worked a miracle of grace upon us asked us to do it. What if I am about to be baptized as a believer? The same one who said, *Believe*, also said, *Be baptized*. He who gave me salvation said, *He that believes and is baptized shall be saved*.

We place the divine authority of Jesus over and against all objections. He, by whose blood we are cleansed and by whose Spirit we are renewed, is Lord and lawgiver to us. His command is our sufficient authority.

If we go to the communion table and critics say, "What is the use of eating a piece of bread and drinking a drop of wine? Why think so seriously of something so small?"

We reply, "He that made us whole, the same said, 'Do this in remembrance of me.'"

We reject what he has not ordained, but we cling to his statutes. If he had commanded a rite even more trivial, or a ceremony even more open to objection in the eyes of carnal man, we would make no further apology than this: He – who has created us anew, given us a hope of heaven, and led us to seek after perfect holiness – has asked us do it. This is our final reply, and although we could find other justifications, they would be superfluous. Our defense is that the Savior commands it.

Doctrines

The same apology applies to all the doctrines of the gospel. I say again, ungodly men will not admit, or if they admit it they ignore it, that the gospel works a marvelous change in men's hearts. If they want proof, we can find them instances by the hundreds and by the thousands, of the reclaiming, elevating, and purifying power of the gospel of Jesus Christ. The gospel is working spiritual miracles daily, but they forget this and go on to find fault with its peculiar doctrines. They often take issue with justification by faith. "Well now," they say, "that is a shocking doctrine. If you teach men that they are to be saved by faith alone, and not by their works, of course they will lead loose lives. If you continually declare that salvation is by grace alone, and not by virtue, the inevitable result will be that men will sin so that grace may abound."

We find a complete answer to this lie in the fact that believers in justification by faith and in the doctrines of grace are among the best and purest of men, and that, in fact, these truths work holiness, but we do not desire to argue this point. Instead, we prefer to remind our adversaries that he who has caused us to be regenerate men also taught us that whosoever believeth in him shall be saved. He expressly declared that the one who believes in him has everlasting life. *For God so loved the world that he gave his only begotten Son, that whosoever believes in him should not perish but have eternal life* (John 3:16).

By the mouth of his servant Paul, he said that by grace are men saved through faith, and that not of themselves, it is the gift of God. *For by grace are ye saved through faith and that not of yourselves: it is the gift of God* (Ephesians 2:8). He has also told us that *by the works of the law shall no flesh be justified*, and he has commanded us to declare that *the just shall live by faith* (Galatians 2:16; Hebrews 10:38). He who is daily by his gospel turning men from sin to holiness has given this for the sum total of the gospel we are to preach: *Look unto me, and be ye saved, all the ends of the earth* (Isaiah 45:22). If this gospel does not make men better and change their evil natures, you may question it if you like, and we understand why you would. But as it continues its purifying work, we won't be embarrassed or hesitate to declare the doctrines which are its essence and life. Our regeneration proves to us our Lord's authority, and upon that we are prepared to base our belief. To us, the best of evidence is his work within us. In that evidence we place our absolute faith.

Precepts

The same applies also to all the precepts which the Christian is called to obey. For instance, if he is true to his colors, he keeps himself separated from all the sinful pleasures, practices, and policies of the world in which others take delight. Because of this position, the ungodly world says that he is strange, narrow-minded, and opinionated. This is how the Christian should respond: "He that made us whole, the same said to us, you *are not of the world, even as I am not of the world* (John 17:16). *Therefore come out from among them, and be ye separate, saith the Lord, and do not touch the unclean thing; and I will receive you* (2 Corinthians 6:17)."

If you follow the precepts of the Lord Jesus Christ, you may answer all charges of narrow-mindedness by presenting the supreme authority of the Savior, whose power has made you a new creature. Where his word is, there is a power to which we bow at once. It is not ours to question our Savior, but to obey him. We are cleansed by his blood. We are redeemed by his death, and we live by his life. Therefore, we are not ashamed to take up his cross and follow him.

This defense should even satisfy those who oppose us, because if they felt as grateful as we do, they would obey also. At any rate, they should say, "We cannot blame these men for doing as Jesus commands them, because he has done so much for them." Surely, the poor man who had been paralyzed for thirty-eight years couldn't be blamed for obeying the command of one who in a moment restored him to health and strength. If he became his servant for life, who would find fault in him? Who would say that he too easily submitted? Shouldn't such a benefactor exert an unlimited influence over him? What could be more natural and proper?

You unconverted people must excuse us, if we, in obedience to our Lord Jesus, do things which to you seem very outside the norm. Although we wouldn't needlessly offend, we cannot please you at the risk of displeasing our Lord. We don't owe as much to you as we owe to him. We don't owe as much to the whole world as we owe to the Lord Jesus. In fact, to tell the truth, we don't feel that we owe *anything* to the world. *For it should suffice us that during the time past of our life we had done the will of the Gentiles* (1 Peter 4:3). When we are asked the question, "What fruit came of those things of which you are now ashamed?" we have to confess that we had no fruit, except the sour grapes which have set our teeth on edge. Like the shipmen who put out to sea against Paul's advice, our only gain has been loss and damage. In serving the world, we found the labor to be weariness and the wages to be death.

> But as for our Lord Jesus, we owe him everything.

But as for our Lord Jesus, we owe him everything. So you must excuse us if we try to follow him in everything. It seems to us that this is an excuse which you should accept from us as thorough reasoning, but if you refuse it, we aren't at all surprised. However, it is quite sufficient for *us*, and even more than sufficient, it makes us glory in what we do. Does Jesus command it? Then it is ours to obey. Objectors may say his commands are unsuitable to the times or outdated or unnecessary, but all this is no concern of ours. If Jesus commanded us to do it, his command stands for us in the place of reasoning. He who made us whole gives us sufficient reason for obedience in that very fact. Some might say, "Oh, but it's contrary to what the fathers teach and to what the church teaches." We care not the snap of our finger for all the fathers and all the churches under heaven if they go contrary to what our Lord teaches, for *they* didn't make us whole, and we aren't under obligation to them as we are to him.

The authority of Jesus is supreme, because it's from his lips that we received the word which healed the sickness of our sin. This satisfies our conscience now, and it will do so amid the seriousness of death. How can we make a mistake if we follow the words of Jesus in all things? My brethren, we can plead our confidence in his command at the last great day – before the Judge of the quick and the dead. What better plea can we have than this: "You made us whole, and you asked us to do this." Such a justification of our conduct will make our death pillow *soft* and our resurrection bright with joy.

Instead of admitting that this isn't an ample justification, let's go further still in the strength of it. If the world considers us vile for obeying our Lord, let us be viler still. Inasmuch as he that made us whole said, *Go ye into all the world and preach the gospel to every creature*, let us make every effort to spread abroad everywhere the delight of his name, devoting ourselves body, soul, and spirit to the extension of his kingdom (Mark 16:15). He who made us whole will make the world whole yet by his own wondrous power. Have we not abundantly shown that our Lord's command is a solid justification of our conduct?

Obligation

Secondly, the cure brought forth an obligation. *He that made me whole, the same said unto me, Take up thy bed and walk.* First, if he made me whole, he is divine, or he could not do this miracle. Or, to say the very least, he must have divine authorization. If he is divine, or divinely authorized, I must be bound to obey the orders which he issues. Isn't that a plain argument which even the poor, simple mind of the paralytic man was able to grasp and put to use? Let us try and feel the force of that argument ourselves. Jesus who has saved us is our God; shouldn't we obey him? Since he is clothed with divine power and majesty, shouldn't we meticulously make every effort to know his will, and attempt to carry it out in every point with passion and zeal, as his Spirit enables us?

In addition to his divine character – which the miracle proved and displayed – there was the goodness which shone in the deed of power and touched the poor man's heart. His argument was, "I *must* do what my great Deliverer commands me. How can you think otherwise? Didn't he make me whole? Would you have *me*, whom he graciously restored, refuse to fulfill his desire? Must I not take up my bed the moment he gives me strength to do it? How can I do otherwise? Is this how I should pay back my good Physician, at once to refuse to do what he asks of me? Don't you see that I'm under an obligation which it would be shameful to deny? He restores these limbs, and I am bound to do with them what he orders me do with them. He says 'walk,' and since these once-withered feet have been restored, shall I not walk? He commands me to roll up my bed, and since I couldn't have used my hands until just now, his word gave them life. Shouldn't I use them to roll up the bed at his command? These poor shoulders of mine were bent with weakness, but he has made me stand upright. Since he now asks me to carry my bed, shouldn't I throw the mattress on my shoulders and bear the easy load which he lays upon me?" There was no good argument to such reasoning. Whatever might have been the claim of Jesus upon others, he clearly had an indisputable right to the loyal obedience of one whom he had made perfectly whole.

Follow me briefly in this, brothers and sisters. If you've been saved by the grace of God, your salvation has put you under obligation from that point forward to do what Jesus asks of you. Are you redeemed? *Know ye not that your body is the temple of the Holy Spirit who is in you, whom ye have of God, and that ye are not your own? For ye are bought with a price, therefore glorify God in your body and in your spirit, which are God's* (1 Corinthians 6:19-20). Have you been blessed by what the Lord has done for you by rescuing you from satanic slavery and adopting you into the divine family? Then it clearly follows that, because you are sons, you should be obedient to the law of the household. Isn't this a first element of sonship, that you should demonstrate your devotion to the great Father of the family?

The Lord has been pleased to put away your sin; you are forgiven. But doesn't pardon demand change? Should we go back to the old sins from which we have been cleansed? Should we live in the iniquities from which we have been washed by the blood of our Lord Jesus? That's horrible to even think of. It would be nothing less than wickedness for a man to say, "I have been forgiven, and therefore I will sin again." There is no remission where there is no repentance. The guilt of sin remains on that man in whom the love of sin still remains. Let us essentially feel the force of this, and follow after purity and righteousness from that point forward.

Brothers and sisters, upon whom Christ has performed his great work, you have experienced the love of God. So if God has loved you in this way, you are bound to love him in return. If God has loved you, you must also love your fellow man. Doesn't our love of God and love of man spring up as *the love of God is poured out in our hearts*? (Romans 5:5). Doesn't everyone see the necessity which calls for the one love to follow the other? Love is the mother of obedience, so everything connected with our Lord places us under obligation to obey him. There isn't a single blessing of the covenant that doesn't entail a corresponding duty. Here, I barely like to say *duty*, because these blessings of the covenant make duty to be our privilege and holiness to be our delight. So, from this point forward, we would no longer live in sin, but having been made heirs of heaven we devote ourselves to leading a heavenly life. So even while we are here below, our conversation can be in heaven, from where we look for the Savior, the Lord Jesus Christ. Brethren, he that made you whole has commanded this to be done by you: Keep the King's commandment.

As Mary said to the waiters at the wedding at Cana, so say I to you, *Whatsoever he saith unto you, do it.* Does he ask you to pray? Then pray without ceasing. Does he ask you to watch as well as pray? Then guard every act, and thought, and word. Does he ask you to love your brethren? Then love them fervently and with a pure heart. Does he ask you to serve them and humble yourself for his sake? Then do so and become the servant of all. Has he said, *Be ye holy; for I am holy*? (1 Peter 1:16). Then aim at this by his Holy Spirit. Has he said, *Be ye therefore perfect, even as your Father who is in the heavens is perfect*? (Matthew 5:48). Then strive after perfection, because he who made you whole has a right to direct your way, and it will be both your safety and your happiness to submit yourselves to his commands.

Constraint

Now I call your attention, in the third place, to the text under the sense of constraint. *He that made me whole, the same said unto me, Take up thy bed and walk.* He made him whole by saying, *Rise, take up thy bed.*

The carrying of the bed was part and parcel of the cure. The first part of the healing word was "rise," but the second was "take up thy bed." Now, it wasn't an ordinary word which Jesus spoke to that man. It wasn't a mere word of advice, warning, or command, but a word full of power, like that which created light out of darkness. When the Lord said to the poor man, "Rise," he meant, "Rise." A thrill went through the man. Those stagnant blood vessels felt the lifeblood stir and flow. Those dormant nerves were aroused to sensations of health, and those withered sinews and muscles braced themselves for energetic action, because omnipotence had visited the impotent man and restored him. It must have been a wondrous joy to his long-paralyzed, nerveless, powerless frame to be capable of healthy motion, to be able to bear a happy burden. The joyful man rolled up his bed, threw it on his back, and marched away with the best of them. The bed-carrying was part of the cure and proof of the cure. The paralytic man had not been called upon to deliberate as to whether he should rise or not. Jesus said, "Rise," and he stood upright. Then he said, "Take up thy bed," and the bed was up at once, and according to the last word, "walk," the man walked with delight.

> When the Lord said to the poor man, "Rise," he meant, "Rise."

It was all done by the power of one thrilling sentence, which didn't linger long enough to be questioned, but accomplished the end for which the Lord had sent it. The restored man didn't carry his bed unwillingly, but he did do it out of constraint, because the same power which made him whole made him obedient. Before the divine energy had touched him, he barely seemed to have any will at all. The Lord had to hunt to find a will in him, saying, Wilt thou be made whole? But after his healing, he cheerfully wills obedience to the one who healed him and carried out the Lord's command.

Taking up his bed, and walking, was done by Christ's enabling and by Christ's constraining, and I pray that you may know by experience what this means. What I want your response to be is this: "I can *only* obey Christ, because by his Holy Spirit he has spoken me into a life which will never die and never be defeated. He has spoken a word in me which has a continuous force over me and thrills me through and through continually. I can no more help seeking to obey Christ than this man could help carrying his bed when the Lord, by a word of power, told him to do so."

Brethren, be instructed and warned. Do you feel reluctant to enter into your Lord's service because of conscious weakness? Has the devil tempted you to draw back from obedience because of your unfitness? Do you hesitate? Do you tremble? Surely, you need to draw near to the Lord again and hear his voice anew. Take your Bible and let him speak to you again out of the Word, and may the same thrill which awoke you out of your death-sleep wake you out of your present lethargy. There is a need for the living Word of God to come home to your inmost soul again with that same miraculous power which dwelt in it at first. "Lord, quicken thou me," is David's prayer, but it suits me every day, and I think most of God's people would do well to use it daily. "Lord, speak life into me now as you did at first. Speak power, speak spiritual force into me."

The charity of the Christ constrains us, says the apostle Paul (2 Corinthians 5:14). This constraint is what we want to feel more and more. We need divine life to carry us forward to acts of obedience. We don't want to destroy willingness, but we desire to have it stimulated into entire subservience to the will of the Lord. Like Noah's ark on dry land, the will keeps its place by its own dead weight. Oh, for a flood of grace to move, to lift, to carry it away by a mighty current. We would be carried before the love of Christ as a tiny piece of wood is drifted by the Gulf Stream, or as one of the specks which dance in the sunbeam would be carried by a rushing wind. As the impulse, which began with Jesus, found the poor man passive and then impelled him on to active movements as with a rush of power, so may it always be with us throughout life. May we forever yield to the divine impulse. To be passive in the Lord's hands is a good desire, but to be what I would call actively passive, cheerfully submissive, and willing to give up our will, this is a higher spiritual state of mind.

We must live, and yet not we, but Christ in us. We must act, and yet we must say, "He that made me whole commanded me to do this holy deed, and I do it because his power moves me to do so. If I have done well, I lay the honor at his feet. If I hope to do well in the future, it is because I hope for strength from him to do well and believe that he will work in me by that same power which converted me in the first place." Beloved, make every effort to dwell under this influence. May the Holy Spirit bring you there!

My last word is a practical lesson. The church of God on earth at this present time anxiously desires to spread her influence over the world. For Christ's sake, we wish to have the truths we preach acknowledged and the precepts which we deliver obeyed. But no church will ever have power over the masses of this or any other land, except in proportion as she does them good. The day has long since passed in which any church can hope to succeed on the plea of history. "Look at what we were" is a vain appeal. Men only care about what we are. The sect which glorifies itself with the faded laurels of past centuries and is content to be inactive today, is near its inglorious end. In the race of usefulness, men nowadays care less about the pedigree of the horse and more about the rate at which it can run. The history of a congregation or a sect is of little value compared to the practical good which it is doing.

Now, if any church under heaven can show that it is making men honest, temperate, pure, moral, holy, that it is seeking out the ignorant and instructing them, that it is seeking out the fallen and reclaiming them, that in fact it is turning moral waste into gardens, and taking the weeds and briars of the wilderness and transforming them into precious fruit-bearing trees, then the world will be ready to hear its claims and consider them. If a church cannot prove its usefulness, the source of its moral strength will have gone, and something even worse than this will have happened, because its spiritual strength will have gone too. It is clear that a barren church is without the fruitful Spirit of God. Brethren, you may, if you want, dignify your minister by the name of *bishop* and give your deacons and elders grand, official titles. You may call your place of worship a cathedral, and you may worship, if you desire, with all the grandeur of pompous ceremony and the adornments of music, incense, and the like, but you will only have the resemblance of power over human minds unless you have something more than these things.

But if you have a church (it doesn't matter by what name it's called) that is devout, holy, living unto God, doing good in its neighborhood, spreading holiness and righteousness by the lives of its members, and that is really making the world whole in the name of Jesus, then you'll find that even the most carnal and thoughtless will eventually say, "The church which is doing this much good is worthy of respect, so let's hear what it has to say." Living usefulness will not screen us from persecution, but it will save us from contempt. A holy church goes with authority to the world in the name of Jesus Christ its Lord, and the Holy Spirit uses this force to bring human hearts into subjection to the truth.

Oh, if only the church of God would believe in Jesus's power to heal sick souls. Remember that this man, thirty-eight years sick, had been ill longer than Christ had lived on earth. He had been afflicted seven years before Christ was born. In the same way, this poor world has been afflicted for a very long time. Years before Pentecost or the birth of the present visible church, the poor, sinful world lay at the pool and could not stir. We must not be hopeless about it, because the Lord is still going to cast sin out of it. Let us go in Jesus Christ's name and proclaim the everlasting gospel and say, *Rise, take up thy bed, and walk*, and it will be done. God will be glorified, and we will be blessed.

Chapter 6

God's Works Made Manifest

Jesus answered, Neither has this man sinned nor his parents, but that the works of God should be made manifest in him. (John 9:3)

Never attribute any sorrow endured by men to some special sin. There is a tendency to think that those on whom the tower in Siloam fell must have been sinners worse than all men who dwelt in Jerusalem. If any have met with a very sudden death, we tend to suppose that they must have been exceedingly guilty – but it is not so. Very godly men have been burned to death in a train; I remember one who came to that terrible end. Many holy men have been drowned on board ship as they've been going about their Master's errands. And some of the most gracious men I've ever met have dropped dead without a moment's warning. You cannot judge a man's state before God by the circumstances which happen to him in this life, and it is very unkind, ungenerous, and almost inhuman, to sit down, like the friends of Job, and suppose that, because Job is greatly afflicted, he must also be greatly sinful. It is not so. All afflictions are not chastisements for sin. There are some afflictions that have quite another end and object. They are sent to refine, sent as a holy discipline, sent as sacred excavators, to make more room in the heart for Christ and his love. You know that it is written, *As many as I love, I rebuke and chasten* (Revelation 3:19).

And, *for whom the Lord loves, he chastens and scourges everyone whom he receives as a son* (Hebrews 12:6).

So it was absurd to suppose that if a man was born blind it was a punishment for the sin of his parents or a punishment sent beforehand for some sin which he might commit at some point in the future. Our Savior asks us to regard infirmities and physical evils as sent to be a space wherein God can display his power and his grace. This was the case in this particular instance. And I'm going to push the fact further and say that even sin itself, existing as it does everywhere, provides the opportunity for what we call "elbow room" for the grace of God. It may even become a platform upon which the wonderful power, patience, and sovereignty of divine grace can be displayed.

We're going to look at how God takes opportunities from the sorrows and sins of men to display his own works and glory. This man was born blind in order that, through his blindness, the power of God might be seen in giving him sight. So I think there are many in whom the power of God can very readily be seen and the works of God be very clearly displayed.

What Works of God Are Seen in the Salvation of Men?

We observe a man who is all out of order; there is nothing right about him. He is a man upside down. His heart loves that which will ruin it, and does not love that which would bless it. His understanding is darkened. He exchanges bitter for sweet, and sweet for bitter. His will has become very domineering and has usurped power which it never ought to possess. If you study him well, you won't make much of him. He is all out of gear, like a piece of machinery in which the wheels don't operate correctly. To describe him briefly in one word, I would say that he is in a state of chaos. Everything is in confusion and disorder, tossed up and down. "Well," says one, "that's my case. I am like that right now."

Creation

The first work of God that we read about in the Bible is the work of creation. *In the beginning God created the heavens and the earth* (Genesis 1:1). When it came time for the event of fitting together the world which we generally call creation, although it was really the arrangement of that which had been created, the Lord came forth. And the Spirit of God, with outspread wings, brooded over chaos and brought order out of confusion. Oh, if only the Spirit of the Lord would come and brood over that man's confused and confounded mind where everything is tossed about in wild disorder! He can't even tell why he was born or for what reason he is living. He seems to have no purpose in life and is tossed to and fro like a log in the ocean. His passions fly from vanity to vanity, and you can't put him into order. His mother tried it, but he despised being tied to her apron strings. Many friends have tried it since then, but he has now taken the bit into his mouth, has run away, and refuses to obey the reins.

Oh God, if you will come and make him a new creature in Christ Jesus, your creating work will be made manifest in him! If you will mold, model, form, and fashion him until he becomes a vessel fit for your use, then the work of God will begin to be clearly seen in him. Oh, that it might be so! There are some of us here who can bear witness that God is a great Creator, because he has made all things new within us and transformed what before was chaos into a world of beauty and delight where he delights to dwell.

Light-making
After the world was created, God's next work was that of light-making. The earth was created, but it was swathed in darkness. *Darkness was upon the face of the deep* (Genesis 1:2). No sun, moon, or stars had yet appeared. No light had yet fallen upon the earth. Perhaps it was because of the dense vapors which shut out the light. God did nothing but say, *Let there be light*, and there was light.

We're discussing one who is not only without form and void, and dreadfully tossed about, but one who is also himself dark and in the dark. He wants the light, but he has none. He doesn't know the way of life, and he doesn't even see a ray of hope that he ever will find the way. He seems shut up in gloomy, thick, Egyptian night. Perhaps, worst of all, he doesn't even know his true condition. He calls darkness light and prides himself that he can see, even though he really can't see anything at all. Lord, speak the word and say, "Let there be light," and the man will see the light and see it at once! I am quite sure that, whether I can speak with power or not, God can speak with power. It is sweet comfort to my heart that he can, at this moment, find the most darkened sinner in the building, wherever he sits or stands, and the light can penetrate into his soul in less time than it takes me to say the words. To this man's own surprise, the darkness will become light around him, and the Egyptian night will be turned into the midday of infinite love and mercy. Pray to God that it may be so, brethren. Lift up a silent prayer to heaven, because this light-giving, this illumination, is a special work of God. There are many, who are now in the dark, in whom it is possible for this work of God to be displayed.

Resurrection

After these two works of God are done, after we've had creation and light-bringing, there is still death, and there is need of the divine work of resurrection. What's the use of a form beautifully fashioned if it's dead, and what's the use of light shining with all its brilliance upon a corpse? Yet, I speak

"Lord, make me live!"

to some who are dead in trespasses and sins. They don't feel the weight of sin, but to a living man it is an intolerable burden. They are not wounded by the two-edged sword of the Lord, though a living man is soon cut and gashed by it. They don't hear the joyous notes of free grace and dying love. Even though they ring out like a peal of silver bells, these dead sinners do not appreciate their sweet music. It is the work of God to make men live. There will come a day, and perhaps sooner than we think, when all the myriads of bodies that lie in our cemeteries and churchyards will rise up from the grave to live again. That will be a glorious display of divine power, but it won't be a greater manifestation of divine power than when a dead heart, a dead conscience, a dead will is made to live with a divine life. Oh, I pray that God would work that mighty miracle of mercy right now!

Pray that it may be so, beloved brethren and sisters in Christ. The dead won't pray for this resurrection, so let's pray for it for them. But if there is a man who does pray for it, one who cries, "Lord, make me live!" that is a proof that there's already a thrill of life shooting through him, or he wouldn't have that living desire.

Cleansing

Brethren, I could continue to build upon the line of the story of the creation and the arranging of the world in due order, but I won't. You can do that for yourselves. Next, I want to speak to you about the divine work of cleansing. There is, in this place of worship, a man who is black with filth. He has done everything he could do in order to rebel against God. Perhaps he is like Mr. John Newton, who describes himself in this way. He says, "I was in many respects like the apostle Paul. I was *a blasphemer and a persecutor and injurious* (1 Timothy 1:13). But there was one point in which I went beyond the apostle Paul. He did these things ignorantly, but I sinned against light and knowledge."

Do I speak to any now who, in sinning, have transgressed very grossly, because they have done what they knew was wrong and have persevered in doing it against the checks of conscience and against the warnings of a better desire within themselves, which they haven't been able to kill? I am amazed, sometimes, when I have had to talk with those whose lives have certainly gone almost to the very extreme of iniquity, but who still have had a certain inward check that would never let them go just that little piece further which would have put them beyond hope. There was always something that they still valued, even when they pretended to disbelieve everything and to blaspheme everything. There was some influence for good operating upon them still, as though God had a line and a hook in the jaws of Leviathan. Even though he ran out so far into the great deep of sin that you couldn't tell where he had gone, he still had to come back again after all. God still does wonders of mercy and grace.

Now, suppose that that black sinner, with all his years of sin, is forgiven outright. Suppose that the entirety of those fifty or sixty years of sin vanish once and for all. Suppose that God forgives, or better yet, that God forgets. Suppose that, with one tremendous fling of his omnipotent arm, he takes the whole mass of that sinner's sin and casts it into the depths of the sea. What a wonder of grace that would be! That is what God will do for everyone who trusts in Jesus. If you will come, cast yourself at his dear feet, and look up to Jesus crucified, bleeding in your place, and believe those words of the prophet Isaiah, *the LORD transposed in him the iniquity of us all* (Isaiah 53:6), or the words of the apostle Peter, *he himself bore our sins in his own body on the tree* (1 Peter 2:24), if you trust Jesus, the great Sin-bearer, then he will make you whiter than snow. And in your case, the works of God will be clearly seen, because none but the almighty God can make scarlet sinners white, and he can do it in a moment. Lord, do it now!

Suppose another thing happens, that a man or a woman who is desperately set on mischief is turned in an entirely opposite direction. That would clearly be a divine work of changing the whole current of life. I have never seen Niagara, and I don't suppose I ever will, but there are some here who have seen it. Down comes the mighty flood with a tremendous crash, forever leaping down from on high. Wouldn't you believe him to be God who, in a moment, makes that waterfall leap upward instead of downward and seek the heights in the same way it now leaps into the depths? Well, the Lord can do that very thing with some big Niagara-fall of a sinner right now. Today, you are determined to go into evil company and commit a filthy sin. Tomorrow, you are determined to grasp the drunkard's cup and not be satisfied until you have turned yourself into something below a beast. You are determined to pursue that evil habit of yours – getting money by gambling, or somewhat worse. Yes, but if my Lord comes forth, determined to save you, then he will make you sing to another tune.

"Oh, but I would never be a Methodist!" says one. I don't know what you will be yet.

"Oh!" says another, "you could never make a convert of me." I did not say that I could, but the Lord can make you what you think you never will be.

There are some here who, if they could have seen themselves ten years ago sitting here and enjoying the Word, would have said, "No, no, Charlie, that's not you, I am sure of it!" and, "No, Mary, that's not you, my girl. You will never be *there*. There's no chance of that."

But you *are* here, you see, and what free grace has done for some of us, it can do for others. Lord, do it according to that mighty power which you worked in Christ when you raised him from the dead! Work in the same manner in the ungodly today and turn them from the error of their ways to run with as much effort after you as they now put into running from you!

I have only one more matter to mention under this topic. I think God's works are sometimes made evident in men, by giving them great joy. For example, let's say there's a person convinced of sin. Mr. Conscience has come up against him. You know Mr. Conscience. He keeps a cat-o'-nine-tails. When he's allowed to do his work and gets a tight hold on a sinner who has long kept him under hatches, he says, "Now it is my turn," and he lets you know it, believe me. Let a man become aware of his conscience with a cat-o'-nine-tails in its possession, and he will never forget it. Every stroke seems to tear off a portion of his quivering flesh. Picture how the nine knotted cords make deep furrows every time they fall.

"You speak," says one, "like a man who knows it."

Knows it? I knew it for years while I was just a child. Neither night nor day could I escape from the sting of those falling cords. Oh, how conscience scourged me, and I could find no rest anywhere until I heard the divine voice that said, *Look unto me, and be ye saved, all the ends of the earth;* and conscience put away his cat-o'-nine-tails (Isaiah 45:22). My wounds were bathed in heavenly balm, they ceased to hurt, and I was glad! Oh, how my heart cried, "Hallelujah!" as I saw Jesus on the cross! Then I understood that God had executed the full vengeance due to my sin upon his Well-beloved, who had kindly bared his shoulder to the lash and bore the punishment of my sin. Then my heart leapt with joy. You'll notice that I'm always preaching the doctrine of substitution. I can't help it, because it is the only truth that brought me comfort. I would never have gotten out of the dungeon of despair if it hadn't been for the grand truth of substitution. I hope no young lady asks me for my autograph this week. I don't know how many days in the week that request is made to me, but I always write this verse:

> "E'er since by faith I saw the stream
>   Thy flowing wounds supply,
> Redeeming love has been my theme,
>   And shall be till I die."

If even once you know the power of that blessed theme, then you will see that it's a work of God to sweep away our ashes and give us the oil of joy, to take from us our robes of mourning and clothe us with garments of beauty, to put a new song into our mouths and to establish our goings. May you all have this blessed work of God worked in you, to the praise of the glory of his grace!

How Are These Works Made Manifest in Some Men?

He Was Totally Blind

For illustration purposes, I'll take this blind man and just go over his life. First, he was totally blind. There was no sham about his blindness. He couldn't see a ray of light. He knew nothing about light. Are any of you totally blind in a spiritual sense? You can't see anything, my poor friend. You don't have a good desire, and you haven't even had a good thought. Ah, you don't know what kind of people we have in this London. We meet with people who, for years, seem never to have had a good thought ever cross their minds. And if someone else were to speak to them about anything that is good, or even decent, he would be talking a foreign language to them! They don't understand it. We have multitudes of that kind in our slums, and in the West End they are just as bad.

When the Lord, in his infinite mercy, comes to these people who are totally blind and makes them see, there is plenty of room for his mighty power to work there, and everybody says, "What a wonderful thing that a person like that should be converted!" I know a man with whom I have often prayed in very sweet fellowship. He was an odd character when I first met him, even though he was a very good man afterwards. He was as eccentric a man as I ever met with, and I'm sufficiently eccentric myself, but he was a dead worldling. His Sundays were the same as any other day. He didn't know any difference between Sunday and Monday, except that he couldn't be in the pub for quite as long on Sundays.

He once said, "I had been out one Sunday morning to buy a pair of ducks, and I put one in each pocket of my coat. As I went along and saw the people going into a place of worship, I thought that I'd see what it was like. I had heard that it was a decent-looking place inside." He went, the Lord met with him, and that day those ducks did not get cooked. They had to wait until Monday, but he was caught and captured for Christ that day. A total change took place in him, and he became a fervent Christian at once, whereas before he had been totally without any kind of religious thought – either of fear or of hope. Here was a case in which the works of God were specially made manifest. That man has gone to heaven now. I remember him well and how I praised God for his conversion.

But the man mentioned in our text was born blind. There are many like that. Indeed, all people are born blind. It is original sin, and we all suffer from it. Sin is a corruption of the blood. We are born blind. There are some who are bred and born in a family utterly destitute of religion. They are brought up to despise it, or brought up in the midst of superstition and taught to say a useless prayer to a crucifix of wood or stone. Can these people, who are brought up in this way, find Christ? They do find Christ. Or rather, Christ finds them, and they hear the gospel, and it testifies of itself to their minds immediately.

> I believe that God is greatly glorified by the salvation of people through the simple preaching of the gospel, the very simplest means that can be used.

I suppose that nobody was ever more superstitious than Martin Luther. I have seen that staircase in Rome which Martin Luther ascended on his knees. It is said to be the staircase down which our Lord came from the palace of Pilate. I have seen the people go up and down on their knees. Just think of Luther doing it, and there came to him, as he was going up the stairs on his knees, those words, *the just shall live by faith*, and he rose up at once, and he did not go on his knees any farther (Hebrews 10:38). Oh, I pray that God would appear in that way to some of you!

He Was Cured by Special Means

Next, this blind man was cured by special means. That was another manifestation of God's works. The Savior spat, stooped down, and with his finger worked that spittle into the dust until he had made clay. Then he took it and began to put it over the man's eyes. I believe that God is greatly glorified by the salvation of people through the simple preaching of the gospel, the very simplest means that can be used. Often men say, when souls are saved in this place, as they are continually, "Well, I can't see anything remarkable in the preacher." No, and if you were to look a great deal longer, you would see less than you see now, because there's not anything to see in him, but there is a great deal in the gospel.

If some preachers would only preach the gospel, they would soon see how very superior it is to all their fine essays! But they prepare their sermons so well. Oh yes! I know, but did you ever hear of the man who used to prepare the potatoes before he planted them in his garden? He always boiled them, but they never grew, because he had prepared all the life out of them. Many boiled sermons are brought out to the people, but they never grow. They are elaborated and prepared so much that nothing will ever come out of them. The Lord loves to bless living words spoken in simple language out of an earnest heart. The man who speaks in this manner doesn't get the glory. All the glory goes to God. In this way, there is room for the works of God to be clearly seen.

He Was Known As a Public Beggar

This blind man was also a specially fit vessel for God to display his works in, because he was known as a public beggar. They used to lead him up in the morning, I suppose, to the gate of the temple, and there he took his place and sat down. He was a man who seemed quick to speak, so I would guess that he often exchanged small talk with those that went by, and they remembered what kind of a man he was. I suspect he was always very sarcastic, and when they spoke to him, and gave him nothing, he knew how to give them something. That blind beggar was a well-known character in Jerusalem, as well known as the blind beggar of Bethnal Green. So the Savior selected him, because he was so well known, and opened his eyes.

You're in the same situation, aren't you? You are well known. But I won't single you out, because I don't like doing that kind of thing. Not long ago, a soldier came in here who had been a professor of religion, but he had turned away from the faith and returned to his former way of life, but he wanted to hear the gospel again. Just over yonder, where there are two pillars, he wisely chose a place where I couldn't see him. But it so happened, on that Sunday night, and he is the witness of this, that I remember saying, "Well, Will, you've got to come back, you know. You've got to come back, and the sooner, the better." Will did come back, and he sent word to me to say that he had come back with a broken heart to find his Lord. I didn't know that his name was Will, I am sure, and I didn't know why he had hidden himself behind the pillars there, but God did, and he adapted the word to the person, and so he fetched Will back again. If there is any Will, or Tom, or Jack, or Mary, or if there are any others who have wandered far from God, oh, sovereign grace, bring them back, whether they are soldiers or civilians, that they may seek and find the Savior even now! This Will was well known, and I trust that his restoration to Christ will clearly display the works of God in him, because he was so well known. Oh, what joy that the Lord would hear the prayer of my friend that morning and convert the Prince of Wales!

We all said "Amen" to that petition. We want the Lord to bring into his church some of those who are well known, whether they be princes or beggars, so that the works of God may be gloriously displayed in them.

He Became a Public Confessor

When this man was converted, instead of remaining a public beggar, he became a public confessor. I like that answer of his: *Whether he is a sinner or not, I do not know; one thing I know, that having been blind, now I see* (John 9:25). Many men can say, "Well, I don't know much about theology, but I know that I was a drunkard, and I know that I'm not a drunkard now. I know that I used to beat my wife, and now, God bless her, she knows how much I love her! Then, I spent time with all manner of sinful company, but now, thank God, his saints are my choice companions! Once, I could have gloried in my own righteousness, but now I consider it refuse and dung, so that I may win Christ and be found in him. There is a great change in me. Nobody can deny that fact, and I praise God's name for it." I pray that the Lord would send out a great company of men who are not ashamed of Jesus Christ! We want many men and women who will come straight out from the world and say, "Christ for me, because he has so touched my heart, that I am for him, and if no one else will confess him, I must do so, because he is my best Friend, my Lord, my Savior, my all." In such cases, the works of God are made manifest.

How May God's Works Be Manifest in Us?

Afflictions

Some of you are very poor. Others are lame or very sickly. You may suffer from tuberculosis, asthma, aches, and pains. Perhaps all this suffering is permitted so that the work of God may be manifest in your afflictions by your holy patience, your submission to the divine will, and your persevering holiness in the midst of all your poverty and trials. All this is sent so that God's grace may be seen in you. Will you look at your afflictions in that light and believe that they are not sent as a punishment, but as a platform upon which God may stand, and display his free grace in you? Endure well all the Lord's will, because your trials are sent for this purpose: that God's works may be clearly seen in you.

Infirmities

The same is true of your infirmities. None of us are perfect, but we may also have physical shortcomings. You must believe – if you are sent to preach the gospel, to teach children, or in any way advance the kingdom of God – that you wouldn't be any better suited for your work if you had all the eloquence of Cicero or all the learning of Newton. You, as you are, can serve the Lord and fill a certain need better with all your drawbacks than you could without those drawbacks. A wise Christian man will make use of his infirmities for God's glory.

There is a strange story they tell about St. Bernard, a tradition believed by some people, but which I look at as an allegory rather than as a matter of fact. He was going over the Alps towards Rome on some business. The devil knew that the saint was about to do something that would greatly injure his kingdom, so he came and broke one of the wheels of the saint's carriage. So Bernard called out to him and said, "You think to stop me in this way, do you, Satan? Now you shall suffer for it yourself!" So he took Satan, twisted him around, made a wheel of him, fastened him to the carriage, and then continued on his way.

The meaning of that allegory is that when infirmities threaten to cripple your usefulness, you are to use those infirmities in God's service. Turn the devil himself into a wheel and carry on all the better because of the hindrance he tried to cause. It might even be an advantage to stammer sometimes to emphasize a word. And if I ever felt myself stuck in a hole by that process, I'd make sure to be stuck somewhere near the cross. Many men have had the power to attract people by a unique characteristic which looked like it must impair their usefulness. All our infirmities, whatever they are, are just opportunities for God to display his gracious work in us.

Oppositions

It's the same with all the oppositions that we come in contact with. If we serve the Lord, we are guaranteed to meet with difficulties and oppositions, but they are only more opportunities for the works of God to be seen in us.

Death

At some point, it will come time for us to die, and even in our deaths, God's work can be displayed. I wonder about what sort of death we will glorify God with. Wasn't it a beautiful expression of John's, when the Savior spoke of Peter? He told Peter how he would die, but John doesn't put it that way. He says, *by what death he should clarify God* (John 21:19). Perhaps it will be by a long, agonizing sickness. Some will be gradually dissolved by tuberculosis. Well, you will glorify God by it. Those pale cheeks and that thin hand, through which the light will shine, will preach many sermons from that sickbed. Or perhaps you'll glorify God in some other way. You may have to die with bitter pangs of pain, but then, if the Lord cheers you and makes you patient, you will glorify God by that kind of death. You will look death calmly in the face, and not fret, and not be afraid. You will have to die somehow, and he will take you home in a way that will somehow or other bring glory to his name, however it may be. So let's begin to rejoice in it even now.

May God bless these words of mine, and may you all be eternal monuments of the boundless, sovereign grace of God. Unto him be glory for ever and ever! Amen.

Chapter 7

The Blind Man's Eyes Opened
or Practical Christianity

Jesus answered, Neither has this man sinned nor his parents,
but that the works of God should be made manifest in him. It
is expedient that I do the works of him that sent me while it is
day; the night comes, when no one can work. (John 9:3-4)

Observe how little our Lord Jesus Christ was bothered by the most violent opposition of his enemies. If the Jews took up stones to stone him, he hid himself from them. But barely a moment later, when he had passed, perhaps, through a single court, and was sufficiently out of range of their sight, he stood still and fixed his eyes upon a blind beggar who had been sitting near the temple gate. I'm afraid that most of us would have had no heart to help even the neediest while we, ourselves, escaped from a shower of stones. And if we had attempted the work, moved by supreme compassion, we would have gone about it blunderingly, in a great hurry, and certainly would not have talked calmly and wisely, as the Savior did when he answered his disciples' question and continued to have a conversation with them. One of the things worthy to notice in our Lord's character is his wonderful, quiet spirit, especially his marvelous calmness in the presence of those who misjudged, insulted, and slandered him. He is insulted often, but never ruffled. Even in the midst of death, he's always full of life. No doubt he felt the weight of all the conflict of sinners against himself. In a passage in the Psalms which refers to the Messiah, we read, *Reproach has broken my heart* (Psalm 69:20). Yet, the Lord Jesus did not permit his feelings to overcome him. He was quiet and self-possessed. He acted with a profound disregard for the assaults and false statements against his character made by his bitter enemies.

He Was Never Enchanted by the Praise of Men

One reason, I take it, for his being so self-contained was that he was never enchanted by the praise of men. Take my word for it, because I know, that if you ever allow yourself to be pleased by those who speak well of you, to the same extent you will be capable of being grieved by those who speak ill of you. But if you have learned (and it's a long lesson for most of us) that you are not the servant of men but of God, then you will not live upon the breath of men's nostrils if they praise you, and you will not die if they denounce you. Then you will be strong and show that you have come to maturity in Christ Jesus. If the great Master's head had been turned by the hosannas of the multitude, then his heart would have sunk within him when they cried, "Crucify him, crucify him!" But he was neither lifted up nor cast down by men. *But Jesus did not trust himself unto them because he knew all men and needed not that any man should give testimony, for he knew what was in man* (John 2:24-25).

His Unbroken Communion with the Father

The innermost reason for this quietness of heart was his unbroken communion with the Father. Jesus dwelt apart, because he lived with God. The Son of Man who came down from heaven still dwelt in heaven. He displayed serene patience, because he was raised above earthly things in the holy contemplations of his perfect mind. Because his heart was with his Father, the Father made him strong to bear anything that might come from men. Oh, I wish that we all could wear this armor of light, the celestial display of communion with the High Eternal One. Then we would not be afraid of evil words or of evil circumstances, because our hearts would be fixed on the sure rock of Jehovah's unchanging love.

His Heart Was So Set upon His Work

There was perhaps another reason for our Savior's wonderful composure when he was attacked with stones. His heart was so set upon his work that he could not be turned away from it, no matter what the unbelieving Jews might do. This ruling passion carried him through danger and suffering and made him calmly defy all opposition. He had come into the world to bless men, and he must bless men. The Jews might oppose him for this reason and for that, but they could not turn the current of his soul from the riverbed of mercy along which it rushed like a torrent. He *must* do good to the suffering and the poor, he couldn't help it. His face was set like a rock towards his lifework. It had become his meat and his drink to do the will of him that sent him. So when they took up stones, although he withdrew himself a little, he returned to his lifework without a moment's delay. Stones could not drive him from his gracious pursuits. We've seen a parent bird chased away from its nest only to return to it the instant the intruder has withdrawn. We also see our Lord return to his holy work almost before he is out of the sight of his would-be murderers. There sits a blind man, and Jesus is at once at his side to heal him.

> "They will overtake thee, O Christ!
>   They will seek to slay thee!
> There are more stones in their cruel hands.
>   Thy haters hurl their missiles fiercely,
>   and they will be upon thee in a moment!
>   What cares he for that?"

No cowardly spirit can make him overlook an opportunity for glorifying the Father. That blind man must be attended to, and even with all the hazards, he stops to deal with him in love. If you and I become completely consumed with zeal for God, and with the desire to win souls, then nothing will deter us. We will bear anything, and not seem to have anything to bear. We will hear slander as though we never even heard it and endure hardship as though there were none to endure. As an arrow shot from a bow by a strong archer defies the opposing wind and speeds forward to the white of the target, so shall we fly forward towards the great object of our compassionate ambition. Happy is that man whom God has launched like a thunderbolt from his hand, who must go on and fulfill his destiny, happy that it is his job to bring sinners to the Savior's feet. Oh, blessed Spirit, lift us up to dwell in God and to sympathize with his fatherly compassion so that we won't care about stones, or sneers, or slanders, but will become absorbed in our self-denying service for Jesus's sake!

The Savior, in his worst and lowest estate, when near to death, thinks of nothing but the good of men. When cruel eyes are watching for an opportunity to slay him, he has an eye for the poor blind man. There is no hardness in his heart towards the sorrowful, even when stones are flying past his ears.

The Worker

Jesus is *the* worker, the chief worker, the example to all workers. He even says that he came into the world to do the will of him who sent him and to finish his work. On this occasion, when he is pursued by his enemies, he is still a worker – a wonder-worker – with the blind man. There are many in this world who ignore sorrow, who pass by grief, who are deaf to cries of pain, and who are blind to distress. The easiest thing that I know of to do with this wicked, wretched city of London is not to know much about it. They say that half the world doesn't know how the other half lives. Surely, if it did know, it would not live as carelessly as it does or be quite as cruel as it is. There are sights in this metropolis that might melt a heart of steel and make Nabal generous.

But shutting your eyes is an easy way to escape from the exercise of benevolence and seeing none of the misery which grovels at your feet. "Where ignorance is bliss, it is folly to be wise," said some easygoing ignoramus of old time. If beggars are demanding, then passersby must be deaf. If sinners are coarse, it is a simple matter to cover your ears and hurry on. If this blind man needs to sit and beg at the gate of the temple, then those who frequent the temple must just slip by as if they were as blind as he was. Crowds pass by and take no notice of him. Isn't that the way with the crowds today? If you are in trouble, if you are suffering heartbreak, don't they just ignore you and continue on their way, even though you lie down and starve?

Rich men find it convenient to remain ignorant of the sores of

Lazarus. It is not so with Jesus. He is quick to see the blind beggar, even if he sees nothing else. He is not enraptured with the massive stones and the beautiful architecture of the temple. Instead, he fixes his eyes upon a sightless beggar at the temple gate. He is all eye, all ear, all heart, all hand, where misery is present. My Master is made of tenderness; he melts with love. Oh, true souls who love him, copy him in this, and let your hearts be touched with the same feeling for the suffering and the sinning.

There are others who, though they see misery, do not diminish it by warm sympathy, but increase it by their cold, logical conclusions. "Poverty," they say, "well, that, of course, is brought on by drunkenness, laziness, and all sorts of vice." I do not say that it is not so in many cases, but I do say that this observation will not help a poor man to become either better or happier. Such a hard remark will exasperate the hardened instead of assist the struggling. Some say, "A great deal of sickness is caused by wicked habits and neglect of sanitary laws," and so on. This also may be sadly true, but it grates on a sufferer's ear. It's not a very kind and pleasing doctrine to teach in the wards of our hospitals! I would recommend you not teach it until you are ill yourself, and then perhaps the doctrine may not seem quite so instructive to you.

> My Master is made of tenderness; he melts with love.

Even Christ's disciples, when they saw this blind man, thought that there must be something particularly wicked about his father and mother, or something especially vicious about the man himself, which God foresaw, and on account of which, he punished him with blindness. The disciples were of the same spirit as Job's three comforters who, when they saw the patriarch on a dunghill, bereft of all his children, robbed of all his property, and scraping himself because he was covered with sores, said, "Of course he must be a hypocrite. He must have done something very dreadful, or he would not be so grievously afflicted."

The world will still stick to its unfounded belief that if the tower of Siloam falls upon any men, they must be sinners above all sinners upon the face of the earth. A cruel doctrine, a vile doctrine, fit for savages, but not to be mentioned by Christians who know that *whom the Lord loves, he chastens*, and even his most beloved have been taken away all of a sudden. Yet, I do hear a good deal of this cruel idea that if men are in trouble, "Well, of course, they brought it on themselves."

Is this your way of cheering them? Cheap, moral observations steeped in vinegar make a poor dish for an invalid. Such criticism is a sorry way of helping a lame dog over a fence. No, it is putting up another fence for him, so he can't get over it at all. I notice this of my Lord, that it is written of him that he *gives abundantly to all, and without reproach* (James 1:5). When he fed those thousands in the wilderness, it would have been most just if he had said to them, "Why did you all come out into the wilderness and not bring your provisions with you? What are you doing out here without something to eat? You are shortsighted and deserve to be hungry."

No, he never said a word of the sort. He fed them, fed them all, and sent them home filled. You and I are not sent into the world to thunder out commandments from the top of Sinai. We are not to make our rounds as if we were judge and hangman rolled into one, to meet all the sorrow and misery in the world with bitter words of censure and condemnation. If we do so, we are very different from that blessed Master of ours who doesn't say a word of rebuke to those who seek him, but simply feeds the hungry and heals all those who have need of healing! It is easy to criticize, it is easy to scold, but ours should be the higher and nobler task of blessing and saving.

There are certain others who, if they aren't indifferent to sorrow and don't proclaim some cruel theory of condemnation, speculate a good deal where speculation can be of no practical service. When we get together, there are many questions which we like to raise and dispute about which are of no practical value whatsoever. There is the question of the origin of evil. That's a fine subject for those who like to chop logic without making enough chips to light a fire for cold hands to warm at. Such was the subject proposed to the Savior – foreseen guilt or hereditary taint? They asked, *Rabbi, who sinned, this man or his parents, that he was born blind?* To what point is it right that the sin of parents should, as it often does, fall upon the children?

I could propose to you many topics equally profound and curious, but what would be the value in that? Yet, there are many in the world who are fond of these topics, spinning cobwebs, blowing bubbles, making theories, breaking them, and making more. I wonder whether the world was ever blessed by as much as one red cent by all the theorizing of all the learned men that have ever lived. Couldn't they all be placed under the heading of vain janglings? I would rather create an ounce of help than a ton of theory. It is beautiful to me to see how the Master breaks up the fine speculation which the disciples set forth. He says somewhat shortly, *Neither has this man sinned nor his parents.* Then he spits on the ground, makes clay, and opens the blind man's eyes. This was work. The other was only worry.

"Father," said a boy, "the cows are in the corn. How did they get in?"

"Boy," said the father, "never mind how they got in, let's hurry up and get them out."

There is common sense about that practical thought process. Here we have people sunken in vice and steeped in poverty. Postpone the inquiries: How did they get into this condition? What is the origin of moral evil? How is it transmitted from parent to child? Answer those questions after the day of judgment, when you will have more light. Now, the important thing is to see how you and I can get evil out of the world, lift up the fallen, and restore those who have gone astray. Never let us imitate the man in the fable who saw a boy drowning, and then and there lectured him on the foolishness of bathing out of his depth. No, let us pull the boy to the bank, dry him and dress him, and then tell him not to go there again, so a worse thing doesn't happen to him.

The Master was no speculator. He was no spinner of theories. He didn't simply proclaim doctrine, but he went to work and healed those that had need of healing. In this, he is the greatest example for us all in this year of grace. What have we ever *done* to bless our fellow men? Many of us are followers of Christ, and oh, how happy we ought to be that we are so! What have we ever *done* worthy of our high calling? "Sir, I heard a lecture the other night," says one, "upon the evils of intemperance." Is that all you did? Has any action come of that brilliant oration and of your careful attention to it? Did you immediately try to remove this intemperance in the world around you by your example? "Well, I'll think about that, sir, one of these days." Meanwhile, what's to become of these intemperate ones? Won't their blood lie at your door?

"I heard the other day," says one, "a very forcible and interesting lecture on political economy, and I felt that it was a very weighty science and accounted for much of the poverty you mention." Perhaps so, but political economy, in itself, is about as hard as brass. It has no bowels, or heart, or conscience, neither can it make allowance for such things. The political economist is a man of iron who would be rusted by a tear. Therefore, he never tolerates the mood of compassion. His science is a rock which will wreck a navy and remain unmoved by the cries of drowning men and women. It's like the sandstorm of the desert which withers everything it blows upon. It seems to dry up men's souls when they get to be masters of it, or rather are mastered by it. It is a science of stubborn facts, which wouldn't be facts if we were not so brutish. Political economy or no political economy, I come back to my point: What have you *done* for others? Let's think about that, and if any of us have been dreaming day after day about what we would do *if,* let's see what we can do now and, like the Savior, get to work.

> He came as he was, and his father received him as he was.

Yet, that is not the point I am driving at. It is this: if Jesus is such a worker, and not a theorizer, then what hope there is for some of us who need his care! Have we fallen? Are we poor? Have we brought ourselves into sorrow and misery? Don't let us look to men or to ourselves. Men will let us starve, and then they will hold a coroner's inquest over our body to find why we dared to die and made it necessary to pay for a grave and a coffin. They will be sure to make an inquiry after it is all over with us. But if we come to Jesus Christ, he will make no inquiry at all, but will receive us and give rest to our souls. That is a blessed text – he *gives abundantly to all, and without reproach* (James 1:5).

When the Prodigal Son came home to his father, according to all moral decency, as people would do nowadays, the father should have said to his son, "Well, you have come home, and I am glad to see you, but what a state you are in! How did you get into this condition? Why, you have scarcely a clean rag on your back! How is it you have become so poor? And you are lean and hungry, how did this come about? Where have you been? What have you done? What company have you kept? Where were you a week ago? What were you doing the day before yesterday at seven o'clock?" His father never asked him a single question, but pressed him to his bosom, and knew all about it by instinct. He came as he was, and his father received him as he was. The father seemed, with a kiss, to say, "My boy, bygones are bygones. You were dead, but you are alive again. You were lost, but you are found, and I inquire no further." That is just how Jesus Christ is willing to receive repentant sinners now.

Is there a prostitute here? Come, poor woman, as you are, to your dear Lord and Master who will cleanse you of your grievous sin. *All manner of sin and blasphemy shall be forgiven unto men* (Matthew 12:31). Is there one here who has violated the rules of society and is singled out as especially sinful? Come and welcome to the Lord Jesus of whom it is written, *This man receives sinners and eats with them* (Luke 15:2). The physician never refuses to go among the sick, and Christ never felt ashamed that he looked after the guilty and the lost. No, write this about his crown: He is the Savior of sinners, even of the very chief, and he counts this his glory. He will work for you, not lecture you. He will not treat you with a dose of theories and a host of bitter accusations, but he will receive you just as you are into the wounds of his side and hide you there from the wrath of God. Oh, blessed gospel that I have to preach to you! May the Holy Spirit lead you to embrace it.

The Work Room

Every worker needs a place to work. Every artist must have a studio. Did Christ have a studio? Yes, he came to do very wonderful works – the works of him that sent him, but what a strange, strange place the Lord found to do his work in! Yet, I don't know that he could have found any other. He resolved to work the works of God, and he selected the most suitable place for doing so.

Creation

If Jesus is to perform the work of creation among men, he must find out where something is missing which he can supply by a creating act. In our text, we have two eyes without the proper light-receiving apparatus. Here, there is room for Jesus to create eyes and sight. He wouldn't have created eyes in my head or yours if we had been present, because eyes are already there, and more eyes would be unsuitable for us. In the case of the blind beggar in the temple, there was room for Jesus to produce that which was lacking in the curious mechanism of the eye. The blind eye was, therefore, his workshop. If there were eyeballs, they were completely sightless and had been so from the man's birth. This presented the opportunity for the Lord to say, *Let there be light* (Genesis 1:3). If that man's eyes had been like yours and mine, clear and bright and full of light, there would have been no space for our Lord's divine operation. But since he was still in the darkness, which had surrounded him from his birth, his eyes provided space where the power of the Almighty might be made abundantly clear by a work so wonderful that since the world began it had never been heard that anyone had opened the eyes of a man who was born blind. The man was blind for this reason: *That the works of God should be made manifest in him.*

That is a blessed thought if you think it over! Apply it to yourself. If there is anything lacking in you, there is room for Christ to work in you. If you are naturally perfect, and there is no fault in you, then there is no room for the Savior to do anything for you. He will not gild refined gold, nor lay enamel on the lily. But if you suffer from some great deficiency, some awful lack that makes your soul sit in darkness, *your* necessity is Christ's opportunity. Your need of grace supplies his need of objects for his pity. Here is room for the Savior to come and display his pity towards you, and you can be sure that he will soon be with you. Even so, come Lord Jesus.

Illuminate

It wasn't only this man's deficiency of sight, but it was also this man's ignorance which required almighty aid. It is a work of God to not only create, but also to illuminate. The same power which calls into existence also calls into light, whether that light is natural or spiritual. It is a divine work to enlighten and regenerate the heart. This man was as dark in mind as he was in body. What a grand thing to enlighten him in a double sense! He didn't know the Son of God, so he didn't believe in him, but asked in wonder, *Who is he, Lord, that I might believe in him?* (John 9:36).

Jesus Christ came to work in this man the knowledge of God, the life of God, in a word – salvation. Because the man was destitute of these things, there was room in him for the Savior's skill and power. Friend, is that your case? Are you unconverted? Then there is space in you for the Redeemer to work by converting grace. Are you unregenerate? Then there is space in you for the Spirit of God to work regeneration. All these spiritual deficiencies of yours – your ignorance and your darkness – shall be turned by infinite love into opportunities for grace. If you were not lost, you could not be saved. If you were not guilty, you could not be pardoned. If you were not sinful, you could not be cleansed. But all your sin and sorrow, by a strange mystery of love, is a sort of qualification for Christ to come and save you.

"That is putting it," says one, "in a new light for me." Accept that new light and be comforted, because it is gospel light, and it's intended to cheer the one in despair. You have said, "There is nothing in me." Therefore, it's clear that there is room for Christ to be your all-in-all. You see there cannot be two all-in-alls. There can only be one, and to the extent that you don't claim that title for yourself, Jesus will wear it. All the space that you occupy in your own self-importance takes so much away from the glory of the Lord Jesus. If you are nothing, then the whole house is left for the Savior. He will come and fill up all your inward vacuum with his own dear self and be glorious in your eyes forever.

I may venture to say that all affliction can be looked at as opening the opportunity for the mercy-work of God. Whenever you see a man in sorrow and trouble, the way to look at it is not to blame him and question how he came to be there, but to say, "Here is an opening for God's almighty love. Here is an occasion for the display of the grace and goodness of the Lord." This man's blindness gave the Lord Jesus opportunity for the good work of giving him his sight, and that work was so great a wonder that all around were obliged to comment on it and admire it. Neighbors inquired about it. The Pharisees had to hold a conclave over it. And even though nearly nineteen centuries have slipped away, here are we at this hour meditating upon it.

That man's opened eyes are enlightening our eyes at this hour. The Bible would not have been complete without this touching and teaching narrative. If this man had not been born blind, and if Christ had not opened his eyes, all generations would have had less light. We ought to be glad that this man was so grievously afflicted, because in his affliction we are graciously instructed. If he had not been sightless, we would not have seen the great sight of birth-blindness chased away by him who is the Light of men. So I think I would say to all afflicted ones, do not kick at your afflictions, do not be excessively troubled by them, or utterly cast down by them, but hopefully regard them as openings for mercy, gates for grace, and roadways for love. That mighty worker of whom I have been speaking will find a workshop in your affliction, and in that workshop he will fashion monuments of his grace. Glory in your infirmities, so that the power of Christ may rest upon you. Rejoice that as your tribulations abound, so also shall your comfort abound by Christ Jesus. Ask him to make all things work together for your good and for his glory, and so it shall be.

I also believe that sin itself has some of the same attributes as affliction, because it also makes room for the mercy of God. I hardly dare to say what Augustine said when speaking of the fall and of the sin of Adam. Looking at all the splendor of grace that followed after it, he said, *Beata culpa* ("happy fault"). As if he thought that sin had furnished such opportunities for the unveiling of the grace of God, and so displayed the character of Christ, that he even dared to call it a happy fault. I will not speculate upon such an expression; I barely dare do more than repeat what that great master in Israel once said. But I do say that I can't imagine an occasion for glorifying God equal to the fact that man has sinned, since God has given Christ to die for sinners. How could that unspeakable gift have been given if there had been no sinners? The cross is a constellation of divine glory brighter than creation itself.

> "For in the grace that rescued man,
> His noblest form of glory shines;
> Here on the cross 'tis fairest writ
> In precious blood and crimson lines."

How could we have known the heart of God? How could we have understood the mercy of God? If it had not been for our sin and misery, how could such patience and love have been displayed? Come, then, guilty ones, take heart and look for grace. As a physician needs the sick so that he may exert his healing power, so does the Lord of mercy need you so he may show what grace he can give. If I were a physician and desired a practice, I wouldn't ask for the healthiest parish in England, but for a position where the sick would fill my surgery. If all I wanted was to do good to my fellow men, I would desire to be in Egypt or some other land visited by cholera, or plague, where I could save human life. The Lord Jesus Christ – looking over this throng here – doesn't look for those who are good, or think themselves so, but for the guilty who know their sinful state and mourn over it. If there's a sinner here, leprous and defiled, if there's a soul sick from head to foot with the incurable disease of sin, the Lord Christ, the mighty worker, looks on him, because in him he finds a laboratory where he can work the works of him who sent him.

The Work-Bell

In the early morning, you hear a bell which arouses the workers from their beds. Observe how they march into the streets, swarming like bees rushing to or from the hive. You see them going to work, because the bell is ringing. There was a work-bell for Christ, and he heard it. Then he said, "I must work." What made him say that? Why, the sight of that blind man. He no sooner saw him than he said, "I must work." The man had not asked anything or even uttered a sound, but those sightless orbs spoke eloquently to the heart of the Lord Jesus and rang aloud the summons which Jesus heard and obeyed, for he himself said, "I must work."

Why must he work? Why, he had come all the way from heaven on purpose to do so. He had come from his Father's throne to be a man, on purpose, to bless men, and he would not cause his long descent to count for nothing. He must work. Why else was he here where work was to be done?

Besides, there were impulses in his heart, which we don't need to stop now and explain, which forced him to work. His mind, his soul, his heart, were all full of a force which produced constant activity. Sometimes, he selected a route when he was travelling, because *it was necessary that he go through Samaria* (John 4:4). Sometimes, he went after men, because he said, *I have other sheep which are not of this fold; it is expedient that I bring them also* (John 10:16). There was a sort of instinct in Christ to save men, and that instinct craved gratification and could not be denied. The sight of those blind eyes made him say, *I must work* (John 9:4 KJV). He thought of that poor man, how for twenty years and more, he had lived in utter darkness and had not been able to enjoy the beauties of nature, look his loved ones in the face, or earn his daily bread. Our Savior pitied the sorrows of the man in life-long darkness. He considered how that man's soul had also been shut up like a prisoner in a dungeon because of gross ignorance. He said, *I must work*. They are after him with stones, but he stops and says, "I must work. They may stone me if they will, but I must work. I hear the summons, and I must work."

Learn this lesson, all you followers of Christ. Whenever you see suffering, I hope you will each say, "I must work, I must help." Whenever you witness poverty, whenever you witness sin, say to yourself, "I must work, I must work." If you are worthy of the Christ, whom you call leader, let all the needs of men prompt you, compel you, force you to bless them.

> "Let the world which lieth in the wicked one arouse you;
> let the cries of men of Macedonia awaken you,
> as they say, 'Come over and help us!'
> Men are dying, dying in the dark.
> The cemetery is filling, and hell is filling too.
> Men are dying without hope,
> and are passing into the eternal night.
> 'I must work.'
>
> They cry, Master, spare thyself;
> incessant labor will wear thee down
> and bring thee to thy grave.
> But see! See! See!
> Perdition swallows crowds;
> they go down alive into the pit!
> Hark to their doleful cries!
> Lost souls are being shut out from God.
> 'I must work.'"

Oh, if only I could lay my hand, or better yet, that my Master would lay his pierced hand on every true Christian here and press it upon him until he cried out, "I cannot sit here. I must be at work as soon as this service is done. I must not only hear, and give, and pray, but I must also work." Well, that's an important lesson, but I don't intend it to be the primary one, because I am looking out for those who long to find mercy and salvation. What a blessing it is for you, dear friend, if you want to be saved, that Christ *must* save! There is an impulse upon him that he must save. I know you say, "I cannot pray." Never mind about that. The matter is in abler hands. You see, this man did not *say* a word. The sight of him was enough to move the heart of the Lord Jesus. As soon as Jesus saw him, he said, *I must work.*

> You will be the workshop of Christ.

Have you ever seen a man in London who has no particular oratory skills, and yet succeeds in obtaining alms on a large scale? I've seen him. He dresses like a laborer. He wears tattered clothes and sits down on a corner where many pass by. His squatting place is a little out of the rush of traffic, but near enough to secure attention from many passersby. He displays a tattered sign, much the worse for the use made of it by somebody else, and on it is written, "I am starving!" He looks gaunt, hungry, and as pale as chalk can make him. Oh, the quantity of halfpence that go into his old hat! How people pity him! He does not sing a mournful ditty. He does not speak a word. Yet, many are moved by the fact that he looks as if it were true that he was starving.

Now, you don't need to be false in what you do if you place your misery and sin before the Lord. When you get home, kneel at your bedside and say, "Lord Jesus, I cannot pray, but here I am. I am perishing, and I put myself within your sight. Instead of hearing my pleas, look at my sins. Instead of demanding arguments, look at my wickedness. Instead of eloquent speech, which I don't have, Lord, remember that I will soon be in hell if you don't save me."

I tell you, the bell will ring, and the great worker will feel that the time has come for him to labor. He will say, *I must work*, and in you the works of God shall be made manifest. You will be the workshop of Christ.

The Work Day

Our divine Master said, *I must work the works of him that sent me, while it is day: the night cometh, when no man can work* (John 9:4 KJV). This is not talking about Christ the risen Savior, but this refers to the Lord Jesus Christ as he was a man here on earth. There was a certain day in which he could bless men. When that day was over, he would be gone. There would be no Jesus Christ on earth to open blind men's eyes or to heal the sick. He would be gone from among men and no longer be approachable as the healer of bodily disease. Our Lord as a man here on earth had a day. It was only a day, a short period, and not very long. He couldn't make it longer, because that matter was settled by the great Lord. The day of his sacrifice was appointed. He himself once said, *My hour is not yet come* (John 2:4). But that hour did come. Our Lord occupied thirty years in getting ready for his lifework. Then, in three years his warfare was accomplished. How much he crowded into those three years! Centuries of service could not equal the labor of that brief period.

Brothers, some of us have had thirty years of work, but we have done very little, I am afraid. What if we have only three years more? Let us feel the weight of the coming eternity! In a little while, I will no longer look into the faces of the throng; they will only remember my name. So I will preach as best I can while my powers remain, and my life is prolonged. Within a little while, brother, you will not be able to go from door to door winning souls. The street will miss you and your tracts. The district will miss you and your regular visits. Do your work well, because your sun will soon set. These words of mine may be more prophetic to some present than we can imagine. I may be speaking to some who are nearing their last hour, and shall soon cash in their account. Up brothers! Up sisters! Say, "We must work, for *the night cometh, when no man can work.*" Life can't be made longer even if we wish to make it so. Predestination will not lengthen out the thread when the hour has come to cut it off. Life will be short at the very longest, and, O how short for those who die young!

If you and I omit any part of our life's work, we can never make up the omission. I speak with solemn reverence for our divine Master, but, if he had not healed that blind man in the day when he lived on earth, he would have missed a part of the business for which the Father sent him. I do not mean that as God, out of heaven, he might not have given the poor beggar sight, but that makes the case the more serious as it pertains to us, since we don't have such a future to expect. If we do not serve men now, it will be out of our power to bless them from the skies. This narrative could never have appeared in the life of the Son of Man if he had forgotten to be gracious to the blind man. His visit here below was the time for our Lord to work. If he had come back from heaven to heal the man, that would have been done in a second coming, and not in the first. Even if he omits anything from his first errand below, it cannot be put in again.

When you and I have written a letter, we add a postscript. When we have written a book, we can write an appendix or insert something that we have left out. But to this life of yours and mine there can be no postscript. We must do our work now or never. And, if we don't perform our service to God now, while our opportunity serves us, we can never do it. If you omitted anything yesterday, you cannot alter the fact of imperfect service on that day. If you are more zealous now, it will be counted as the work of today. Yesterday will remain just as incomplete as you left it. So we must be on the alert to do the work of him that sent us while it is called today.

In conclusion, if our Lord Jesus Christ was so diligent to bless men when he was here, I feel certain that he is not less diligent to hear and heal them now in that spiritual sense in which he still works upon men.

Oh, I wish that I knew how to lead you to seek my Lord and Master, because if you seek him, he will be found by you as surely as you seek him. Christ has not lost the bowels of his compassion. He is not cold in heart or slack in hand. Go to him at once. I just spoke to some of the chief of sinners, and I say to them again, "Go to Jesus!" Let me speak to some of you who are *not* the chief of sinners, you who have been hearers of the gospel and have only failed because you do not believe in Jesus. Go to him at once. *You* are backward, but he is not. He must still work, and still work while the gospel day lasts, because that gospel day will soon close. He is waiting and watching for you. Come to him even now.

"I do not know what it is to come," one might say.

Well, to come to Christ is simply to trust him. You are guilty. Trust him to pardon you.

Another says, "If I do that, can I still live as I did before?"

No, you cannot.

If a ship needed to be brought into harbor, and they took a pilot on board, he would say to the captain, "Captain, if you trust me, I will get you into harbor all right. There, let that sail be taken down." And they do not reef it. "Come," he says, "attend to the tiller, and steer as I command you." But they refuse. "Well," says the pilot, "you said you trusted me."

"Yes," says the captain, "and you said that if we trusted you, you would get us into port. But we have not got into port at all."

"No," says the pilot, "you do not trust me, because if you trusted me, you would do as I ask you."

A true trust is obedient to the Lord's commands, and these commands forbid sin. If you trust Jesus, you must leave your sins and take up your cross and follow him. Such trust will surely have its reward: you shall be saved now and saved forever.

God bless you, dear friends, for Christ's sake.

Chapter 8

Work

I must work the works of him that sent me, while it is day: the night cometh, when no man can work. (John 9:4 KJV)

A very speculative question had been put to our Lord, and his answer to that very speculative question is, *I must work.* His disciples wished to know something about the mysterious fact that some people are born in an unhappy condition – blind, deaf, or dumb – and why they were sent into the world under such disadvantageous circumstances. Wouldn't you also like to know? Don't you wish that the Savior had expounded on that mystery? There are so many points of controversy connected with that question, that he could barely have had a more controversial topic. Surely, he could have enlightened us far more than Socrates or Plato. Why didn't he, with such a perfect opportunity, plunge into the labyrinth of metaphysics, expound on predestination, and touch on the points which agree or disagree with free agency? Here was a perfect opportunity for interpreting all the marvels of divine sovereignty. Why didn't he immediately open all this up to the people? Instead, he turns to them and says, "I must work; *you* may think; *you* may talk; *you* may argue, but *I* must work. *You* may be consumed by, if you know no better, the inferior occupation of wrangling about words, but *I* must work. I have to obey a nobler cause than those which come to your carnal ears."

We gather from this that the Savior has a greater respect for work than he has for speculation. That when he comes into the world, he will go to all the mighty thinkers, the gentlemen who are constantly producing new ideas, and put them into the same category as rubbish. But when he finds a single worker, a poor widow who has given her two mites, a poor saint who has spoken for Christ and been the means of the conversion of a soul, he will receive these works which were done for him as precious grains of costly gold. We may say of work done for Christ, like the land of Havilah, *the gold of that land is good*," and Christ thinks it to be so. He estimates the work of faith and labor of love done for him at a great price.

A Necessity to Labor

The first thing we observe in our text is a necessity to labor: *I must work*. With Christ, it wasn't, "I may if I want"; or, "I can if I like." We don't see the mere possibility of work, but a necessity – *I must*. He couldn't help himself. If I may use such words concerning one who is no less divine than he was human, he was under restraint. He was bound. He was compelled. The cords which bound him, however, were the cords of his deity. They were the cords of love which bound him who *is* love. It was because he loved the sons of men so much that he couldn't sit still and see them perish. He couldn't come down from heaven and stand here robed in the same mortal flesh as us and be an impassive, careless, idle spectator of so much evil, so much misery. His heart raced with desire. He thirsted to do good. And his greatest and grandest act, his sacrifice of himself, was a baptism with which he had to be baptized, and he was distressed until it was accomplished.

> He must let his soul run out in hot consecration and devotion to the cause of those whom he came to save.

His great soul within him felt as if it could not stop. It was like the troubled sea that cannot rest. Each of his thoughts was like a mighty wave that could not be still. His whole soul was like a volcano when it begins to swell with the lava and wants to vent. He must let his soul run out in hot consecration and devotion to the cause of those whom he came to save. He says, *I must work*.

Not only was it the love within which drove him, but it was also the sorrow around him which compelled him. That blind man had touched the secret chord which set the Savior's soul to work. If that blind man had not been there, or, rather, if it had been possible for the Savior to forget the cases of misery which existed around him, then he might have been quiet. But because he saw the multitudes perishing like sheep without a shepherd perishing before his soul, because, far more vividly than you and I have ever done, he realized the value of a soul and the horror of a soul being lost, and he felt as though he could not be still, he said, *I must work.*

Picture yourselves standing on the beach when a ship is being broken on the rocks. If there were anything that you could do to contribute towards the rescue of the mariners, wouldn't you feel within yourselves, "I *must* work"? It is said that sometimes when a crowd sees a vessel going to pieces, and hears the cries of the drowning men, they seem as if they were all seized with madness, because they don't know what to do and are ready to sacrifice their own lives if they could possibly do something to save others. Men feel that they *must* work in the presence of so dreadful a need. And Christ saw this world of ours quivering over the pit. He saw it floating, as it were, in an atmosphere of fire, and he wished to quench those flames and make the world rejoice. Therefore, he must work to that end. He could not possibly rest and be quiet. He didn't know how to relax even at night.

> "Cold mountains and the midnight air
> Witnessed the fervor of his prayer."

When he was faint and weary and needed to eat, he would not eat, because the zeal of God's house had eaten him up, and it was his meat and his drink to do the will of him that sent him. The love within and the need around him acted towards one common end and formed an intense necessity, so that the Savior must work.

He also came into this world with a purpose which wouldn't be achieved without work, but which was a passion with him. So he must work, because he desired to accomplish his purpose. The salvation of the many whom the Father had given to him, the gathering together of those who were scattered abroad, the finding of the lost sheep, and the restoration of the fallen – he *must* accomplish these objectives. Eternal purposes must be fulfilled. His own promises must be honored. He had loved his own which were in the world, and he loved them so that he could not leave the world until all his work was completely done, and he would be able to say, *It is finished* (John 19:30).

Hopefully – looking forward to the reward, anticipating the glory of bringing men from the imprisonment of their sins, and carrying them into the tower of salvation – he longed and panted to work. The soldier who is desirous of promotion scorns peace and longs for war, so he may have an opportunity of ascending in the ranks. The young man who wants to carve out a position for himself in the world is not satisfied to vegetate in a country village. He wants work. He wants it because he knows that work is the way of rising in the world. It is true enough, if a man has an honorable ambition, that he should seek the means by which that ambition may be attained.

The Father's desire was that the Son be crowned with the gems of the souls which he had saved, to be the great friend of man, the great Redeemer of mankind, and consequently, the Son must work. He must be men's Savior, and he can't be their Savior without working. Therefore, the passion within, the need around him, and the great and all-absorbing purpose which drove him onward, furnished three cords which bound him, like a sacrifice, to the horns of the altar. *I must work.*

Without going into more detail on a theme so tempting, let me ask whether you and I feel the same compulsion. Because if we are as Christ was in the world, if we are worthy to be called his followers at all, we must be compelled with his compulsion. We must feel the weight of his load. Do we feel as if we *must* work? Oh, there are so many who profess Christ who feel that they must be fed. They don't even get so far into effort as to desire to feed, but they must be fed as with a spoon. They desire to have certain precious gospel truths broken down, dissolved into baby food, and put into their mouths while they lie in bed almost too idle to digest the food after they have received it.

There are some other Christians who feel as if they must always find fault with other people's work, as if it were a passion with them to criticize and judge. There are others who believe they must be excused from working. They will use any excuse to get out of any task, and do their best to escape giving to any charitable or Christian need, and, if they can, they avoid exposing their own precious selves to any kind of sorrow or toil in the service of the Lord Jesus. I trust *we* are not of such a weak spirit as this. If we are, then let us stop bearing the name of the gospel. As one said, "Either be a Stoic, or give up being called a Stoic." So I would either be a Christian, or give up being called a Christian. It is not to be a Christian and to shun work for Christ.

However, I trust that we have felt this compulsion – *I must work.* Why *must* I work? That I may be saved? Oh no! God forbid! I am saved, if I am a Christian, not through my own works, but through Christ's works. I have heard the gospel which tells me that there is life if I look to the Crucified One. I have looked to Christ, and I am saved. Then why must I work? *Because* I am saved. If he bought me with his blood, I must spend myself for him who bought me. If he sought me by his Spirit, I must give myself to him who sought me. If he has taught me by his grace, I must tell to others what I have learned from him. The motive which dictates Christian activity is not so worthless and selfish a one as that of obtaining heaven through that activity. Why, even a Romanist (a masterly Romanist, however strange an anomaly, that so sweet a song should come from so foul a cage of unclean birds!) could sing:

> "My God, I love Thee;
>   not because I hope for heaven thereby,
> Nor yet because who love thee not
>   Must burn eternally.
>
> Thou, O my Savior, thou didst me
>   Upon the cross embrace;
> For me didst bear the nails and spear,
>   And manifold disgrace."

Our love is caused by Christ. His love for us makes us feel that we must work for him. When we were little children, a kind friend made us very happy one day, and yet a second and a third time did that same friend make our little hearts leap for joy. And when we went to bed we said, before we fell asleep, "I wish we could do something for Mrs. So-and-so. I wish I could give her something." Perhaps we had no money. But the next morning, we got a few flowers out of the garden and set off so pleased to take our little bouquet to our kind friend, and we said, "Please accept this little present, because you have been so kind to me." We felt as if we couldn't help it, and we were only afraid that our little present wouldn't be received. We felt that if we could have done ten, twenty, or fifty times as much, we would have thought it all too little. But it was our happiness to do what we did, and to wish to do more.

The same spirit prompts us to desire to do something for the Lord Jesus. Oh, will he accept anything from me? Will he let me try to increase his glory? Will he permit me to feed his lambs, to be a shepherd to his sheep, to look after three or four girls in a Sunday school, to watch over one child as for him, to give a tract away, or to give of my resources to any of his interests? Oh, then, how good it is of him to let me! How I wish I could do more! Oh, how I wish that I had a thousand hands to work for him, a thousand hearts and a thousand tongues, so that I might use all for him!

Brethren, I hope you feel the love of Christ in you which makes you say, "I must work." Then, if you live in this neighborhood, and most of us, I suppose, do live this side of the water, can you go through the courts and streets, can you go into the darker parts of the neighborhood, those close by which you know, without feeling, *I must work*? I wish, sometimes, that some of you people who have been successful in the world and who live a little farther out in the country, where the air gets a little purer, I wish you could be made to sniff the air in which poverty always lives in this city of ours. Then, I think, you would feel as if you must work. Our city missionaries must sometimes feel marvelously enthusiastic, I think, from the sights which they see and the sounds which they hear. They must feel as if they must work, because men are dying, hell is filling, the gospel is not taken to the people, and the people do not come to the gospel. The multitude go their way as though there were no Christ and no heaven. I wish to God I could have said, no hell after they died, but that is their portion, and they live as if they were preparing themselves to inherit it.

A Specialty of Work

Secondly, let us notice that there is a specialty of work – *I must work the works of him that sent me*. There are plenty of people who say, "I must work," but there are very few who say, *I must work the works of him that sent me.* Oh, the work – the brain-work and head-work – that is done in London to get rich! It is very proper, of course. If a man wants to get on in the world, he must work. It is very well. I would not say to any young man, "Be idle." If you want to prosper in anything, throw your whole soul into it and work as hard as you can. Many, many people feel the drive of working to be successful or to support a family. Very proper indeed, but I don't need to exhort you to do it, because, I believe, as honest and moral men you will feel that obligation without any exhortation from me. Some work in order to get fame. Well, that is not such a bad thing on its own, but I don't need to speak about it, because those who choose that path will fall into it without my advice.

> It was not a work of his own devising.

Here is the point: *I must work the works of him that sent me.* Christ came into this world neither to be a king among kings nor to be famous among the famed, but to be a servant of servants and to fulfill the will of God. *Then said I, Behold, I come; in the volume of the book it is written of me, I delight to do thy will, O my God; thy law is within my bowels* (Psalm 40:7-8). He came to do it, and, having come, he did it.

Observe the character of the work which Christ performed. It was not a work of his own devising. It was not a work which he had set to himself of his own will, but it was a work which had been ordained of old and settled by his Father. *I came . . . not to do my own will, but the will of him that sent me.* Observe too, that Christ made no picking nor choosing about this work. He says, *I must work the works* – not some of them, but all of them – whether they're works of drudgery or works of honor, bearing reproach for the truth or bearing testimony to the truth, works of suffering himself or works of relief to those that suffered, works of silent, secret groaning or works of ministry in which he rejoiced in spirit, works of prayer on the mountainside or works of preaching on the mountain's brow. Christ had given himself up unreservedly to do for God whatever the Father asked him to do. All these works were works of mercy, works of soul saving, and unselfish works. He saved others, but he would not save himself. They weren't works by which he increased his own treasure. Instead, he distributed to the needy. They weren't works by which he lifted up himself; he humbled himself to men of no position. His works did not earn him honor among men. Instead, he offered his back to those who beat him. The dishonor of those who dishonored fell upon him. His works were works of pure generosity to men and entire devotion to God.

I wonder whether you and I, as Christians, have ever fully and thoroughly experienced a compulsion to do these types of works. *I must work the works of him that sent me.* Brethren, it's so easy to work our own works, even in spiritual things, but it is so difficult to be brought to this: *I must work the works of him that sent me.* There are ten thousand actions good in themselves, which it might not be right for me to choose as my occupation in life. I know many people who think it is their business to preach, but who really should make it their business to hear for a little while longer. We know some who think it's their job to take the headship of a class, but who might be amazingly useful by giving away some tracts or by taking a seat in a class themselves for a little while.

The fact is, we are not the ones who pick and choose the path of Christian service which we are to walk in, but we are to do the work of him that sent us. Our objective should be, since there is so much work to be done, to find out what part of the work the Master would have us to do. Our prayer should be, "Show me what you would have me to do" – have me to do in particular, not what is generally right, but what is specifically right for me to do. My servant might think it's a very proper thing for her to arrange my papers for me in my study, but I would feel only a small amount of gratitude to her. If, however, she will have a cup of coffee ready for me early in the morning, when I have to travel to a distant country town to preach, I will be much more likely to appreciate her services. So some friends think, "I could do so well if *I* were in such-and-such a position, if I were made a deacon, if I were elevated to a certain position."

Follow the path laid out before you and work as your Master would have you. You will do better where he puts you than where you put yourself. You are no servant at all when you pick and choose your service, because the very spirit, the very essence of service consists in saying, "*Not my will, but thine, be done* (Luke 22:42). I wait for orders from the throne. Teach me what you would have me to do."

However, on this point there is less need of insisting than there is of insisting upon the other. We must feel ourselves impelled to some form or other of spiritual effort for the good of others. I ask you Christian men and women, do you all feel this? Oh, what wonders were performed by two or three hundred people after our Lord went up to heaven. They were enough to evangelize the whole world! Here is this great city of London of ours, with its more than three million inhabitants. I don't know how many Christian souls there are in it, but there must be many thousands. Yet, up to this day, we have been insufficient for the evangelization of this city. Instead of our meeting its demands, it is a simple matter of statistics that ten years ago London was better provided for than, with all our efforts, it now is!

Is this to be tolerated? If there were a good reason for this, we might accept this grim reality. But since there is none, and the fault must be with us, let us ask, What is the cause of the mischief? It is that all Christians haven't yet learned the truth that each Christian is personally to do the work of him that sent him. We are not to delegate our ministers to do it or think that we can discharge the service of God by proxy. Each man and woman must personally give himself and herself to the service of Christ, feeling that he can read this text for himself: "*I, I, I* must work the works of him that sent me. I must do it even if nobody else does. I must feel a compulsion. I must in some form or other commit myself to those works which are specifically the works of God, who sends his people into this wicked world on purpose, so they may do them."

I will say here, as an illustration, to prove to you that progress is not impossible if we are only willing to make the effort. There is probably no religious movement in England which is so overwhelming, which has advanced so rapidly, as the movement of Ritualism, which we sometimes call Puseyism. It is advancing wonderfully, and it is advancing in two quarters, two quarters which ought to shame us forever, because they are the two most inaccessible quarters. You will find rampant Puseyism laying hold upon the upper classes and getting into the drawing rooms which we thought could not be entered. It's storming what we thought to be impregnable citadels of rank and lofty respectability. It's finding them in such a style and getting them into its grip so wholly and completely that the resources of the rich are given far more exceedingly to their false faith than our resources are given to our true faith.

The next greatest advance of this system has been made among the poorest of the poor, those people who, it is said, will not come to hear the gospel. Oh, but that is a lie, because they will come to hear the gospel if the gospel is preached so that they can understand it. But it is the scandal of many Christian churches that these poor people will not go to them. Yet these very same people are affected by Puseyism and get converted to it too. They go down on their knees as earnest worshippers and are thorough believers in the whole thing!

Now, how is this done? Well, I will tell you. The priests who believe in this thing, honestly believe in it. They believe it to be the truth, and they hold it with a grip that is not relaxed. They are not ashamed to suffer reproach for it, but come out boldly in their own colors, not hiding, and playing, and shuffling, as some others have done, ashamed to confess what they have done, but they have come out boldly. And let me say, all honor to them for the honorable courage they have displayed in their dishonorable work! I like to give the devil his due. If you see courage even in a foe, you can still let it be called courage. I reverence the courage of those who will stand up for Rome in the midst of deception, and Protestantism, as well as the courage of the Protestant, who stands up against Rome in the midst of a Roman superiority.

If they have done all this, and they have done it mostly through the real devotion of the priests, don't we have some such courage and devotion among our ministers? I hope, that if the ministers have failed here, each one will begin to correct himself, and that we will become as devoted and as bold in our cause as they can be in theirs.

But the next thing is this: they make all their members and all their admirers devoted missionaries. You will find them reading their little tracts, dropping their books, saying a word to those young men in the shop, talking a little to that young lady in the drawing room. You will find them everywhere sending their sisters of mercy around.

A minister I know went into the house of one of his members and said, "There is a Sister of Mercy going around near here. Does she call at this house?"

"Oh yes," was the answer, "certainly. She goes into every room in the house."

"Well," he said, "I did not know that I even dared to go into every room. Does the Sister of Mercy really go into every room here in the house?"

"Oh yes, sir, and into every room on our street."

"Well, how is that?"

"Oh, I don't know, sir, but she gets in somehow or other."

And why shouldn't we get in somehow or other? Why can't we do what they can do? Should they do what we dare not do and cannot do? Oh, it's a fine thing that the soldiers of the pope should be braver than the soldiers of the cross. Should it be so? Oh! God forbid. May the old spirit, and the old courage, and the old enthusiasm come back to the Christian church, and there is enough to save London yet. There is enough for us to push back the tide of popery yet. There is still enough to prove the gospel and to show that it is still a thing of power, *mighty through God for the destruction of strong holds* (2 Corinthians 10:4). But we must come to this conclusion, that our work, our activity, must drive itself into the special channel of doing the work of him that has sent us, and doing it at once.

A Limitation of Time

I must work the works of him that sent me, while it is day. This limitation of time sounds very weighty to my ears, coming from the lips of Christ. Jesus Christ, the immortal, the everliving, says, *I, I must work while it is day!* If anyone could have postponed work, it was our eternal Lord. He is in heaven, but he is working still. There are a thousand ways in which he can serve his church. We believe not in the intercession of the saints, but in the intercession of the saints' Master, because the saints can't work for us in that land of rest after they quit this world of labor, but he can. He can continue to pray for us. The Head of the church is always active, and yet he said, *I must work while it is day.* See the importance placed on you and me? We can do nothing further with our hands once the turf has covered our head. All time to work is over then, so consider it a warning when it says, *while it is day.*

How long will it be *day* with us? Some days are very short. These wintry days are soon over. My young brother and sister, your day may be very brief. Work while you have it. Is there a sign of tuberculosis? Work then. Don't make that an excuse for idleness, but an argument for labor. Work while it is day. Or, if there is no sign of illness, remember that your sun may still go down before it reaches its noon. Young man, don't wait until your skills are fully developed and your opportunities are large. Instead, say, *I must work the works of him that sent me, while it is day.* You may never live to be twenty-one. Be a soul winner before you are a man!

Dear sister, seek to be a mother in Israel, a mother for Jesus Christ while you are still just a girl. Seek to win souls for Jesus while you yourselves are but lambs in Jesus's fold – *while it is day.* Some of you are getting gray, and your day can't be very much longer. Evening has come, and the shadows are drawn out. You must not make the infirmities of old age an excuse for being altogether out of harness. The Master doesn't ask from you what you are unable to give, but what strength you still have, give it to him *while it is day,* feeling that you must work the works of him that sent you.

While it is day. If I had a prophet's eye and could pick out the people here for whom the bell will toll during the next month, how this text might affect them! *While it is day!* Dear mother, if you had only another thirty days – another month to live – and you knew it, how you would pray for your children during that month! How you would talk to those dear boys about their souls, but you have never taken them aside and spoken to them yet! Sunday school teachers, if you knew that you would only go to class one, two, three, or four more Sundays, how seriously would you begin to talk with those children in your class! This is the way we ought to live and work always. You know Baxter's words:

> "I preach as tho' I ne'er preach again,
> And as a dying man to dying men."

Let us do the same. Suppose you live ten, twenty, or thirty years longer. Those years seem very brief, and when they are gone, they seem like yesterday! So let me even ring the bell myself. Let me sound the text like a warning bell in your ear: "*While it is day! While it is day! While it is day!*"

And, since I just reminded you of your own mortality, let me give the text another sound, as I ask you to remember that the *day* may soon be passed, not to you, but *to the objects of your care.* Let me remind you that there are two lives here to be insured, another life as well as your own. *While it is day.* You will not have the opportunity to speak to some people in London tomorrow, because they will die tonight. It is impossible for you to have an opportunity of speaking to two thousand of them next week, because they will die this week. The bills of mortality will demand, and the insatiable hunger of death will call for them. They must go. Oh, do your work *while it is day* with them!

With some, it is *day* only for a very short time, even though they may live long, because with some men their *day* is only the one occasion when they go to a place of worship; the one occasion when there is sickness in the house, and the missionary enters; the one occasion when a Christian comes across their path and has a fair opportunity to speak to them of Christ. Many of our friends here in London don't have a day of mercy, in a certain sense. They do not hear the gospel. It never crosses their path. A bishop once said that it would have been better for some people in London if they had been born in Calcutta, India, because if they had been born in Calcutta, Christian devotion might have found them. But living as they do, in some of the back slums of London, no one cares about their souls at all. Therefore, since their day may be so brief, and yours is so brief too, let each gird up his loins tonight and say, *I must work the works of him that sent me, while it is day.*

You came over Blackfriars Bridge tonight, and you may drop down dead on it as you go back! You came from your house tonight, and you left at home a dear friend to whom you wish to speak about his soul. Do it tonight, because he may die in the night. I think I read it in the life of Dr. Chalmers, that on one occasion he spent an evening with a number of friends, and there was present a Highland chieftain, a very interesting character. They spent the evening telling amusing stories of their lives and travels. And after an enjoyable evening, they went to bed. At midnight, the whole family was startled from their sleep. The

Highland chieftain was in the pangs and agonies of death. He went up to his chamber in sound health, but died during the night. The impression upon Chalmers' mind was this: "Had I known that he would have died, wouldn't the evening have been spent differently? Then shouldn't it have been spent in a very different manner by men all of whom might have died?" He felt as if the blood of that man's soul in some measure fell upon him. The experience itself was a lasting lesson to him. May it also be to us in the hearing of the story. From this time forth, may we work with all our might *while it is day*.

Reminder of Our Mortality

Now we come to the last words of the text: *the night cometh, when no man can work.* Here is the reminder of our mortality. *The night cometh.* You can't put it off. As sure as night comes in its due season to the earth, so death comes to you. There are no maneuvers by which night can be deferred or prevented, nor by which death can be postponed or altogether stopped. *The night cometh,* however much we may dread it, or however much we may long for it. It comes with sure and steady steps in its appointed time. *The night cometh.* The night cometh for the pastor, who has labored for his flock; for the evangelist, who has preached with earnestness; for the Sunday school teacher, who has loved her charge; and for the missionary, who has worked for souls. *The night cometh.* The night cometh for the sitters in the pews – the father, the mother, the daughter, the husband, the wife. *The night cometh.* Will you need to be reminded that the night cometh for you? Will you embrace it for yourself, or will you, nursing man's delusion, think all men are mortal but yourself? The night cometh when the eyes are closed, when the limbs grow cold and stiff, when the pulse becomes faint and, finally, will stop its beating. *The night cometh.*

Solomon thought this out for all mankind: *There is no man that has power over the spirit to retain the spirit; neither does he have power over the day of death, and weapons are of no use in that war; neither shall wickedness deliver those that are given to it.* (Ecclesiastes 8:8). To the Christian worker it is sometimes a dreary thought. I have plans in action for the cause of God, some of which I've just begun, and sometimes I think I would really like to live long enough to see them mature.

Perhaps I will, but daily, I feel like I will not. Constantly, it haunts me – I may begin these things, but if I don't do all I can do today, I may never have tomorrow. So I say again what I've said a thousand times in my own soul, that I will do all I can *now*. As for the years that are to come, they must manage for themselves. It is no use when starting plans to look forward at what they may grow into in years to come and then to write down as our work what might spring out of our work. No. We must do immediately and at once all that has to be done. God can afford to wait with his work, but we can't afford to delay with ours. We must work now, *while it is day: the night cometh, when no man can work.* The coming of the night, though always comfortable to the Christian when he remembers that he will see his Master, is sometimes still a very heavy thought to us who are engaged in many works for Christ, and who would like to live to see some of those works prosper.

How dreary the conclusion! *When no man can work.* Mother, you can't bend over your children and teach them the way of life when you have departed. If you desire to have them taught in the things of God, your voice will never teach them of the love of Jesus when you're gone. Missionary, if that district of yours is unattended and souls are lost, you can never make up for the damage you've done, for the mischief you've caused. Your memory and your love are past. You are gone. The place that knew you once knows you no more. Among the deeds of the living, you can take no share. If, by your example, you lifted the floodgates of sin, you cannot return to let them down again, or to stem the current.

> If you missed opportunities to serve Jesus here, you can't come back again to retrieve them.

If you missed opportunities to serve Jesus here, you can't come back again to retrieve them. If one were a warrior and lost a battle, one might long for another day to dawn and for another conflict to save the campaign. But if you lose the battle of life, you will never have it to fight again. The tradesman may have claimed bankruptcy once, but he trusts that, with more careful decisions, he may still achieve success. But bankruptcy in our spiritual service is bankruptcy forever, and we have no chance of retrieving our loss. It is a night in which no man can work.

The multitude before the throne can do no service here. They cannot alleviate the poverty of London or remove its shame and sin. They can praise God, but they cannot help man. They can sing unto him that loved them and washed them, but they cannot preach of him, nor proclaim to those who need to be washed at the fountain that is filled with his blood. It would almost be desirable if they could, because surely, they would do the work so much better than we can do it! But the Master has decreed otherwise. They must fight no more. They must only stand and look on at the battle. They must work the field no longer. They will eat the fruit, but they cannot till the soil. The work is left to those who are still here. Let us have no regrets, because they can't join in. Instead, let us thank God that he reserves for us all the honor as well as all the labor. Let us plunge into the work now.

Like the British soldiers in battle, when few were told by their king that he hoped there was not one man there who desired to be more, for, said he, "the fewer the men, the greater each man's share of the honor." So let us wish for helpers from the skies. With the might of God upon us; with the Word still full of precious promises; with the mercy seat still rich in blessing; with the Holy Spirit, the irresistible Deity, still dwelling in us; with the precious name of Jesus, which makes hell tremble, still to cheer us, let us proceed, feeling that we *must work . . . while it is day: the night cometh, when no man can work.* Let us work as long as the day lasts. As we hear the chariot wheels of eternity behind us, we will speed on with all our might.

But all that I've been saying applies very little to some of you, because you've never given yourselves to God. You are still servants of Satan, and you cannot serve God. Poor souls, do you know why we want Christian people to be devoted? It's in order that you may be saved. We wouldn't need to stir up Christians if it weren't for you. You are without God; you are without Christ. Some of you are on your way to everlasting ruin. Others, who have heard the gospel for many years and know as much about it as I do, know nothing about its power within your own souls. Isn't it strange that we are so devoted to you, but you aren't devoted to yourselves?

If there was a woman's child out there in the street, and a dozen women tried to grab the child before it was run over by a cab, you would think it was a very strange thing if the mother stood by calm and cool, unexcited, or, as it were, uninterested about it. Yet, here is your soul, and there are just as many people in this chapel who feel anxious about you and wish they could save you, yet you do not care about your own soul! So if you are lost forever, it will be no surprise, will it? You do not value yourself at anything. You throw yourself away. Who should be blamed for this? Will this be one of the thorns in your pillow forever: "I took no thought about my soul. I set no value on it, and I carelessly threw it away"? Will this sobering remorse keep up the flame unquenchable that shall forever torture your conscience: "I refused to think about everlasting things. I played the fool, and danced my way into hell. I wasted my time where God was devoted. I was careless where ministers wept. I was frivolous where Christ bled"?

I beg you to consider your ways and remember that whoever believes in the Lord Jesus Christ will be saved! Believe in him. Trust him. That is the way of salvation. Rest upon him. And when you've been saved, I pray that the Lord would cause you to feel the impulse of my text and say, "I too must join with the band of workers saved by Christ. I too must say as Christ said, *I must work the works of him that sent me, while it is day: the night cometh, when no man can work.*"

Chapter 9

The Spur

I must work the works of him that sent me, while it is day:
the night cometh, when no man can work. (John 9:4 KJV)

If this ninth chapter of John is intended to be a continuation of the history contained in the eighth, as we think it is, then it brings to our attention a very extraordinary fact. We observe in the eighth chapter that our Lord was about to be stoned by the Jews. Then, he withdrew himself from the circle of his infuriated foes and passed through the crowd, not in a hurried manner, but in a calm and dignified way. He was not at all disconcerted, but wholly self-possessed. His disciples, who had seen his danger, gathered around him while he quietly retreated. The group went their way with firm footsteps until they reached the outside of the temple. At the gate, there sat a man well known to have been blind from his birth. Our Savior was so little affected by the danger which had threatened him that he paused and fixed his eye upon the poor beggar, attentively surveying him. He continued in his forward progress and worked the miracle of this man's healing. If it's true that the two chapters make up only one narrative, and I think it is, though we aren't absolutely sure, then we have before us a most memorable instance of the marvelous calmness of our Savior in the face of danger. When the Jews took up stones to stone him, he didn't needlessly expose his life, but after he had withdrawn a very little distance from the immediate danger, he was stopped by the sight of human misery and maintained a calm head to perform a deed of mercy.

Oh, the divine majesty of benevolence! How brave it makes a man! It leads him to forget himself, despise danger, and become so calm that he can coolly perform the work which is given to him to do. I see our Savior as being considerate of others and unmindful of himself. There is a lesson here for us, not only for us to imitate but also to bring us comfort. If he, while flying from his enemies, still stopped to bless the blind, how much more will he bless us who seek his face now that he is exalted on high and clothed with divine power and glory at the right hand of the Father? There is nothing to hurry him now. He is exposed to no danger now. Send up your prayer, breathe out your desires, and he will reply, *According to your faith be it unto you* (Matthew 9:29).

As we read about this cure of the blind man, we are struck again with the difference between the disciples and the Master. The disciples looked at this man, blind from birth, as a great mystery, a strange phenomenon, and they began, like philosophers, to suggest theories as to how it was consistent with divine justice that a man could be born blind. They saw that there must be a connection between sin and suffering, but they couldn't trace the connection in this instance. So they were all speculating on the wonderful problem in front of them, which they didn't know how to solve.

This reminds us of theories on another difficulty which never has been explained yet: the origin of evil. They wanted to sail on the boundless deep and were impatient for their Master to pilot them, but he had other and better work to do. Our Lord gave them an answer, but it was a short and curt one. He wasn't looking at the blind man from their point of view. He wasn't considering how the man came to be blind, but how his eyes could be opened. He considered less the various metaphysical and moral difficulties which might arise out of the case, and considered more what would be the best method to remove from the man his suffering and deliver him from his piteous plight. A lesson to us, that instead of inquiring how sin came into the world, we should ask how can we get it out of the world. Instead of worrying our minds about how this set of circumstances is consistent with justice, and how the event can work together with kindness, we should see how both can be turned into something useful to God.

The Judge of all the earth can take care of himself. He does not experience any difficulties for which he needs any of our advice. Only presumptuous unbelief ever dares to suppose the Lord to be perplexed. It will be much better for us to do the work of him that sent us, than to be judging divine circumstances or our fellow men. It is not ours to speculate, but to perform acts of mercy and love according to the intent of the gospel. So let us be less inquisitive and more practical, less for cracking doctrinal nuts and more for bringing forth the bread of life to the starving multitudes.

> The Judge of all the earth can take care of himself.

Once again, our Lord tells us the right way of looking at sorrow and at sin. It was a dreadful thing to see a man shut out from the light of the sun from his very birth, but our Savior took a very encouraging view of it. His view was not in despair and contained nothing that could suggest complaining. It was most encouraging and stimulating. He explained the man's blindness in this way: *Neither has this man sinned nor his parents, but that the works of God should be made manifest in him.* The man's calamity was God's opportunity. His distress was an occasion for displaying divine goodness, wisdom, and power.

I see sin everywhere – in myself, in others, in this great city, in the nations of the earth, and very obvious sin and suffering in war. But what should I say about it? Should I sit down and wring my hands in utter despair? If so, I would be incapable of service. No. If I am going to do good, as Jesus did, I must take his brave and hopeful view of things. In this way, I will keep my heart whole and be prepared to work. The Master's view of it is that all the distress in the world provides, through the infinite kindness of God, a platform for the display of divine love.

I remember in the life of Dr. Lyman Beecher, he tells of a young convert who, after finding peace with God, was heard by him to say, "I rejoice that I was a lost sinner." You might think it's a strange thing to be glad about, because of all things it is most to be mourned. But here was her reason: "Because God's infinite grace, and mercy, and wisdom, and all his attributes, are glorified in me as they never could have been had I not been a sinner and had I not been lost." Isn't that the best light in which to see the saddest things? Sin, somehow or other, desperate evil as it is, will be overruled to display God's goodness. Just as the goldsmith sets a foil around a sparkling diamond, the Lord has allowed moral and physical evil to come into this world to cause his infinite wisdom, grace, power, and all his other attributes to be seen better by the whole intelligent universe.

Let's look at it in this light, and the next time we see suffering, we will say, "Here's our opportunity to show what the love of God can do for these sufferers." The next time we witness abounding sin, let us say, "Here is an opportunity for a great achievement of mercy." I suppose great engineers have been very glad for Niagara, that they might span it; very glad for the Mont Cenis, that they might bore it; very glad for the Suez Isthmus, that they might cut a canal through it – glad that there were difficulties, that there might be room for engineering skill. Were there no sin, there would have been no Savior; if no death, no resurrection; if no fall, no new covenant; if no rebellious race, no incarnation, no Calvary, no ascension, no second advent.

That is a fantastic way of looking at evil and marvelously stimulating. Though we don't know, and perhaps will never know the deepest reason why an infinitely gracious God permitted sin and suffering to enter the universe, yet we can at least encourage this practical thought: God will be glorified in the overcoming of evil and its consequences. Therefore, let us gird up our loins in God's name for our part of the conflict.

The Master Worker

The text is a portrait of the great Master Worker. Let's read it again: *I must work the works of him that sent me, while it is day: the night cometh, when no man can work.*

First, this Master Worker takes his own share in the work. He says, *I must work.* I, Jesus, the Son of Man, for two or three years working here on earth in public ministry, I, I must work. There is a sense in which all gospel work is Christ's. As the atoning sacrifice, he treads the wine press alone. As the great Head of the church, all that is done is to be credited to him. But in the sense in which he used these words, speaking of his human nature, speaking of himself as tabernacling among the sons of men, there was a portion of the work of relieving this world's woe and scattering gospel truth among men, that he must do, and nobody else *could* do. "I must work, preach, pray, and heal, even I, the Christ of God." In salvation, Jesus stands alone. In life-giving, he has no human coworker. But in light-giving – which he refers to in the fifth verse: *As long as I am in the world, I am the light of the world* (John 9:5) – he has many companions. All his saints are the light of the world, even as Jesus Christ while in the world was the world's light.

He cured some who could not be cured by Peter, or James, or John. Some had the good news brought to them who couldn't receive it from any lip but his own. Our Lord, when he became the servant of servants, took his share in the common labors of the elect brotherhood. How this should encourage us! It is sufficient for the general to stand in the place of observation and direct the battle. We don't usually expect that the commander will take a personal share in the work of the conflict. But with Jesus this is not so. He fought in the ranks as a common soldier.

As God-man and Mediator, he rules and governs all the distribution of grace. Yet, as partaker of our flesh and blood, he once bore the burden and heat of the day. As the great Architect and Master Builder, he supervises all. Yet, there is a portion of his spiritual temple which he humbled himself to build with his own hands. Jesus Christ has seen actual service and actually resisted to the point of blood in the midst of the dust and turmoil of strife.

It is said that this same aspect made Alexander's soldiers brave, because if they were worn out by long marches, Alexander did not ride but marched side by side with them. If a river had to be crossed in the heat of opposition, in the midst of all the risk was Alexander himself. Let this be our encouragement – Jesus Christ has taken a personal share in the evangelism of the world. He has not only taken his own part as Head, Prophet, High Priest, and Apostle, in which he stands alone, but he has also taken his part among the common builders in the erection of the New Jerusalem.

Next, our Lord placed great emphasis upon the gracious work which was laid upon him. *I must work the work of him that sent me*; whatever else is not done, I must do that. As his servant, I must faithfully do the work allotted to me by God. Those against me may be close at my heels, their stones may be ready to fall upon me, but I must fulfill my lifework. I must open blind eyes and spread the light around me. I can forget to eat bread; I can forget to find shelter for myself from the dew that falls so heavily at night, but this work I must do.

Beyond all things, the Redeemer felt a force upon him to do his Father's will. *Knew ye not that it behooves me to be about my Father's business?* (Luke 2:49). *For the zeal of thy house has consumed me* (Psalm 69:9). Everything in the Savior's life yielded to his master passion. There were some works our Savior would not do. When someone asked him to speak to his brother to divide their inheritance, though that might have been a useful thing, Christ did not feel a call to it. *And he said unto him, Man, who made me a judge or a divider over you?* (Luke 12:14). But when it came to the work of giving light, *that* he must do. It was the specialty of his life, and to this he bent all his strength. He was like an arrow shot from a bow, not speeding toward two targets, but with undivided force hurrying towards one single end. The unity of his purpose was never for a moment broken. No second object ever eclipsed the first. Certain works of grace, works of benevolence, works of light-giving, works of healing, works of saving – these he must do. *He* must do them. He must perform his own part of them. He rightly describes this work as the *works of him that sent me.* Note that.

If ever there lived a man who might have taken a part of the honor of the work for himself, it was the Lord Jesus. Yet, over and over again, he says, *The Father that dwells in me, he does the works* (John 14:10). As man, he is particularly careful to set us the example of acknowledging constantly that if any work is done by us, it is the work of God through us. So, though he says, *I must work*, notice the next words: *the works of him that sent me.* They are still my Father's works when most think they are mine. Though I must work them, they will still be credited to him, and he shall gain honor from them. If I don't say much about this in respect to Christ, it is because it seems so much easier to apply this to us than to him, and if so easily applied, let it be humbly and practically remembered by us today. If you win a soul by your work, it is God's work. If you instruct the ignorant, you do it, but it is God that does it through you if it's rightly done. Learn to acknowledge the hand of God, and yet don't pull back your own. Learn to put your hand out, and yet feel that it is powerless unless God extends his own. Combine in your thoughts the need of the all-working God and the duty of your own exertion. Don't make the work of God an excuse for your idleness, and don't let your earnest activity ever tempt you to forget that the power belongs to him.

The Savior is a model to us in putting this in just the right form. It is God's work to open the blind eye. If the eye has been sealed in darkness from birth, no man can open it. God must do it, but the clay and spittle must still be used, and Siloam's pool must be made use of, or the light will never enter the sightless eye. So, in grace, it is God's work to illuminate the understanding by his Spirit. It is his work to move the affections, his work to influence the will, his work to convert the entire nature, his work to sanctify, and his work to save.

> He was not ashamed to tell others about his submission to the Father.

Yet you, believer, are to work this miracle. The truth you spread will illuminate the intellect; the arguments you use will influence the affections; the reasons you give will move the will, and the precious gospel you teach will purify the heart. But it is God who does it – God dwelling in the gospel. Only as you see and understand these two truths will you work correctly. *I* must work personally, and this holy work must be my special business, but I must do it in a right spirit, humbly feeling all the while that it is God's work in and through me.

Our Lord, in this portrait of himself as the master worker, is clearly seen as owning his true position. He says, *I must work the works of him that sent me.* He had not come from the Father on his own account. He was not here as a principal, but as a subordinate, as an ambassador sent by his king. His own witness was, *I can of my own self do nothing; as I hear, I judge, and my judgment is just because I seek not my own will, but the will of the Father who has sent me* (John 5:30). He often reminded his hearers in his preaching that he was speaking in his Father's name, and not in his own name. For instance, when he said, *The words that I speak unto you I speak not of myself; but the Father that dwells in me, he does the works* (John 14:10). He took upon himself the form of a servant. God gave him a mission and gave him the grace to carry out that mission, and he was not ashamed to tell others about his submission to the Father.

In his divine nature, he was God over all, blessed forever, whose praises ten thousand harpers are overjoyed to sound upon that glassy sea. Yet, as the Mediator, he lowered himself to be sent, a commissioned agent from God, a servant to do Jehovah's bidding. Because he was such, it was proper for him as a servant to be faithful to him that sent him. Jesus felt this as a part of the divine obligation, which impelled him to say, "I must work. I am a sent man, and I have to give an account to him that sent me."

Brothers and sisters, I wish we all felt this. Because just as the Father sent Christ, in the same way Christ sent us, and we are acting under divine authority as divine representatives. We must, in joy, be faithful to the communion with which God has honored us by trusting us with the responsibility of the gospel of Christ. No man shall serve God correctly if he thinks he stands on an independent footing. It is recognizing your true position that will help to drive you onward in incessant diligence in the cause of your God.

Dwelling very briefly on each of these points, I must remind you that our Lord did not regard himself merely as an official, but he threw hearty enthusiasm into the work he undertook. I see unyielding zeal glowing like a subdued flame in the very center of the live coal of the text. *I must work the works of him that sent me.* Not, "I will," "I intend," or "I ought," but "I must." Even though he was sent, the commission was so compatible to his nature that he worked with all the enthusiasm of a volunteer. He was commissioned, but his own will propelled him forward, not out of obligation, but willingly the Lord Jesus became a Savior. He couldn't help it. It was within his very nature that he must be doing good. Was he not God, and isn't God the fountain of kindness?

Doesn't Deity, perpetually like the sun, send forth beams to gladden his creatures? Jesus Christ, the God incarnate, by irresistible instinct must be found doing good. Besides, he was so tender and so compassionate that he had to bless those in sorrow. He felt for that blind man. The blind man grieved in his darkness, but not more than the Savior grieved for the poor sufferer's sake. The eyes which Christ fixed on that man were eyes brimming with tears of pity. He felt the miseries of humanity. He was not stonehearted, but tender and full of compassion towards all the suffering sons of men.

So our Savior was self-impelled to his labors of grace. His love forced him – he must do the work that he was sent to do. It is a right thing when a man's business and inclinations run together. If you put your son as an apprentice in a trade which he doesn't like, he will never make much of it. But when his duty and his own desires run in the same channel, then he is likely to prosper. So Jesus was sent of God, but not as an unwilling ambassador. He came as cheerfully and joyously as if it was by his own voluntary wish. He cried in gracious enthusiasm, "I must, I *must*."

No man does a really good and great work until he feels he must. No man preaches well except he who *must* preach. The man sent of God must come under irresistible pressure, even like the apostle of old who said, *For though I preach the gospel, I have no reason to glory, for it is an obligation laid upon me; for woe is me, if I do not preach the gospel!* (1 Corinthians 9:16). Or, he must be like the eloquent Eliphaz in the book of Job who spoke first and only spoke at all because he felt like a vessel needing to vent. Our Savior became so grand a worker because desire kindled, burned, and flamed within his soul until his nature was all aglow. He was like a volcano in full action which must pour forth its fiery flood. But in his case the lava was not that which destroys, but that which blesses and makes rich.

Another point regarding our Savior as a worker is that he clearly saw that there was a fitting time to work and that this time would have its end. In a certain sense, Christ always works. For Zion's sake he does not rest, and for Jerusalem's sake he does not remain silent in his intercessions before the eternal throne. But, my brethren, as a man – preaching, healing, and relieving the sick on earth – Jesus had his day, just like every other man, and that day ended at the set time. He referenced a common Eastern proverb which says that men can only work by day, and when the day is over, it is too late to work, and he meant that.

He had an earthly lifetime in which to labor, and when that was over, he would no longer perform the kind of labor he was then doing. He called his lifetime a day in order to show us that he took seriously the shortness of it. We too often look at life as a matter of years, and we even think of the years as though they were very long, even though every year seems to spin around more quickly than the last. Men who are growing gray will tell you that life seems to pass by at a much faster rate than in their younger days. To a child, a year seems like a long time. To a grown man, even ten years is just a short space of time. To God, the Eternal, a thousand years are like a single day.

Here, our Lord sets us an example of estimating our time at a high rate, on account of how brief it is. The longest you have is a day. That day, how short! Young man, is it your morning? Are you just converted? Is the dew of repentance still trembling upon the green blade? Have you just seen the first radiance which streams from the eyelids of the morning? Have you heard the joyous singing of birds? Up with you, man, and serve your God in love! Serve him with all your heart!

Or have you known your Lord so long that it is noon with you, and the burden and heat of the day are on you? Persevere, make good speed, because your sun will soon decline. And have you been a Christian long? Then the shadows lengthen, and your sun is almost down. Quick with you, man, use both hands. Strain every nerve, and put every muscle to work. Do all at all times, and in all places, that your mind can think of or your enthusiasm can suggest to you, because *the night cometh, when no man can work.*

I love to think of the Master with these furious Jews behind him, yet stopping because he must do the work of healing, because his day was still unended. He cannot die until his day is over. His time is not yet come, and if it were, he would close his life by doing one more act of mercy. So he stops to bless the wretched and then passes on his way. Be quick to do good at all times. *Be ye steadfast, unmovable, always abounding in the work of the Lord* (1 Corinthians 15:58). Knowing that the time is short, redeem the time, because the days are evil. Press much into little by continuous diligence. Glorify your God greatly while the short day of your life burns on, and may God accept you as he accepted his Son.

Ourselves As Workers Under Him

First, I'll remind you that there rests on each of us a personal obligation – individual, distinct, personal obligation. *I must work the works of him that sent me.* We are in danger nowadays of losing ourselves in societies and associations. We must labor to maintain the uniqueness of our dedication to Christ Jesus. History is rich with records of deeds of personal daring. We can't expect modern warfare to exhibit much of the same, because the fighting is done so much by masses and machinery. In the same way, I am afraid our mode of doing Christian work is getting to be so mechanical, so much *en masse,* that there is barely room in ordinary cases for personal deeds of daring and individual acts of bravery. Yet, the success of the church will lie in that very daring and bravery. It's in each man feeling that he has something to do for Christ, which an angel couldn't do for him and that the strength of a church exists in that, before God. He must believe that God has committed to him a certain work which, if it's not done by him, will never be done. A certain number of souls will enter heaven through his influence, and they will never enter in any other way. God has given his Son power over all flesh to give eternal life, to as many as he has given him. We must believe that Christ has given us power over some part of the flesh, and by our instrumentality they will get eternal life, and by no other means. We have work to do, and we must do it.

> We have work to do, and we must do it.

Brothers and sisters, our church will be grandly equipped for service when you all have this same outlook, when there is no throwing the work on the minister, or on the more gifted brothers, or leaving it all to be done by distinguished sisters, but when each one feels, "I have my work, and to my work I will bend my whole strength, to do it in my Master's name."

Secondly, the personal obligation in the text compels us to do the same type of work as Christ did. I explained to you what it was. We are not called to save souls, for he alone is the Savior, but we are called to enlighten the sons of men. That is to say, sin is not even known to be sin by many. Our teaching and example must make sin apparent to them. The way of salvation by the substitutionary sacrifice of Christ is quite unknown to a large part of mankind. It is our work to simply and incessantly be telling that soul-saving story. This work must be done, no matter what else we leave undone.

Some men spend their time making money, and that is the main object of their lives. They would be just as usefully employed if they spent all their lives collecting pins or cherry stones. Whether a man lives to accumulate gold coins or brass nails, his life will be equally pointless and end in the same disappointment. Moneymaking, or fame-making, or power-getting, are only pieces of play. They are sports and games for children. But the work of him that sent us is a far nobler thing. It is permanent gain. If I gain a soul, it is lasting treasure. If I win the Lord's approval, I am forever richer. If I give a man one better thought of God, if I bring to a darkened soul the light from heaven, or lead one erring heart to peace, if one spirit quickly rushing downward to hell is by my means directed to a blissful heaven, then I have done some work worth doing. And such work, brethren, we *must* do, whatever else we leave undone. Let's make everything else in this world subservient to this which is our lifework. We have our callings, we ought to have them, for *if anyone desires not to work neither should he eat* (2 Thessalonians 3:10).

Our earthly calling is not our lifework. We have a high calling of God in Christ Jesus, and this must take priority. Poor or rich, healthy or sick, honored or disgraced, we must glorify God. This is necessity. All else *may* be, this *must* be. We resolve, sternly resolve, and desperately determine, that we will not throw away our lives on playthings, but God's work must and will be done by us. Each man will do his own share, God helping him. May the ever-blessed Holy Spirit give us power and grace to turn our resolves into actions.

Let us not forget the truth which I shared earlier: that it is God's work which we are called upon to do. Let us look at the text again. *I must work the works of him that sent me.* I can discover no greater motivation in all the world than this, that the work I have to do is God's work. We have the example of Samson. The strength which existed in Samson was not his own, it was God's strength. Was that a reason for Samson to lie still and be idle? No, it was the very sound of a mighty trumpet which stirred the blood of the hero to fight for the people of God. If the strength of Samson was more than the force of sinew and muscle, force given to him by the Almighty One, then to the work with you, Samson, and smite the Philistines! Slay again thy thousands!

Do you dare to sleep with God's Spirit upon you? Up, man! Feel free to sleep if you are just a common Israelite, but when God is in you and with you, how can you remain idle? No, use your strength and conquer the enemies!

When Paul was in Corinth, God performed special miracles by his hands, so that even handkerchiefs which were taken from his body healed the sick. Was that a reason for Paul to withdraw himself to some quiet retreat and do nothing? To my mind, there appears to be no stronger argument for why Paul should go from house to house and lay his hands on all around and heal the sick. It's the same with you. You have the power to work miracles, my brother. The sharing of the gospel, accompanied by the spirit of God, works moral and spiritual miracles. Since you can work these miracles, should you say, "God will do his own work"? No, man, but right and left, at all times and in all places, go and proclaim the soul-saving story, and God will prepare your way! God works by you, so you must work.

A small vessel, lying idle in dock without freight, is useless to its owner. But a great ship with much horsepower cannot be allowed to remain unemployed. The greater the power at our command, the more urgently we are bound to use it. The indwelling power of God is extended to us in reply to faith and prayer, so shouldn't we work to obtain it? The fact that the church's work is God's work rather than hers, is no reason for her to indulge in sloth. If she had only her own strength, it might not be such a crime for her to waste it; but being surrounded with God's strength, she dares not loiter. God's message to her is, *Awake, awake; put on thy strength, O Zion; put on thy beautiful garments, O Jerusalem, the holy city* (Isaiah 52:1). God desires that this message be heard by every heart, so that all of us would arise, because God is in our midst.

Next, we see in the text our obligation resulting from our position. We are all sent just like Jesus was if we are believers in Christ. Let us feel the weight of our obligation pressing us into action. What would you think of an angel who was sent from the throne of God to bear a message, and who lingered on the way or refused to go? It was midnight, and the message came to Gabriel and his fellow songsters, "Go and sing o'er the plains of Bethlehem where shepherds keep their flocks. Here is your sonnet: Glory to God in the highest, on earth peace, good will towards men." Could you imagine if they didn't act, or if they wished to decline the task? It would be impossible with such music and with such a mission given from such a Lord! They sped joyously on their way. Your mission is not less honorable than that of the angels. You are sent to speak of good things which bring peace and good will to men and glory to God. Will you stand around and do nothing? Can you remain silent? No, as the Lord Jesus sends you, go forth. I pray that you go at once and proclaim the story of his love with joy. I could imagine an angel almost being tempted to linger, if sent to execute vengeance and to deluge fields with blood for the iniquity of nations. But I don't think he would even hesitate then, for these holy ones do the Lord's bidding without question. If the mission was of mercy, the loving spirit of an angel would leap for joy and be excited by the sweetness of the errand as well as by the mission of his Lord.

> As the Lord Jesus sends you, go forth.

We, too, if we are sent by God on a difficult mission, are bound to go. But if we're sent on so sweet a mission as proclaiming the gospel, how can we delay? To tell the poor criminal shut up in the dungeon of despair that there is liberty, to tell the condemned that there is pardon, to tell the dying that there is life in a look at the crucified One – do you find this hard? Do you call this toil? Shouldn't it be the sweetest aspect of your life that you have such blessed work as this to do? If tonight, when you are in your chamber alone, you suddenly see a vision of angels who speak to you in celestial voices and appoint you for holy service in the church, you would surely feel impressed by such a visit. But Jesus Christ himself has come to you, has bought you with his blood, and has set you apart by his redemption. You have confessed his coming to you, because you have been baptized into his death and declared yourself to be his. Are you less impressed by Christ's coming than you would have been by an angel's visit?

Awake, my brother, the hand of the Crucified has touched you, and he has said, "Go in your strength." The eyes that wept over Jerusalem have looked into your eyes, and they have said with all their ancient tenderness, "My servant, go and snatch dying sinners like brands from the burning, by proclaiming my gospel." Will you be disobedient to the heavenly vision and despise him that speaks to you from his cross on earth and from his throne in heaven? Blood-washed as you are, blood-bought as you are, give yourself up more fully than ever to the delightful service which your Redeemer assigns to you. Be quick to say, "I, even I, must work the work of him that sent me while it is day."

You have no idea the amount of good you may do, my brethren, if you always feel the burden of the Lord as you should. I was led to think of that fact from a letter which I received, which did my heart good as I read it. The dear friend who wrote it is present, and I know he won't mind my reading an extract. He had fallen into very great sin even though he often attended this tabernacle. Being frequently convicted in heart, his conversion wasn't brought about until one day he was riding by railway to a certain town. He says, "I entered into a compartment in which were three of the students of the Tabernacle College. Although I did not know them at first, I began speaking on the subject of temperance. I found two of them were total abstainers, and one was not. We had a nice, friendly chat, and one of the abstainers asked me if I enjoyed the pardon of my sins and peace with God. I told him I regularly attended the tabernacle, but I could not give up all my sins. He then told me how, in his own case, he had found it very desirable to be much in prayer and communion with God, and how in this way he was kept free from many sins which had previously held him prisoner. I concluded my business in the town and was returning home. I was rather foolish, because I had no money with me to pay for my ride home and consequently, had to walk all the way. I heard some singing at a little chapel. I entered and was invited to a seat. It was H-- Baptist Chapel. It turned out that the three students with whom I had travelled on the train a few hours before were there. It was an occasion of deep concern to many, because one of the students, who was their pastor, was saying good-bye to his flock that evening, and many were in tears, including him. I asked one of the students to pray for me. He did so, and I tried to lift up my whole heart to God, and, as it were, leave all my sins outside. I found them a heavy weight. At last I believed in Jesus and exercised a simple faith, the kind I never knew before. I became quite remorseful and humiliated. I found the Lord there; he is sweet to my soul. God has for Christ's sake forgiven me of all my sins. I am happy now. I will always pray for the students at the Pastors' College and never, I hope, withhold my finances for the support of the same. God be praised for the students!"

Do you see that a casual word about Christ and the soul will have its reward? I heard once of a clergyman who used to go hunting. When he was reproved by his bishop, he replied that he never went hunting when he was on duty. But he was asked, "When is a clergyman off duty?" It is the same with the Christian – when is he off duty? He ought to be always about his Father's business, ready for anything and everything that may glorify God. He feels that he is not sent on Sunday only, but sent always, not called now and then to do good, but sent throughout his whole life to work for Christ.

The greatest obligations seem to me to lie upon each one of us to be serving Christ, because of the desperate case of our ungodly neighbors. Many of them are dying without Christ, and we know what their end must be, an end that has no end, a misery that has no bounds. Oh, the sorrow which sin causes on earth! But what is that to the never-ending misery of the world to come! Our time in which to serve the Lord on earth is very short. If we are going to glorify God as dwellers on earth, we must do it now. We will soon be committed to the grave, or they whom we are able to bless may go there before us. Let us then challenge ourselves! I felt much weight on my mind yesterday from the consideration that we, as a nation, are enjoying peace, an unspeakable blessing, the value of which, none of us can rightly estimate. Now, if we don't make, as a Christian church, the most diligent attempt to spread the gospel in these times of peace, before long this nation may also be plunged into war. War is the most unquestionable of curses. Among its other mischiefs, it turns the minds of the people away from all religious thoughts.

Now, while we have peace, and God spares this land from the horrors of war, shouldn't the church of God be intensely eager to use their opportunities? The night is coming, and I don't know how dark that night may be. The political atmosphere seems heavily charged with evil elements. The result of the present conflict between France and Prussia may not be what some would hope, because it may again crush Europe beneath a despot's heel. Now, while we have liberty – a liberty which our fathers bought at the stake and sealed with their blood – let us use it. While it is day, let us work the works of him that sent us, and let each man take for his motto the verse that comes right after my text, *As long as I am in the world, I am the light of the world* (John 9:5). Take care that your light is not darkness. Take care that you don't conceal it. If it is light, take care that you don't despise it, because even if it's a little light, it is what God has given you. Make sure that you will be able to give God a joyful account of even your little light. If you have any light, even if it's only a spark, it is for the world that you have it. It has been given to you for the benefit of the souls of men. Use it, use it now, and God help you.

Oh, that our light as a church would shine upon this congregation! How I long to see all my congregation saved! Let believers be more in prayer, more in service, more in holiness, and God will send us his abundant blessing for Jesus's sake. Amen.

Chapter 10

The Blind Beggar of the Temple and His Wonderful Cure

As long as I am in the world, I am the light of the world. When he had thus spoken, he spat on the ground and made clay of the spittle, and he anointed the eyes of the blind man with the clay and said unto him, Go, wash in the pool of Siloam (which is by interpretation, Sent). Then he went and washed and came back seeing. (John 9:5-7)

Our Savior had been dealing with the Jews and the Pharisees, who had bitterly opposed and even taken up stones to cast at him. He felt much more at home when he could fix his eyes upon poor, needy beings and bless them with healing and salvation. It is the lot of some of us to be in constant controversy with the carnal professors of the present day. It is a great relief to us to get away from them and their stones, find individual sinners, and preach the gospel to them in the name of God, which spiritually opens the eyes of the blind.

At the gate of the temple sat a blind beggar who must have been a memorable character. He was very clever and possessed quick wit. From having been there so long, he must have been well known to all who regularly frequented the temple and even to those who came from far away to the great yearly gatherings. This man could not see Jesus, but Jesus could see him. We read in the opening of the chapter, *And as Jesus passed by, he saw a man who was blind from his birth* (John 9:1).

There were many other blind men in Israel, but Jesus saw this man with a special eye. I can picture the Savior standing still and looking at him, taking stock of him, listening to his quaint speeches, noting what kind of man he was, and exhibiting special interest in him.

This morning there is someone in the tabernacle who cannot see Jesus because he has no spiritual eyes. But I am convinced that my Master is looking at him, searching him from head to foot, and reading him with his discerning eyes. He is considering what he will make of him, because he has the great and gracious intent that he will take this sinner, who is spiritually like the blind beggar, enlighten him, and allow him to behold his glory.

I suppose that the blind beggar of the temple hardly valued sight, because he had been blind from his birth. Those who have seen must greatly miss the light of day, but those who have never possessed sight at all can hardly understand what that sense must be like. Therefore, it can't be as much of a loss to them. The person I am talking about at this time has no idea of the joy of true religion, because he has no sense of spiritual life and light. He has never seen. So he doesn't know his own misery in being blind. He has been blind from his birth, and in all probability, he is content to be so, because he doesn't know the delight which waits for a heaven-illumined eye. To him, spiritual things are an unknown region of which he has no understanding. He is with us here, but he isn't looking for salvation or even desiring it. But Jesus knows the value of sight. He knows the glories which heavenly light would bring home to the mind, and he will not be limited in his action by human ignorance, but will dispense his gracious blessings according to his own mind, which is as large as the boundless sea.

This beggar did not pray for sight. At least, it isn't recorded that he did. He was a beggar, it was his trade to beg, but among all his petitions, he didn't ask for sight. Yet, Jesus gave him sight. Remember that glorious declaration of free grace: *I was found of those that did not seek me* (Isaiah 65:1). Isn't it a wonderful thing that Jesus often comes to those who didn't seek him? He comes all of a sudden to them in the sovereignty of his infinite compassion, and before they have begun to pray for the blessing, he has given it to them. His free love precedes their desires for it. When they become fully aware of the value of salvation, they find themselves already in possession of it, and so their first prayers are mingled with praises. I am persuaded that there are some here who are like the man born blind. They don't know what they want, they are not yet aware of the value of the blessing, and, because of these reasons, they have not sought it, but they are going to receive it today.

The blind beggar had this one circumstance in his favor: he was in the path where Jesus was likely to go, because he was at the temple gate. My friend, you too are on hopeful ground, because you are sitting in the place where my Lord has often been, and where he is very likely to come again. We have prayed him into this house hundreds of times, and we have done so today. He has been glorified in this tabernacle, and his friends have welcomed him so warmly that he delights to come here. I pray that as Jesus passes by he stops and looks upon you with his eyes of infinite mercy!

> The desperate needs of the sinner are the opportunities for the Savior.

What was our Lord doing? To tell the truth, he was under a divine compulsion. He said, *I must work the works of him that sent me.* He was looking out for material to work upon, in which the works of God would be made manifest. Here was the very man prepared for Christ as clay is prepared for the modeler. Let him receive his sight, and all Jerusalem would see the work of the Lord. Even those who dwelled in far-off lands would hear of it. This blind beggar was the very person the Savior was looking for.

My Master walks up and down these aisles, and he finds many who can see, or who think they can. These he passes by, because *those that are whole need not a physician* (Matthew 9:12). But as he continues to walk, he comes at last to a poor, dark creature, hopelessly, helplessly blind from his birth, and he stops and says, "This is the man. There is room for a miracle here." It is true, O Lord. There is space for healing power to exhibit itself. In that hard heart and stubborn will, there is room for renewing grace. The desperate needs of the sinner are the opportunities for the Savior. And you, poor, guilty, lost, and ruined sinner, you are the raw material for Christ's grace to work upon. You are the very man his forgiving love is looking for.

You who cannot see spiritual things, you who barely know what heavenly sight can mean, and hardly have a desire to know, you are the very person in whom there is elbow room for omnipotent grace – space and scope for the matchless skill of our Savior's love. My Lord stops and looks at you. "This will do," he says. "This is the kind of man I want. I can work out my mission and life purpose here. I am the Light of the World, and I will deal with this darkness, removing it at once."

O Lord Jesus, you are in the highest heaven now, and yet you hear your servants' prayers from this poor earth. Come into this tabernacle and repeat the wonders of your love! We don't ask you to open the natural eyes of the blind, but we ask you to give spiritual sight to the inwardly blind, understanding to those in error, and salvation to the lost. Prove yourself to be the Son of the Highest by saying, "Let there be light." These poor blind ones don't pray to you, but *we* ask for grace for them, and surely your own heart prompts you to answer us. Come without delay and bless them, to the praise of the glory of your grace!

This case of the blind beggar is eminently instructive. Therefore, let us examine it in the hope that while we are considering this model case we may see it repeated in spiritual form in our midst. Holy Spirit, bless our discourse to that end.

The Great Healer Was Made Obvious

First, in this man's healing, and in the salvation of every chosen soul, we will see that the Great Healer was made obvious. If anyone among us is ever to be saved, the Savior will be made great by it. If we are pardoned, *we* will not be honored by the forgiveness, but the royal hand which signed and sealed the pardon will be greatly magnified. If our eyes are opened, we will not be made famous for sight, but he who opened our eyes will be made renowned by the cure. It was like that in this case, and rightly so.

In this man's mind, as soon as he received sight, a man named Jesus came to the forefront. To him, Jesus was the most important person in existence. All he knew of him at first was his name. With only that limited information, Jesus filled the whole horizon of his vision. He was more to him than those learned Pharisees or all his neighbors put together. Jesus was exceedingly great, because he had opened his eyes. By fixing his mind upon that figure, he saw more in it, and he declared, "He is a prophet." He boldly said this when he was running great risks by doing so. To their faces, he told the carping Pharisees, "He is a prophet." A little further on he came to this: that he believed him to be the Son of God and worshipped him.

Now, my dear friend, if you are saved by Jesus, your star must set, but the star of Jesus must rise and increase in brilliance until it becomes no longer a star, but a sun, making your day and flooding your whole soul with light. If we are saved, Christ Jesus must and will have the glory of it. No one on earth or in heaven can rival Jesus in the honor of souls brought from darkness to light; he is everything to them. Do you dislike this? Do you want a share of the spoils, a fragment of the glory? Go your way and be blind, because your condition can never change as long as you refuse to honor the Savior. He who opens a man's eyes deserves his grateful praises forever.

After this man received sight, his testimony was all about Jesus. It was Jesus who spat, it was Jesus who made the clay, and it was Jesus who anointed his eyes. It will be the same way in your mind with the gospel of your salvation: it will be "only Jesus." It is Jesus who became the guarantee of the covenant, and Jesus who became the atoning sacrifice. Jesus is the High Priest, the Mediator, and the Redeemer. We know Jesus as Alpha, and Jesus as Omega. He is the first and last. In your salvation, there will be no mistake about it and no mixture in it. You will have nothing to say about man, or man's worth, or man's will. You will put all your crowns on the head which was once wounded with the thorns. Jesus did it, did it all, and he must be praised.

The authority of Jesus issued the saving command, "Go, wash." These were not the words of Peter, or James, or John, but the words of Jesus. Therefore, the man obeyed them. The gospel message, "Believe and live," is not obeyed until you perceive that it is proclaimed by the supreme authority of King Jesus, the Savior. He that asks you to believe is that same Lord who can and will give you healing through your obedience to his command. Trust him because he commands you. The assurance of the gospel is the authority of Christ. Obey his command, and you have obtained his salvation. The success of the gospel command is produced by him that spoke it. It accomplishes its work, because it comes from *his* mouth. *The word of the king is his power*, and the gospel is the word of the great King (Ecclesiastes 8:4). Therefore, those who listen to it find it to be the power of God unto salvation.

This man, when he had received sight, attributed it most distinctly and undividedly to Jesus. He said, *he has opened my eyes* (John 9:30). Whenever he delivered his testimony, whether to his neighbors or to the Pharisees, there was no uncertainty about it. He had been enlightened by Jesus, and by Jesus alone. To him, he gave all the glory, and he was right to do so.

So listen to what I'm saying. You who desire to find light today, give me your attention now! Attempt to realize that Jesus Christ is a living and acting person. He is not dead. He rose long ago. Being alive and exalted to the highest heavens, he is clothed with infinite power and majesty and is mighty to save. In a spiritual way, he is still among us and working according to his gracious nature. To us, he is not an absent Christ, nor a sleeping Christ. He is still doing what he did when he was on earth, only he now works in the spiritual as he once worked in the physical world. He is now present to save, present to open the eyes of the spiritually blind, and present to bless you.

Understand that he is looking upon you at this moment. Standing in front of you, his shadow is now falling upon you. He is considering your case. Are you praying? He is hearing. Has it not even progressed as far as a prayer? Is it only a desire? He is reading that desire. As it passes like a shadow across the camera of your soul, he is thinking upon you. At this moment, he is able to say the word that will remove the film from your eyes and let in the everlasting light of grace. Do you believe this? If so, then cry to him, "Lord, grant me to receive my sight!" He will hear you. Perhaps, while I am speaking, he will send the light. To your intense delight you'll find yourself in a new world. Escaping from darkness, you will enter into his marvelous light.

You must realize that the great change you need in order to obtain salvation is beyond all mortal power. You cannot accomplish it yourself, nor can all the help of men and angels joined together accomplish it for you. It is even beyond your own understanding. As a carnal man, you don't know what spiritual things are, and you can't grasp the idea of them. A dead man can't know what life is. If he could live again, he would have some knowledge of life derived from his former life. But as for you, it would all be new and strange, because you've never lived unto God. You cannot comprehend what heavenly sight is, because you were born blind. May the Lord do a new thing in you at this moment and bring you into a new heaven and a new earth where righteousness dwells!

You must have this miracle worked upon you. If the blind man had remained blind, he might have continued as a tolerably happy beggar. He seems to have had very considerable mental resources, and he might have made his way in the world as well as others of the begging community. But *you* cannot be happy or safe unless the Lord Jesus opens your eyes. Nothing remains for you except the black- ness of darkness forever, unless light from heaven

> You must have Christ, or die.

visits you. You must have Christ, or die. Here is the blessedness of it: right now, he is still in the midst of us and able to save completely. He is willing to repeat the miracles of his mercy to those who will trust in him to do so. I think I can almost hear the prayer struggling in your bosom. Silent, and unclothed in words, it sits on your lips. Let it speak. Say, "Lord, open my eyes this day." He will do it! Blessed be his name! He intentionally came to open the eyes of the blind.

The Special Means Were Made Observable

We've touched on the great Healer as he stands central to the miracle. Now, I'll direct your thoughts to the special means observable in the miracle. Jesus could have healed this man without means, or he could have healed him by other means. But he chose to work the cure in a manner which to all ages will remain a grand sermon, an instructive parable of grace. He spat on the ground, made clay of the spittle, and anointed the eyes of the blind man with the clay. This is a picture of the gospel.

This picture meets with many modern criticisms. In the first place, the mode of cure seems very eccentric. He spat and made clay with the spittle and the dust! Very unique! Very odd! In the same way, the gospel is odd and unique in the judgment of the worldly-minded. They say, "It seems so strange that we are to be saved by believing." Men think it's so odd, that fifty other ways are immediately invented. Though not one of the new methods is worth describing, yet everybody seems to think that the old-fashioned way of *Believe on the Lord Jesus Christ* might have been greatly improved upon.

The way of justification by faith is particularly prone to criticism, and it's about the last way this wise world would have selected. Yet, eccentric as it may seem for Christ to heal with spittle and dust, it was the best and wisest way for his purpose. Suppose, instead, he had put his hand into his pocket and taken out a gold or ivory box, and out of this box he took a little crystal bottle. Suppose he had taken out the stopper, poured a drop on each of those blind eyes, and they had been opened. What would have been the result? Everybody would have said, "What a wonderful medicine! I wonder what it was! How was it made? Who wrote the prescription? Perhaps he found the charm in the writings of Solomon, and he learned to distill the matchless drops."

So the attention would have been fixed on the means used, and the cure would have been credited to the medicine rather than to God. Our Savior used no such rare oils or choice spirits. He simply spat and made clay of the spittle, because he knew that nobody would say, "The spittle did it," or "It was the clay that did it." No, our Lord may seem to be eccentric in his choice of means, but he is extremely wise. The gospel of our Lord Jesus – and there is only one – is the wisdom of God, however strange it may seem in the judgment of the worldly. Some may think it strange, but it is the sum of all wisdom. Those who try it, find it to be so. It would be impossible to improve upon it. Its adaptation to man's case is marvelous. Its suitability to its design is matchless. It blesses man while it gives all glory to God. No one makes the gospel a rival to Christ. In every case, by the gospel, the power which blesses men is demonstrated as the power of God.

The means may also appear offensive to some. Oh, I think I can picture some of the fine gentry. How they turn up their noses as they read, *He spat on the ground and made clay of the spittle*. It turns the stomachs of those delicate ones. It's the same way with the gospel. The Agags who live delicately don't like it. How the men of "culture" sneer at the gospel for which our fathers died. Hear how they criticize the ever-blessed word of our salvation. They say that it's only fit for old women, idiots, and such fossils of the past ages as the preacher who is now addressing you. We are all fools except these men of progress, and our gospel is disgusting to them. Yes, but stop a minute, and disgust may come to an end. In this miracle, the means used was spittle. But from whose mouth? It was the mouth of Jesus – which is most sweet. No fragrant perfume, made of the rarest spices, can ever equal the spittle of his divine mouth! Clay! What if it's just clay? Clay made by the spittle of the mouth of the Son of God is more precious than *a marvellous crystal* or the rarest powders of the merchant (Ezekiel 1:22). It's the same with my Master's gospel. It is offensive to those who are proud of themselves. It is offensive to carnal thinking and to the idiotic self-complacency of those who consider themselves to be wise, but have become otherwise. But to you who believe, he is precious. How precious? No tongue can tell.

> "What if we trace the globe around,
>> And search from Britain to Japan,
> There shall be no religion found
>> So just to God, so safe for man."

The gospel is still a stumbling block to the Jews and foolishness to the Greeks, but to us who are saved it is that *Christ is the power of God, and the wisdom of God* (1 Corinthians 1:24).

Still others object that the Lord healed this man in such a commonplace way! To spit and make clay of the spittle, why, anybody could do that! Why not use an impressive ceremony? Why not practice an eclectic method? If it had been one of the doctors of the age, he would have made a great performance of it. His prescription would have been a treat for learned men. Did you ever read *Culpeper's Complete Herbal*? I hope you have never taken any of the medicine which that learned herbalist prescribes. In one mess, you will find a dozen articles, each one of them monstrous. In many prescriptions, you will find twenty or more herbs most curiously combined. Such were the prescriptions of even earlier times. If they did no good, at least they confused the patient.

Today, what is the new gospel that is proposed to us? It is the gospel of "culture." Culture! This, of course, is the monopoly of our superiors. It is only to be enjoyed by very refined people who have been to college and who carry inside of themselves a whole university, library and all. The gospel, which is made to be plain enough for poor beggars, is for that reason despised. That Jesus Christ came into the world to save sinners is too commonplace a teaching. That he bore our sins in his own body on the tree is rejected as an outrageous dogma, unfit for this intelligent age! Oh yes, we know the men and their stares of contempt.

Yet, as commonplace as our Lord's medicine was, it was unique. All the philosophers of Greece and all the wise and rich men of Rome couldn't have created another drop of this healing application. Only the Christ possessed that matchless spittle. Only his fingers could make that special clay. Even so, if the gospel seems commonplace, we must remember that there's not another like it! Tell me, you who are wise, can you find anything that compares with it? Christ in the sinner's place, became sin for us, so we might be made the righteousness of God in him. Can you match this? Jesus redeeming his people from the slavery of sin. You may call it a mercantile atonement, if you want, and grow red in the face in your rage at the substitutionary sacrifice, but you cannot equal it. The more you ridicule the gospel, the more we will cling to it, and the more we will love it, because the very spittle of Christ's mouth is dearer to us than the deepest thoughts of your profoundest philosophers.

I think I hear another objector say that the remedy was quite inadequate. Clay made out of spittle would be positively inert, and could exercise no healing power upon a blind eye. The clay alone has no healing properties, but when Jesus uses it, it will accomplish his purpose. The man, after he had washed the clay into the pool, came up seeing. The gospel may appear as if it couldn't possibly renew the heart and save from evil. To believe in the Lord Jesus Christ seems an unlikely means of producing holiness. Men ask, "What can evangelical preaching do to remove sin?" We point to those who were once dead in sin who are made alive by faith. In this way, we prove the power of the gospel by facts.

"Oh," they say, "can faith transform the character? Can belief conquer the will? Can trust transport the mind to a high and elevated life?" It can and does do so. And even though in theory it appears inadequate, as a matter of fact, it has made men into new creatures and has turned sinners into saints.

Another wise gentleman judges that clay upon the eyes could even be harmful. "To stick clay over a man's eyes would not make him see, it would add another impediment to the light." I've even heard it said that to preach salvation by faith goes against good morals and may even encourage men in evil. They are blind bats! Can't they see that reality is the very reverse? How often harlots are made chaste, thieves are made honest, and drunkards are made sober by the gospel! By this very gospel of faith, which they say is against good morals, the best of morals are produced. And in the next breath, they denounce believers as Puritans, too precise and religious. Nothing creates as many good works as that gospel which tells us that salvation is not of works, but by the grace of God.

> Nothing creates as many good works as that gospel which tells us that salvation is not of works, but by the grace of God.

Another objector declares that our Lord's way of cure was opposed to the law. Here is this man named Jesus actually making clay on the Sabbath. Wasn't this a shocking infringement of the law? It is insinuated that our gospel of faith in Jesus makes men think lightly of the law. We preach against the idea of merit, and we say that good works cannot save men. Therefore, we are charged with lowering the dignity of the law. This is not true. Our gospel establishes the law and promotes true obedience. When the Savior said, "Go, wash," the blind man went and washed. The Lord Jesus had taught him the best kind of obedience – the obedience of faith. Even though it seems that we are in conflict with the law when we declare that by the works of the law shall no living flesh be justified, we also establish the law, because faith brings with it the principle and source of obedience. To trust God is the very essence of obedience. He who believes in Jesus has taken the first step in the great lesson of obeying God in all things. To see how Jesus suffered the law-penalty and how he honored the law for us is to see that which makes the law most glorious in our thinking.

So do not try to find fault with the gospel. We sometimes tell servants that it's never wise to quarrel with their bread and butter. I would emphatically say to every anxious person: do not quarrel with the gospel of salvation. If you are in a right state of mind concerning your condition, I'm sure you won't. When I found the Lord, I was driven into such a corner. Whatever salvation might have been, I would have accepted it on God's terms without a question. If you are the man that

I'm looking for, if you want to receive spiritual sight, you will make no conditions with Jesus. You won't ask for a perfumed ointment for your eyes, but you will gladly accept an anointing with clay from your Savior's hands. Whatever the Lord prescribes as the way of salvation, you will joyfully accept. In that cheerful acceptance lies a great part of the salvation itself, because your will is now one with God's.

Let's pray for the Holy Spirit to reveal the gospel to our hearts and make us love it, receive it, and prove its power.

The Plain Command

Our Lord said to his patient, "Go, wash in the pool of Siloam." The man could not see, but he could hear. Salvation comes to us not by sight or ceremonies, but by hearing the Word of God. The ears are the best friends a sinner has remaining with him. It is by way of Ear-gate that the Prince Emmanuel comes riding into Mansoul in triumph. "Hear, and your soul shall live."

The command was specific: "Go, wash in the pool of Siloam." The gospel is also specific: *Believe on the Lord Jesus Christ, and thou shalt be saved.* It is not: do this or that work, but believe! It is not: believe in a priest or in any human being, but in Jesus. If this man had said, "I will wash in Jordan, because it was there that Naaman lost his leprosy," his washing would have been useless. It was a little, insignificant affair, that pool of Siloam whose waters flowed softly. Why must he go there? He didn't ask for reasons, but he obeyed at once. And in obeying, he found the blessing.

My hearer, you have to believe in the Lord Jesus Christ, and you shall be saved. There aren't twenty things to be done, but only this one. The very longest form of the gospel goes like this: *He that believes and is baptized shall be saved* (Mark 16:16). The faith is to be openly confessed by obedience to the Lord's prescribed baptism, but the first matter is the faith. He that believeth on him has everlasting life. This is very specific! You can make no mistake in the matter.

It was also intensely simple. "Go, wash in the pool." Go to the pool and wash the clay into it. Any boy can wash his eyes. The task was simplicity itself. So is the gospel as plain as a pikestaff. You don't have to perform twenty genuflections or posturings, each one peculiar. Nor do you have to go to school to learn a dozen languages, each one more difficult than the other. No, the saving deed is one and simple. Believe and live. Trust Christ, rely upon him, and rest in him. Accept his work upon the cross as the payment for your sin, his righteousness as your acceptance before God, and his person as the delight of your soul.

But the command was also clearly personal. "Go, wash." He couldn't send a neighbor or a friend. His parents couldn't go for him. It would have been useless for him to have said, "I will pray about it." No, he must go and himself wash in the pool. So too the sinner must himself believe in Jesus. Only your own faith will achieve the goal. Your own eyes want opening, so you must go yourself and wash in the pool in obedience to Jesus. You must personally believe unto eternal life. Some of you are under the impression that you may sit still and hope that God will save you.

I have no authority to encourage you in such a rebellious inactivity. Jesus commands you to go and wash, and how dare you sit still? When the Father comes to receive his prodigal child, he finds him on the road. He was still a great way off when his Father saw him, but his face was turned in the right direction, and he was making his way to the Father's house. He says to you, *Awake thou that sleepest and arise from the dead, and the Christ shall shine upon thee* (Ephesians 5:14). Up with you, man! The pool of Siloam won't come to you – you must go to it. The waters won't leap out of their bed and wash your eyes. You must stoop to them, and wash in the pool until the clay is gone and you see. It is a very personal direction. Make sure that you treat it as such.

It was a direction which involved obedience to Christ. Why must I go there and wash there? Because he tells you. If you want Jesus to save you, you must do as he commands you. You must take Jesus to be your Lord if you take him to be your Savior. Dear heart, yield to Jesus Christ today. A servant has never had such a master. Your desire will be to bow down and kiss those dear feet which were nailed to the cross for you. Yield yourselves to the rule of Jesus at once. The act of faith is even more acceptable, because it is the heart's obedience to Jesus. Submit to him by faith, I beg you.

The command was for the time present. Jesus didn't say, "Go, wash in the pool tomorrow or in a month's time." If the beggar had been blind inwardly as well as outwardly, he might have said, "My blindness brings me in money. I'll make a little more as a blind beggar, and then I'll have my eyes opened." He valued sight too much to delay. Had he delayed, he would have remained blind until doomsday! If any of you think it would be inconvenient to be converted right now, I have no hope for you. I can preach no salvation to you but a present one. He who refuses to be saved today isn't likely to be saved at all. Go, blind beggar, go and be blind forever unless you agree to sight today. It may be "now or never" with you. Today is the day of salvation, and tomorrow is nothing but the devil's net. You will be hopelessly lost if you continue to delay.

The command in the blind man's case was very noteworthy: "Go, wash," and so is the spiritual command which is its parallel: *Believe in the Lord Jesus.* I beg you to hear the word which commands you to trust the Savior. He cries, *Look unto me, and be ye saved, all the ends of the earth* (Isaiah 45:22). Oh, may God help you to do so this very instant! Will you not? Blessed Spirit, lead them to do so, for Jesus's sake!

The Delightful Result Certified

Finally, I invite you to see the delightful result certified. I can picture this man, attended by his neighbors, going to Siloam. They had seen Jesus place the clay upon the man's eyes and had heard him say, "Go to Siloam."

They volunteer to go and act as guides to the blind. Curiosity inspires them. He reaches the pool and descends the steps. He is close to the water. He stoops his head and washes his eyes. What will come of it? The clay is gone, but what else has happened? Suddenly the man lifts up his face and cries, "I can see! I can see!"

What a shout must have come from them all. "What a wonder! What a marvel! Hosanna! Blessed be God!"

The man cries, "It's true! I washed, and I can see!"

This man could see at once. He washed, and his blindness was gone. Eternal life is received in a moment. It doesn't take the tick of a clock to justify a sinner. The moment you believe, you have passed from death to life. Quick as a flash of lightning the change takes place, and eternal life enters and casts out death. Oh, I pray that the Lord would work salvation now! This man could see immediately. We read of another blind man in Scripture who first saw men as trees walking, and only after a time saw every man clearly (Mark 8:24). But this man saw clearly at once. I pray that you who hear me would believe and live at once!

This man knew that he could see. He had no question about that, because he said, *one thing I know, that having been blind, now I see* (John 9:25). There's the possibility that some of you have been decent people all your lives, and yet you don't know whether you're saved or not. This is poor religion – cold comfort! Saved, and not know it? It must be as lean a salvation as that man's breakfast when he didn't know whether he had eaten it or not. The salvation which comes through faith in the Lord Jesus Christ is conscious salvation. Your eyes will be so opened that you'll no longer question whether you can see. He could see, and he knew that he could see. Oh, if only you would believe in Jesus and know that you have believed and are saved! I pray that you would get into a new world and enter into a new state of things altogether! May that which was totally unknown to you before be made known this very hour by almighty grace.

And other people noticed that he could see. It was like they couldn't quite grasp it. Some said, *This is he.* Others would only say, *He is like him.* A man with opened eyes is very different from the same man when he is blind. If we were to take someone we know who has no eyes, and suddenly eyes were placed in his appearance, we would probably find his expression so altered that we would hardly think him to be the same person. Therefore, the cautious neighbors only said, *He is like him.* Yet they were *all* sure he could see. None of the Pharisees said to him, "Are you sure you can see?" Those twinkling eyes of his – so full of fun, wit, and sarcasm – were obvious proof that he could see.

In the same way, your friends at home will know that you are converted if it is really true. They will hardly need telling, because they will find it out. The very way you eat your dinner will show it. It will! You eat it with gratitude and ask for a blessing on it. The way you will go to bed will show it. I remember a poor man who was converted. He was dreadfully afraid of his wife – not the only man in the world that lives in that fear – so he was fearful that she would ridicule him if he knelt to pray. He crept upstairs in his stockings, so she wouldn't hear him, and so he could have a few minutes of prayer before she knew he was there. His scheme broke down. His wife soon found him out. Genuine conversion is no easier to hide than a candle in a dark room. You cannot hide a cough. If a man has a cough, he must cough. And if a man has grace in his heart, he will show grace in his life. Why should we want to hide it? Oh, may the Lord give you such an eye-opening this day that friends and relatives will know that your eyes have been opened!

The restored one never lost his sight again. Christ's cures are not temporary. I have heard of many cases lately of people who have been extremely happy because they imagined that they were perfectly restored. The cure lasted a week, and then they were as bad as ever. Imagination can do great things for a season, but Christ's cures last forever. Any eye that Christ opened never went blind again. We believe in being born again, but not in becoming unborn. I know that whatever the Lord does will be forever. My friends, I have nothing to preach but eternal salvation! Come to Christ, and he will work an effective cure in you. Trust him completely, because in him there is everlasting life.

This man, when he received sight, was willing to lose everything as a consequence. The Jews cast him out of the synagogue. But when Jesus found him, the man wasn't upset about the Jews. I can picture his face when Jesus found him – how happy he was as he worshipped his benefactor!

"Poor soul, poor soul, you've been cast out of the synagogue!"

"Oh," he says, "don't pity me. They may cast me out of fifty synagogues now that Christ has found me. What do I care about synagogues now that I have found the Messiah? When I was in the synagogue, I was a blind man. Now, I'm out of the synagogue, but I have my sight."

When you become a Christian, the world will hate you and criticize you. But what about it? Some will have no more to do with you. This may be the best favor they can do you. We had a lady of title in our membership once, and a very gracious sister she was. I had a little apprehension about her at first, that the other "great ones" would draw her away from the truth. Soon after her baptism, she remarked that a certain noble family had given her the cold shoulder, and others who were very close friends had stopped visiting. She took it as a matter of course, and only remarked that it made her own course easier, because she no longer had the pain of hearing their ungodly conversation or even the responsibility of severing the relationship.

The world has done its best for the child of God when it casts him out. His excommunications are better than its communications. The outside of the world's house is the safest side of it for us. That we love the brethren and that the world hates us are two good evidences of grace for which a man may be grateful. "Let us join Christ outside the camp, bearing his reproach."

What a wonderful thing the Lord Jesus had done for this man, and what a wonderful thing he is prepared to do for all who trust him! It was a work of creation. The man's eyes were useless, and Jesus created sight in them. To heal a limb is one thing, but to create an eye, or to enable that which was only the mere form of an eye to become an organ of perception is a greater thing by far. To save a soul is a work of creation. We are created anew in Christ Jesus. It was also a work of resurrection. Those eyes had been dead, and the Lord Jesus raised them from the dead. The Lord God Almighty can work creation right now, and he can produce resurrection today. And why shouldn't he?

Today, we commemorate both of these divine works. This first day of the week was the beginning of the creation of God. It is also the day in which our Lord rose from the dead, as the firstfruits of those who slept. This Lord's Day commemorates the beginning of creation and of resurrection. Let's pray for the almighty Lord to display among us the works of God this day. Oh Lord, regenerate, illuminate, pardon, and save those who are here and glorify your Son! Amen, and amen.

Chapter 11

Speak for Yourself, A Challenge!

He is of age, ask him; he shall speak for himself. (John 9:21)

Our individuality and the personal responsibilities which fall upon us in reference to Christ must not be lost sight of. If, for instance, a spiritual miracle has been performed upon us, we are obliged to confess – no, we are *delighted* to confess that he has opened our eyes. We are bound, especially those of us who are of a more mature understanding, to carry our own personal testimony for him. The allegation and the appeal may apply to each one of us: *He is of age, ask him; he shall speak for himself.* Jesus Christ *bore* our sins. He gave *himself* for us. He served us, not by proxy, but by personal devotion. Not by alms doled out pitifully, but by his life surrendered as a sacrifice to God cheerfully. In this way, he has entrusted his love to us, so what less can we do in return than bear our own brave, bold, personal testimony for him?

What a parallel there is between this man's case and our own. He had suffered from a grievous, personal evil. He was born blind. So we were born in sin. Sin has cast its blindness over the fabric of our existence from our very birth. We will never forget the midnight of our nature. We couldn't even see the beauties of Christ himself – though as bright as the noonday sun – because we were so blind. This man was personally delivered from his ailment, and so have we been delivered, I trust. I know many here who can say that. They were blind, but now they see.

You have received, as the blind man did, a personal blessing – being gifted with sight. The blemish that blighted your life has been healed. It's not that somebody sees for you and tells you what he sees, but you see for yourself. It's not merely assigned to you that you see because you have been told what somebody else saw. You have no proxy in the matter, no sponsor in the business. You yourself are conscious that a work of grace has been performed on you. You were blind, but now you see, and you know it.

The blind man was cured through personal obedience to Christ's command. He heard a special call addressed to him: "Go, wash in the pool." He went and came back seeing. Many here have heard the voice which says, "Believe and live," and it has come to you, not as a general exhortation, but as a specific command. You have believed, and you live. You have washed and have come back seeing. Well now, all this is personal. Therefore, your Lord and Master has a right to expect a personal testimony from you of his power to save. You are of age. When anyone asks you, I trust you will speak for yourself. Speak up and speak out for your Master without hesitation or fear.

Saved Men Are Compelled to Speak

There are times when saved men are positively compelled to speak for themselves. They must, out of necessity, carry the full weight of their personal witness. What else can they do when friends desert them? Father and mother were quite willing to claim that this young man was their son and quite willing to bear their witness that he was born blind, but they wouldn't go any further. They could have gone further if they liked, but they were afraid of the sentence of excommunication which the Jews had already agreed upon: that if any man confessed that Jesus was the Christ he would be put out of the synagogue. So, feeling very little regret in declining to take any responsibility themselves, because they had great confidence in their son's power to take care of himself, they abandoned him. They threw upon him the stress and full responsibility of giving a plain answer, which would bring about such disgrace. They backed out of it. They had no desire at all to become the subjects of persecution because their blind son had been blessed with sight. The young man who had been blind was required to do battle himself for the good Lord who had bestowed such a great blessing on him. *Ask him,* said his parents, *he shall speak for himself.*

With many young people, there are times when their parents frown upon their religion, or at least turn the cold shoulder to them. They show no sympathy with their faith or their feelings. However, some of us rejoice when our children are converted. We are not ashamed to stand by them, defend them, and protect them, whatever comes of it. But there are fathers and mothers who themselves have no love for the things of God, so their children, if they are converted, have a hard time of it. I've even known some who profess to be disciples of Christ take a step back and leave others to stand alone in the Master's cause when things become difficult. For example, in a conversation when you expected to hear an old gentleman speak up bravely for the truth of the gospel, but he didn't. You knew he was a member of a Christian church, but he very cautiously held his tongue for a long time. Then he quietly said something about not casting pearls before swine. Probably, he

> It is tragic how many seem afraid of being compromised themselves.

didn't have any pearls, or possibly, he was a swine himself. How else could you account for such awful cowardice? But some know what it is to be compelled by youthful passion to come out so boldly as to risk the charge of forwardness, because everybody else seemed to be deserting the doctrine whose duty it was to defend. It is tragic how many seem afraid of being compromised themselves. They say, *ask him; he shall speak for himself,* while they safely retreat behind the bushes out of rifle range, never coming forward unless, perchance, you win the victory. Then they would most likely come forward to share the spoils. Whenever a man is placed in such a position where he finds himself deserted in the battle for Christ by those who ought to be at his back, let him despise retreat and say gallantly, "I am of age, I will speak for myself. In the name of God, I will bear my witness."

Christian men, however reserved and awkward their natural disposition may be, are compelled to speak out when they are pressed. These Pharisees took this man and questioned him rather closely. They presented questions to him by way of examination and cross-examination. "What did he do to you? How did he open your eyes?" and so on. He does not appear to have been disturbed or disconcerted by the questions. He acquitted himself grandly. Self-contained, quiet, shrewd, immoveable, his mind was made up. And with a thorough mastery of the situation, he was ready for them. He did not hesitate.

I trust if you and I are ever required to answer questions asked of us, even though it might be with intent to entangle us, we will never be ashamed to own our Lord or to defend his cause. We could even expect to be struck with muteness if we were ever ashamed to speak of Christ when we are commanded to do it. If it comes to a challenge as to whose side I'm on, could I ever hesitate to say, "I am with Immanuel, the crucified Savior"? If they ever back us into a corner and say, *thou also wast with Jesus of Nazareth* (Mark 14:67), oh, may God give us grace to be prompt and not think twice.

> "Of course I was, and of course I am still.
> He is my Friend, my Savior, my all in all;
> and I never blush to own his name."

Christians must come out and each man must bear for himself a clear and distinct testimony. When others revile and slander our Lord Jesus Christ, it becomes necessary for us to commend and sing the praises of him. They said to this man, *Give glory to God; we know that this man is a sinner* (John 9:24). Then he spoke gratefully with a heart bubbling up with thankfulness. "He has opened my eyes." *One thing I know, that having been blind, now I see* (John 9:25). Then, when they went one step further, saying, *as for this fellow, we do not know where he is from*, he spoke up more heroically still (John 9:29). He turned upon his assailants and outwitted them with their own marvelous ignorance. *Indeed this is a marvellous thing that ye do not know where he is from, and yet he has opened my eyes* (John 9:30). He fought for his Master so decisively that they were willing to throw away the weapons of debate and take up stones of abuse with which to stone him.

Oh, if they speak ill of Christ, will we be quiet? Shouldn't we have a word of rebuke for the blasphemer? Should we stand by as we hear the cause of Christ denounced in society, and for fear of feeble man refrain our tongue or smooth the matter over? No, let us throw the gauntlet down for Christ and say at once, "I cannot and I will not restrain myself.

Now the very stones might speak. When my dear friend – my best of friends – is abused, I must and will proclaim the honors of his name."

I think Christian people in this country don't take half the liberty they might. If we speak a word of religion or open our Bibles on a train or anything of that kind, they say, "It's all for show!" They can play cards, I suppose, in a public space with no consequence. They can make the night hideous with their howling. They can utter all sorts of profanities and sing lascivious songs at their sweet will, but we are accused of being "holier than thou" if we take our turn. In the name of everything that is free, we will have our turn. And every now and then, I like you to sing, to their annoyance, one of the songs of Zion, because they sing the songs of Babylon loud enough to annoy us. Let's tell them that as long as we live in a land of liberty and rejoice that Christ has made us free, we will be no more ashamed of his testimonies than they are ashamed of their iniquities. When they begin to sin in private and blush to utter a profane word, then that may be the time – no, and not even then – for us to keep our religion to ourselves.

So you see there are times when men – quiet, reserved men – must speak. They will be traitors if they don't. I don't think this blind man was at all talkative. The briefness of his replies seems to indicate that he was rather a concise speaker, but they drove him to it. He was like the stag at bay. He must fight, however gently disposed. And I think there is not likely a Christian man who has been able to go all the way to heaven while he quietly hides himself as he runs from bush to bush, skulking into glory. Christianity and cowardice! What a contradiction in terms. I think there must have been times when you've felt inclined to say to yourself, "Well now, cost what it may. I may be tabooed in society. I may be ridiculed by the rough, and I may lose respect among the polite, but for Jesus Christ and for his truth I must bear witness." Then it becomes true of you: *He is of age, ask him; he shall speak for himself.*

Be Prepared to Speak for Yourself

It is always good to be prepared to speak for yourself, and this man was evidently ready to do so. When his parents said, *ask him; he shall speak for himself,* I think there was a little twinkle in the father's eye as he spoke, meaning to say, "You'll get more than you bargained for. He *can* speak for himself. We've known him a good many years, and he has always had a pretty sharp reply for anybody who thought him a fool. If you think that you will get much out of him now, you are mightily mistaken. He will be more likely to upset you than you are to upset him."

And as they handed him over to the inquisitors, though they were unkind, I suppose they didn't feel that he was a tender chicken that needed much of their care. So they seemed to say, "He is of age, he's a grown man, ask him. *Only ask him.* He will speak for himself, we give you permission." And so he did.

I want to have a band of Christian people here, of that same sort, who, when asked anything about their holy faith, can answer in such a way that they aren't likely to be the butts of ridicule and scorn, because they will prove more than a match for their adversaries. But how, you will ask, are we to be prepared to speak for ourselves?

To start with, it's good to cultivate a general habit of openheartedness and boldness. We have no need to intrude and push ourselves into people's lives in such a way that we become a nuisance and a bore to them. Far from it. Let us walk through the world as those who have nothing to conceal, conscious of the integrity of our own motives and the rightness of our heart before God. We don't need to wear our armor and sleep in it like the knights of old. Instead, we know that truth is the best apparel. Let us show that we have nothing to hide or cover, nothing to disguise or keep secret. Let us display that the gospel has worked in us to create such an honesty and frankness of spirit that no gossip can make us blush and no foe can cause us fear. Let us tell what we believe as true, because we can vouch for its accuracy. Let us silence those who find fault with these things, but not as much by our battles as by our character. Let us prove to them that we have a solid reason for our simple protest – that we have actually received the grace in which we earnestly believe. Our words will have weight when they see that the fruit of our lives matches the flower of our profession. There is great power in this manner of answering the adversary.

However, be careful when you do speak, to be sure of your ground. This man was. *Whether he is a sinner or not,* he says, *I do not know.* So he offered no opinion on a subject of which he couldn't be quite positive. But where he had hard fact on his side, there was nothing vague in his statement: *One thing I know, that having been blind, now I see.* This is an argument which the most astute critic would find difficult to answer. As the blind man looked them full in the face, it was enough to bewilder them.

There are some of you in whom such a drastic change of character has been worked in you that you could honestly say, "I know I'm not the man I used to be. My manner of life from my youth is well known to many, if they would testify. But now God, by the gospel of his Son, has opened my eyes, renewed my heart, cleansed my leprosy, and set my feet in the way of peace." Even those who scoff at the gospel are, in the cases of many of us, unable to deny the remarkable and beneficial change it has brought about. There is a righteousness here about which we need be very uncompromising. Put your foot down and say, "No, you cannot misjudge this. You may philosophize, if you like, but it was the old-fashioned, simple gospel of the children that changed me, and made me love that which I used to hate, and hate that which I used to love. That is a thing you cannot disagree with. It's one thing I know without any doubt."

> Let them have it with the thrill you had when you first heard it.

And it is well, like this man, to have the facts ready to point out. *A man that is called Jesus made clay and anointed my eyes and said unto me, Go to the pool of Siloam, and wash; and I went and washed, and I received sight* (John 9:11). Give them the plan of salvation just as you first understood it, and present it to them very simply and plainly. It's often the very best answer you can give to those who question in order to criticize and discuss with an intent to find fault. Let them have it with the thrill you had when you first heard it. Tell them how the Lord has dealt with your soul and what he has done for you. He would have to be a hard-hearted man who can sneer at the simple statement of your own conversion. The change it has brought about in you will be a fact which he cannot dispute. Though he might think you're deluded and call you an enthusiast, there is nothing as difficult for him to grapple with as your honesty and confidence. "He opened my eyes." There's the point. "If he opened my eyes, then he was of God. God must have been in such a thing as that, because I was born blind." Give a reason for the hope that is in you, with meekness and fear, to all those who oppose you.

Christian men should at all times also be ready to bear abuse. *Thou wast altogether born in sins* (John 9:34). I don't suppose the blind man cared one bit what they had to declare or insinuate on that score. Their scorn could not deprive him of his sight. He merely shook his head and said, "I can see. I was blind, but now I see. Pharisees may abuse me, but I can see. They may tell me I am this, that, and the other, but I can see. My eyes are open." So, child of God, you may often say to yourself, "I may be ridiculed. I may be mocked as Presbyterian, Methodist, Baptist, or schismatic, or whatever they like. It doesn't matter – I am saved. I am a changed man. The grace of God has renewed me. Let them call me whatever they like."

Some people are very sensitive to ridicule. They shrink from and seem irritated at a joke, and what men call teasing grates upon them. What a baby a man is who cannot brave a fool's laugh! Stand upright, and when you go back to work, show a bold front. You that go to work at some of the big factories, and have been quizzed and poked fun at because of your religion, bolster your courage and say, "Here I am, five feet ten high, or six feet, or whatever else it may be, and should I be ashamed to be laughed at for Christ?" You're not worth the boots you stand upright in if you allow yourself to be rendered useless by their play. I have no doubt that many soldiers in the barrack room find it hard to keep up their spirits when comrades taunt them with scoff and scorn in their rough way. But after all, dear friends, shouldn't common manliness supply us with the necessary fortitude? When we've got ahold of a thing that we believe to be right, we would be showing our inexperience to let it go for fear of a giddy prank or a paltry grimace. Let them laugh. They will be tired of teasing us when they find out that our patience triumphs over their senseless tricks. Let them find some enjoyment if they can, poor simpletons. I sometimes feel more inclined to smile than to be upset over the jokes that are coined at my expense. Their playful antics may relieve some of the pitiful sorrows that burden their lonely hours. Melancholy holds carnival in this mad world. Ghosts and goblins haunt the happiest brain. What if for once they get a living object for their sport, and I become the butt of their buffoonery? There is no fear that it will harm me. The only danger is that it will hurt them. Be of that mind, dear friends, and don't care about any of their teasing.

This born-blind man, whose eyes were opened, was prepared to meet the Pharisees and speak up for himself, because he felt intense gratitude to him who had granted him the priceless gift of sight. You see, all through the narrative, even though he didn't know much about Jesus, he felt conscious that he was his true friend, and he stuck to him through thick and thin. Now, you and I may not know much about our Lord – not one tenth of what we hope to know – but he has opened our eyes. He has forgiven our sins. He has saved our souls. And by his grace we will stick to him, come what may. If your gratitude to him is always at its full heat, whenever you are taunted, whenever at any time you are put to the test, you will be faithful to your friend and able to say with a sound conscience:

> "I'm not ashamed to own my Lord,
>   Or to defend his cause;
> Maintain the honor of his word,
>   The glory of his cross."

Willingly Speak for Christ

Every saved man should willingly speak for himself about Christ. I've said that you will be driven to it. I have also asked you to be prepared for it when you are driven to it. Now, I have to urge that you should willingly do it.

Aren't we all indebted to Christ if, indeed, he has saved us? How can we acknowledge that debt if we are ashamed of him? His testimony is: *He that believes and is baptized shall be saved* (Mark 16:16). Does the baptism save us? No, but he who believes is bound to be baptized so that he may in this way confess his Lord, because baptism is the answer of a good conscience towards God. It is the disciple's grateful response to his Master's gracious call. You know how it is written: *if thou shalt confess with thy mouth the Lord Jesus and shalt believe in thine heart that God has raised him from the dead, thou shalt be saved* (Romans 10:9). I have no right to refuse to confess if I inwardly believe. Why should I? If I owe so much to him, should I, can I, think of not confessing him?

If there were a commandment issued that we were not to own our Lord, that we were to tell no man, that we must hide the secret from family, friends, and neighbors, it would be most distressing to me. But he does command us to own him and bear our testimony to him. We honor the command, we consider it most appropriate and fitting, and we cheerfully obey it. Is it not so?

We should each willingly speak up for Christ, because each one of us knows most about what he has done for us. No one here knows all that he has done for me. I think I hear you say, "That's true, but then you don't know what he did for us." No. We are over head and ears debtors to him. Oh, what mercy he has shown to some of us. If the world could know our state before conversion, it might almost make our hair stand on end to read the story of our lives. How the grace of God has changed us! Oh, what a change! If ravens become doves, and lions become lambs, your theologians might expound or mystify the phenomenon in a word or two of Greek terminology. But this conversion is what we see every day, and scientific men are silent, while scoffers only want to ridicule it. The change is infinitely greater than when dry bones are raised and clothed with flesh. When stones begin to melt and run into streams is nothing compared to the regeneration we have experienced. We must tell it; we must talk about it. We know more about it than others, and we are bound to be the honest narrators of the wondrous narrative.

The more individual testimonies are attributed to Christ, the more weight there is in the accumulated force of the great aggregate. If I bear witness for Christ in the name of you all, saying, *The LORD has done great things with us, of which we shall be glad*, I hope there is some honor to Christ and some influence to take effect (Psalm 126:3). But if ten, twenty, thirty, or fifty were to rise one after the other and say, "The Lord has done great things for me," and each one were to tell his own tale, how much more conviction would be demonstrated.

I heard of a lawyer in the United States who attended an experience meeting among his neighbors. He was a skeptic, if not a thorough unbeliever, when he entered the place. But he sat with his pencil and took notes of the statements of his neighbors. When he reviewed the evidence afterwards, he said to himself, "If I had these twelve or thirteen people in the witness box on my side, I would feel quite sure of winning my case.

I live among them. They aren't the most educated people I've ever met, but they are very honest, trustworthy, and plain-spoken people. And even though each one has told his tale, they all come to the same point and all bear witness to one fact, that there is such a thing as the grace of God, and that it does change the heart. Well, I'm bound to believe it after all this testimony." And he believed and became a Christian. Of this I am certain, that if Christian people shared their testimony regarding the power of Jesus Christ in their hearts more often, the cumulated witness would influence many thoughtless minds, and multitudes would come to believe in Jesus. The Holy Spirit delights to own and bless the true stories only you can tell.

Some of you will probably say, "They can do without my story." No, my friend, we can't discard your evidence, because the different experiences are as numerous as the individuals converted, although there is unity in the operation of the Holy Spirit. Our Lord opened the eyes of many blind men, and he unstopped the ears of many deaf people. He loosed the tongues of many who were dumb, and we can't even count how many lepers he cleansed. But each patient could tell you his

> The Holy Spirit delights to own and bless the true stories only you can tell.

own symptoms and the tiniest details of his own healing. Your story too has its special appeal as it contributes to the general narrative. Minimally, *you* would be sorry if it were not so. *The LORD shall count when he writes up the peoples that this one was born there* (Psalm 87:6). I know you would like your name to be mentioned then, and I think it would be worth your while now to mention the mercies you've received in just the manner you received them.

To speak for myself, I believe that God, in converting me, revealed a way of his own that exactly suited my need. My case was enough like yours to produce sympathy, and so unlike yours as to be uniquely special, and I'm sure it was the same with each one of you. Your career, your character, your circumstances are each different. As a great master seldom paints the same picture twice, so the Master artist, God, seldom, I think never, works precisely the same in any two hearts. There is a difference, and in that difference, there is an illustration of the manifold wisdom of God. This is why we want your story.

Besides, your testimony may touch the heart of somebody like you. Little Mary over there says, "Well, I am nobody. I'm only a nursemaid. The Lord Jesus Christ has cleansed me and made me his, it's true, but you can do without my tale." No, Mary, we can't. Perhaps your testimony will be exactly what another little lass like yourself needs to hear. A little maid waited on Naaman's wife. Who but she could have told her mistress that there was healing for Naaman or that he could go to a prophet in Israel and be made whole? Tell your story gently, quietly, and at the proper times, but let it be known.

"Oh," says the old man, "but I am so feeble now. You could get along without my saying anything." No, father William, we cannot. You are just the man whose few words have full weight. You are presented every now and then with choice opportunities of leading souls to the Savior.

"I am too old to think about these things," says one. But you could tell how the Lord has dealt with you in your old age, and maybe it will strike home.

You working men, if you were all to speak up for Christ, as I know many of you do, what an effect would be produced, and what an influence you would have on others like you. Of course, when they hear us preach they say, "Oh well, you know, he is a parson. He says it professionally. It is his business to say it." But when you tell of what the Lord has done for you, it becomes what people talk about. It is repeated over and over again. I know what Tom says when he gets home. He says to his wife, Mary, "What do you think of that Jack that I've been working with? Why, he has been talking to me about his soul. He says his sin is forgiven him, and he seems to be such a happy man. You know that he used to drink and swear the same as I do, but he is a wonderfully different man now, and from what I see, there must be something to it. Well, he asked me to his home the other night, and I noticed that his place is very different from ours."

"There, you hold your tongue," Mary will answer up pretty sharply. "If you brought your wages home to me regularly every week, I could budget them for you better."

"Ah," he says, "and that is what I have been thinking. It is just because he is a religious man that he brings his wages home. I think there's something real about his conversion. Do you know he doesn't drink like I do? He does not involve himself with all manner of foolishness. I wouldn't have thought so much about it if the parson had spoken to me. But now I really do think there is something good and genuine in the *grace* he talks about. You and I had better go next Sunday evening to the tabernacle, or somewhere else, and hear about it for ourselves."

There are many, many souls brought to Christ in that way. We can't do without your testimony, Jack, because your conversation is suitable to others like you.

And you, your ladyship, you say, "I love the Lord, but I don't think I could possibly say anything in my circle and walk of life."

Couldn't you? Ah, but *I* am sure you will easily surmount this little difficulty if you attain a little more growth in grace. We had one among us whose rank entitled her to move in an upper sphere of society, but she preferred the humble companionship of the church. Her silvery locks some of you well remember. She has left us now and has gone home to glory. Her lot was cast among the aristocracy, but with gentle, quiet, bland simplicity she introduced the gospel wherever she went. Many have come to these pews to listen to your minister who would have never been here if it weren't for her calm, beautiful, unobtrusive, holy life, and the nerve with which, anywhere at any time, she could say, "Yes, I am a Christian. What is more, I am a Nonconformist, and what you will think is even worse, I am a Baptist. And what you will think is worst of all – I am a member of the tabernacle." She never blushed to own our blessed Redeemer's name or to acknowledge and befriend the lowliest of his disciples. You would do well to follow the example of her faith. In whatever circle we move, let us strive to become centers of influence.

So I have tried to show you, dear friends, that each one has a witness to bear. It's a privilege to be prized and a duty to be fulfilled, because the gift you have received qualifies you for the service you are asked to render. Suppose the soldier when he marched to battle were to say, "I don't need to load my gun. I don't need to fire in the day of battle, because I see that on the right and on the left, there are good marksmen picking off the enemy." Yes, but when you are in full battle, your bullet has got its barrel and the barrel for your bullet is not the barrel for any other bullet, so let it go, let it go. We must all fire, brethren. Not some, but all must fire, and our charge must be this: *"One thing I know, that having been blind, now I see.* For this reason, I bear witness to my Lord. Let anyone who wants, criticize, but he has opened my eyes."

Intend to Do It

Finally, just as every Christian, being of age, has to speak for himself, we intend to do it. For my own part, I intend to do so. That which I believe to be true, I have spoken to you from my youth up. There have been times when I have offended a good many. I will offend a good many more, I hope, because that's not a matter I have ever taken into consideration. Is this true? Is it a necessary truth? Is it essential that it be spoken plainly and published widely? Away it goes like a hand grenade flung into the midst of the crowd. May every minister of Christ – and I trust the rightness of this approach will be more and more recognized – take courage to speak for his Master. I pray that they would speak without restraint in the name of him that sent him – in the name of God – with a courage that befits his commission. A trembling lip and a cowardly countenance in a minister shows him to be unworthy of the office which he pretends to hold. We must set our faces like a flint and bear testimony to the truth – to the whole truth and nothing but the truth – as far as God shall teach it to us.

> We must set our faces like a flint and bear testimony to the truth.

And won't you also take up this resolution: "We are of age, and we intend to speak for ourselves"? You can't all preach, and I hope you won't all try. What a world of turmoil and disorder we would have if every man and woman felt a call to preach. We would have a church of all mouth, and then there would be a vacuum somewhere. There would be no hearers left if everybody became a preacher. It is not to seek recognition in public assemblies, but to exert influence in private society that you are called. By good conversation, with a speech seasoned with salt, at home among friends, family, or companions – to a dozen or to one – make known what love has done, what grace has done, what Christ has done. Make it known among your servants, among your children, among the people you do business with. Wherever you go, make it known.

Wear your uniform wherever you go. I do not like to see a Christian soldier ashamed to show the scarlet. Oh no, put it on. It is an honor to serve his Majesty. If there is anything in Christianity that you are ashamed of, get out of it. Don't pretend to believe if you are afraid of betraying your profession. But if you do receive the gospel, and believe it, as the revelation of God, never be embarrassed to own it, but be brave to proclaim it at all times and in all places.

"Well," says one, "I am so passive." I know you are, brother. Come, then, drop a little of your modesty and distinguish yourself a little more for your manliness. I've told you about the soldier who was passive in the day of battle – they shot him for being a coward. It's not acceptable to be passive when duty calls or where danger summons you to the front. I have heard of a man with the face of a lion and the heart of a deer. Beware of a too-passive disposition. Disreputable things are sometimes disguised in polite words. So reserve may be dastardly, and caution may be cowardly. Be valiant for your Lord and Master. Don't play the traitor's part by your silence.

> "Ashamed of Jesus, that dear Friend,
>   On whom my hopes of heaven depend!
> No; when I blush, be this my shame,
>   That I no more revere his name."

Break the ice now and speak to somebody about this blessed message. Will you resolve to do so? Take care that you don't put it off until your heart grows cool, and the words you plan to say freeze on your lips. Do it, and it will grow on you. You will come to greet the opportunity as much as you now shrink back from the necessity. It will bless your life. I think it is Horatius Bonar who says:

> "He liveth long who liveth well;
>   All else is being flung away;
> He liveth longest who can tell
>   Of true things truly done each day.
>
> Be what thou seemest; live thy creed;
>   Hold up to earth the torch divine;
> Be what thou prayest to be made;
>   Let the great Master's steps be thine.

Fill up each hour with what will last,
   Buy up the moments as they go;
The life above, when this is past,
   Is the ripe fruit of life below.

Waste not thy being; back to him
   Who freely gave it, freely give;
Else is that being but a dream,
   'Tis but to *be* and not to *live*."

Dear friends, some of you who are believers in Christ have never yet confessed him. I hope that you will resolve from this moment to proclaim yourselves to be his disciples and become his faithful followers. You are of age. "Yes," one says, "I am of rather full age, for I am over fifty." Others of you are older than that, and even though you are believers in Christ you have never confessed him. It will not do, brother. It will not do to die with, and it doesn't do to think of now.

When he comes, they will be happy who were not ashamed of him. But when he comes in his glory with all his holy angels, trembling will take hold of those who thought and said they loved him but never dared to bear reproach for his name's sake or to suffer shame for the gospel. I hope these reflections will make you very uneasy and prompt you to say, "Please, God, I will join a Christian church before this week is over." If you are a believer in Christ, I urge you not to play games with the voice of conscience, but to pay your vows to the Most High.

Sadly, there are some of you who can't speak for Christ in any way at all, because you don't know him. He never opened your eyes. Never try to talk of matters you do not understand, or pretend to bear witness to mercies you have not experienced. The Christ we preach is not only the Christ of history who was crucified, dead, and buried. He is also a living Christ, right now, among us still by his Spirit, changing our natures, turning and guiding the direction of our thoughts and our lives, purifying our wishes and motives, teaching us to love each other, admonishing us to be pure, entreating us to be gentle, and giving us a heart to aspire after those things that are above, instead of groveling among those things that are below. If you have never met this Christ, you can't bear witness as to his power. But he is to be found. Trust in him. He is divine – the Son of God. His blood is the blood of the great sacrifice of which Moses spoke and all the prophets bear witness. He is the last great sacrifice of God. Come and trust him. And when you trust him, that trust will be like the woman touching the hem of his garment. No sooner had she touched him, than she was made whole, because power went out of him. That power still proceeds from his sacred person whenever the simple touch of faith brings the sinner into contact with the Savior. I pray that the Lord would lead you to believe in Jesus, and when you have believed through grace, come forward and confess his name. In this way, you will be numbered with his saints now and in glory everlasting.

Chapter 12

The Healing of One Born Blind

Since the world began it has not been heard of that anyone opened the eyes of one that was born blind. (John 9:32)

It was quite true that there was no instance recorded in Scripture or in secular history at the time when this man spoke, of any person who was born blind having obtained his sight. I believe it was in the year 1728 that the celebrated Dr. Cheselden, of St. Thomas's Hospital, for the first time in the world's history achieved the marvel of giving sight to a man who had been blind from his youth up. Since then, some successful operations have been performed on persons who were born blind. However, this man was quite correct in the statement that then, and in his day, neither by skillful surgery or even by miracle had birth-blindness been healed.

No doubt this man was a great student in the matter of blindness. It touched so close to home because he dwelt beneath its perpetual shadow. He was the one man in the city who understood the subject thoroughly, but in all his research, he found no ground for hope. Having learned the whole history of blindness and its cure, this man had come to the assured conviction that none ever had been healed who shared his condition – certainly a mournful conclusion for him. Our Lord Jesus did for him what had never been done before for any man. This pleasing fact seems to be full of consolation to any people here who labor under the idea that theirs is a most peculiar and hopeless case. It probably isn't so unique and special a case as you think. But even if it is, there is no room for despair since Jesus delights to open up new paths of grace. Our Lord is inventive in love. He creates new modes of mercy. It is his joy to find out and relieve those whose miserable condition has baffled all other help. His mercy isn't bound by precedents. He preserves a freshness and originality of love. If you can't find an instance in which a person like yourself has ever been saved, you should not conclude that you must inevitably be lost. Rather, you should believe in him who does great wonders and marvels unsearchable in the way of grace.

He does as he wills, and his will is love. Have hope that inasmuch as he sees in you a unique sinner, he will make you into a unique trophy of his power to pardon and to bless. That's how it was with this man's eyes. If eyes that had been born blind were never opened before, Jesus Christ would do it, and greater would be the glory brought to his name by the miracle. Jesus doesn't need to be shown the way; he loves to cut paths for himself. The greater the room for his mercy, the better he likes the road.

It is the church's business to spread light on all sides.

Let's gather instruction from the particular expression which the healed man used here. May the Holy Spirit make the meditation truly profitable to us.

The Peculiarity of His Case

It wasn't an instance of a desire for light that could have speedily and easily been remedied. There was plenty of light all around him, but the poor creature had no eyes. Now, there are millions of people in the world who have little or no light. Darkness covers the earth, and gross darkness covers the people. It is the church's business to spread light on all sides. For this work, she is well qualified. We should not permit any person to perish due to a lack of knowing the gospel. We cannot give men eyes, but we can give them light. God has placed his golden candlesticks among us and expressly said, *Ye are the light of the world* (Matthew 5:14). Now, I believe that there are some people who have eyes, but only see a little, because they need light. They are children of God, but they walk in darkness and see no light. God has given to them the spiritual ability of sight, but they are still down in the mines, in the region of night and death shade. They are imprisoned in Doubting Castle, where only a few feeble rays struggle into their dungeon. They walk like men in a mist, seeing, yet not seeing. They hear doctrines preached which are not the pure truth, just the scattered corn of the covenant. And while their eyes are blinded with chaff and dust, they themselves are bewildered and lost in a maze. Too many in this murky light weave theories of doubt and fear for themselves which increase the gloom. Their tears defile the windows of their soul. They are like men who hang up blinds and shutters to keep out the sun. They cannot see, even though grace has given them eyes. May we by explanation and example – by teaching with our words and the louder language of our lives – scatter light on all sides so that those who dwell in spiritual midnight may rejoice, because for them light has sprung up.

This was not the case of a man blinded by accident. If that were the case, the help of man might have been of some service. People who have been struck with blindness have recovered. Notable is the instance in Bible history when Elisha struck a whole army with blindness, but afterwards he prayed to God for them and they received their sight at once. *And when the Syrians came down to him, Elisha prayed unto the LORD and said, Smite these people, I pray thee, with blindness. And he smote them with blindness according to the word of Elisha. And Elisha said unto them, This is not the way, neither is this the city; follow me, and I will bring you to the man whom ye seek. And he led them to Samaria. And when they came into Samaria, Elisha said, LORD, open the eyes of these men, that they may see. And the LORD opened their eyes, and they saw; and, behold, they were in the midst of Samaria* (2 Kings 6:18-20).

There is more that we can do in cases where the blindness is traceable to circumstances rather than to nature. For instance, everywhere in the world, there is a degree of blindness caused by prejudice. Men judge the truth before they hear it. They form opinions about the gospel without having studied the gospel itself. Put the New Testament into their hands, beg them to be honest and to investigate it with their best discernment and to seek guidance from the Holy Spirit, and I believe many would see their error and correct their thinking.

There are some true spirits whose thoughts are blinded by prejudice, who would be helped to see the truth if we would tenderly and wisely place it before them. The prejudices of education sway many in this country. We are to the very core a conservative people, unyielding to established error, and suspicious of any long-neglected truth. Our countrymen are not quick to receive the most obvious truth unless it has been in vogue for ages. Perhaps it is better that we are like this, than whirled about with every wind of doctrine and running after every new idea, as some other nations do. But because of this, the gospel has to combat a mass of prejudice in this country. It's not uncommon to hear, "Such were my fathers, such ought *I* to be." Or again, "Such our family has always been, therefore such will I be and such shall my children be."

No matter how obvious the truth may be that is presented to some men's minds, they will not even give it a hearing, because old men, good men, and men in authority have decided otherwise. Such people assume that they are right by inheritance and approved by ancestry. They can't learn anything, they have reached the fullness of wisdom and that's where they plan to stop. The church of God should try to remove all prejudices from human eyes from whatever sources they may come. We may be able to cure such blindness, and it is within our responsibility to attempt it.

Like Ananias, we may remove the scales from the eyes of some blinded Paul. When God has given eyes, we may have the opportunity to wash the dust out of them. Mingle with your fellow men, tell them what the faith is that has saved you, and let them see the good works which the grace of God produces in you. And as the gospel first removed from men's eyes the scales of Judaism, Greek philosophy, and Roman pride, there is no doubt that in this land and in this age, it will make short work of the prejudices which some are doing their best to nurture. But this was not the case of a man who was blind by accident, so it wasn't a type of understanding darkened by prejudice. The man was blind from his birth, so his was the blindness of nature. Therefore, it baffled all surgical skill.

Concerning the blindness caused by human depravity, the blindness that comes with us at our birth, and continues with us until the grace of God comes and causes us to be born again, I'll say that since the beginning of the world it hasn't been heard that any man has opened the eyes of one whose spiritual blindness was born with him and is a part of his nature. If it is something external that blinds me, I may recover. But if it is something from within which shuts out the light, who is he that can restore my vision? If from the beginning of my existence I am full of foolishness, if it's a part of my nature to be without understanding, how dense is my darkness! How hopeless is the dream that it can ever be removed except by a divine hand! Let us think and say what we will, but every one of us is by nature born blind to spiritual things.

We are not capable of understanding God, not capable of understanding the gospel of his dear Son, and not capable of understanding the way of salvation by faith in such a practical way as to be saved by it. We have eyes, but we cannot see. We have understandings, but those understandings are perverted. They are like a compass which forgets the pole. We judge, but we judge unrighteously. By our nature, we exchange bitter for sweet, and sweet for bitter; we replace darkness for light, and light for darkness. This is inbred in our nature, worked into the very fabric of our being. You can't get it out of man, because it is a part of the man – it is his nature.

If you ask me why man's understanding is so dark, I reply, because his whole nature is disordered by sin. His other abilities, having been perverted, act upon his understanding and prevent its acting in a proper manner. There is a coalition of evil within, which deceives the judgment and leads it into captivity to evil affections. For instance, our carnal heart loves sin. The course of our unrenewed soul is towards evil. We were conceived in sin and shaped in iniquity, and we as naturally go after evil as a swine seeks out filth. Sin has a fascination for us, and we are captured by it like birds with a lure or fish with bait.

Even those of us who have been renewed have to guard against sin, because our nature is so inclined to it. With much diligence and great labor, we climb the ways of virtue, but the paths of sin come easy to the feet. Isn't that because our fallen nature leans in that direction? You only have to relax your efforts and to release your soul from its anchor-hold, and it drifts immediately downward towards iniquity, because that's the direction the current of nature runs. It requires much power to send us upward, but downward we go as easily as a stone falls to the ground. You know it is true. Man is not as God made him. His affections are corrupt. Since it is clear that the affections often sway judgment, the balances are held unfairly, because the heart bribes the head.

Even when we imagine that we are very honest, we have unconscious leanings. Our affections, like Eve, seduce the Adam of our understanding, and the forbidden fruit is judged to be good for food. The smoke of the love of sin blinds our mental eye. Our desire is often father to our conclusion, we think we are judging fairly, but we are really indulging our depraved nature. We think a certain thing to be better, because we like it better. We won't condemn a fault too severely, because we have a leaning that way. Neither will we commend an excellence, because it might cost our flesh too much to do what is required to reach it, or not reaching it might strike too severe a blow upon our ego. As long as our natural love of sin covers the mind's eye with cataracts and even destroys its optic nerve, we shouldn't be surprised that the blindness is beyond removal by any human surgery.

In addition to all this, our natural pride and self-reliance rebel against the gospel. Every one of us sees ourselves as very important individuals. Even if we sweep a street-crossing, we have a dignity of self which must not be insulted. A beggar's rags may cover just as much pride as an alderman's gown. Self-importance is not restricted to any one position or grade of life. In the pride of our nature, we are all accounted by ourselves to be both great and good. And anything which would in any way lower us, we reject as unreasonable and absurd. We can't see it and are angry that others do.

He who makes us suspect our own nothingness teaches a doctrine hard to be understood. Pride will not and cannot understand the doctrines of the cross, because they ring her death knell. A consequence of our natural self-sufficiency is that we all desire to enter heaven by our own efforts. We may deny human merit as a doctrine, but flesh and blood everywhere lust after it. We want to save ourselves by feelings if we cannot by doings, and we cling to this as for dear life.

When the gospel comes with its sharp axe and says, "Down with this tree! Your grapes are gall, your apples are poison, your very prayers need to be repented of, your tears need to be wept over, your holiest thoughts are unholy, you must be born again, and you must be saved through the merits of another, by the free, undeserved favor of God," then immediately all our manliness, dignity, and excellence stand up in indignation, and we resolve never to accept salvation on such terms. That refusal assumes the shape of a lack of power to understand the gospel. We do not and cannot understand the gospel, because our opinions of ourselves stand in the way. We start with wrong ideas of self, so the whole business becomes confusion, and we ourselves are blinded.

Another reason why our understanding does not and cannot see spiritual things is because we judge spiritual things by our senses. Imagine a person who makes a foot rule as his standard of everything which exists in nature, and assume that this man with his foot rule in his pocket becomes an astronomer. He looks through the telescope and observes the fixed stars. When he takes out his foot rule, he is told that it is quite out of place in connection with the heavens. He must give up his feet and inches and calculate by millions of miles. He is indignant. He won't be fooled by such enthusiasm. He is a man of common sense, and a foot rule is a thing which he can see and handle. Millions of miles are mere matters of faith, no one has ever travelled them, and he does not believe in them. The man effectually closes his own eyes, and his understanding cannot develop within such limits.

> We will never be able to reach the thoughts and things of God as long as we continue judging after the sight of the eyes.

In the same way, we measure God's corn with our own bushel. We can't be brought to believe that *as the heavens are higher than the earth, so are my ways higher than your ways, and my thoughts more than your thoughts* (Isaiah 55:9). If we find it hard to forgive, we imagine that it's the same with God. Every spiritual truth is acted upon in the same way. We intend to measure the ocean of divine love with measuring cups, and we estimate the sublime truths of revelation by drops in the bucket. We will never be able to reach the thoughts and things of God as long as we continue judging after the sight of the eyes, according to the measure of an earthbound, carnal mind.

Our understanding has also become empty and out of gear from the fact that we are at a distance from God, and because of this, we don't believe in him. If we lived near to God and habitually recognize that *in him we live and move and have our being*, then we would accept everything he spoke as being true, because he spoke it (Acts 17:28). Then our understanding would be clarified immediately by its contact with truth and God. But now, we think of God as a distant person. We have no love for him by nature, nor any care about him. It would be the best news some sinners could hear if there was an announcement that God was dead. They would rejoice at the thought that there was no God. The fool always says, "There is no God" in his heart, even when he doesn't dare say it with his tongue. In our nature, we would be glad to be rid of God. It's only when the Spirit of God comes and brings us near to God and gives us faith in our heavenly Father that we rejoice in him and are able to understand his will.

So you see, our entire nature, fallen as it is, operates to blind our eyes. Therefore, the opening of the eye of the human understanding towards divine things remains an impossibility to any power short of the divine. I believe there are some brethren whose belief is that you can open a sinner's blind eyes by convincing them with words. You might as well hope to sing a stone into sensibility. They imagine that you must enchant men with splendid discourse, and then the scales will fall from their eyes. The climax is a marvelous motivator, and the conclusion is more wonderful still. If these won't convince men, what will? To finish a discourse with a blaze of fireworks, won't that enlighten? Sadly, we know that sinners have been dazzled a thousand times by all the pyrotechnics of oratory, and have remained as spiritually blind as they ever were.

A belief has been held by some that you must argue the truth into men's minds. They believe that if you can present the doctrines of the gospel to them in a clear, logical, demonstrative form, they must give way. But, truly, no man's eyes are opened by logic. Reason alone gives no man power to see the light of heaven. The clearest statements and the most simple presentations are equally in vain without grace. I bear witness that I have tried to make the truth "as plain as day," but my hearers have not seen it for that. The best declaration of truth will not of itself remove birth-blindness and enable men to look unto Jesus. Nor do I believe that even the most enthusiastic gospel appeal, nor the most passionate testimonies to its truth will convince men's understanding.

All these things have their place and their use, but they have no power in and of themselves to enlighten the understanding in a way that saves.

I bring my blind friend to an elevated spot, and I ask him to look at the distant landscape.

"See how the silver river threads its way amid the emerald fields.

See how yonder trees make up a shadowy wood;

How wisely yonder garden, near at hand, is cultivated to perfection;

And how nobly yonder lordly castle rises on yon knoll of matchless beauty."

He shakes his head, because he has no admiration for the scene. I borrow poetical expressions, but he still doesn't join in my delight.

I try plain words and tell him, "There is the garden, and there is the castle, and there is the wood, and there is the river. Don't you see them?"

"No," he says. He can't see a single one of them, and doesn't know what they are like. What ails the man? Haven't I described the landscape well? Have I been inaccurate in my explanations? Haven't I given him my own testimony that I have walked those glades and sailed along that stream?

He shakes his head, and my words are lost. His eyes of his heart alone are to blame. Let's come to this conviction about sinners, because if we don't, we will hammer away and do nothing. Let us be assured that there is something the matter with the sinner himself which *we* cannot cure. Let's do what we can with him, but we can't get him saved unless he is cured. Let's embrace this, because it will drive us away from ourselves, and lead us to our God. It will drive us to the strong for strength and teach us to seek power beyond our own. It is then that God will bless men, because then we will be sure to give all the glory to his name.

The Specialties of the Cure

Secondly, we will dwell a little on the specialties of the cure, not exactly of this man's cure, but of the cure of many whom we have seen. First, it is usually accomplished by the most simple means. This man's eyes were opened with a little clay put into them, and then washed out at the pool of Siloam. God blesses very small things to the conversion of souls. It is very humbling to a preacher who thinks, "Well, I preached a pretty good sermon that time," to find out that God doesn't care one bit about him or his sermon, and that a stray remark he made in the street which he hardly thought was of any value whatsoever was what God blessed. When he thought he had done his best, he had done nothing, and when he thought he had done nothing, God blessed him.

Many souls have had their eyes opened by an instrument which never dreamed of being so useful. Indeed, the whole way of salvation is in itself extremely simple, so it's a good comparison to the clay and spittle which the Savior used. I don't find many souls converted by bodies of divinity. We have received many into the church, but we have never received one who became converted by a profound theological discussion. We very seldom hear of any great number of conversions under very eloquent preachers, very seldom indeed. We appreciate eloquence, and don't have a word to say against it by itself, but evidently it has no power spiritually to enlighten the understanding, and neither does it please God to use the excellency of words for conversion.

When Paul laid aside human wisdom and said he wouldn't use the excellency of speech, he only laid aside what wouldn't have been of much use to him. When David put off Saul's armor and took the sling and the stone, he slew the giant. And giants aren't to be conquered today any more than they were then by champions dressed in Saul's armor. We must keep to the simple thing, to the plain gospel, plainly preached. The clay and the spittle was not an artistic combination, inclination was not charmed by them, or culture gratified, yet by these and a wash in Siloam, eyes were opened. In this way, it pleases God through the foolishness of preaching to save them that believe.

Secondly, in every case it is a divine work. In this case, it was clearly the Lord Jesus who opened the man's eyes literally, and it is always his work by the Holy Spirit spiritually. He gives a man the ability to know spiritual things and embrace them by faith. No eye is ever opened to see Jesus except by Jesus. The Spirit of God works all good things in us. Don't let us lose sight of this belief for any reason. The complicated nature of some men's doctrinal systems requires them to attribute some measure of power to the sinner, but we know that he is dead in sin and entirely without strength. Beloved, change your belief structure, and don't reject the truth before us now, because it stands confirmed by our own daily experience and is revealed in the Word of God. It is the Spirit that brings life and enlightens. A blind soul only yields to that voice which of old said, "Let there be light."

Next, this opening of the eyes is often instantaneous, and when the eye is opened, it often sees just as perfectly as if it had always been seeing. A few hours ago, I saw what I believe was the opening of the eyes of one seeking soul. Two sisters came and inquired of me in the sanctuary. They had been hearing the gospel here for only a short time but had been impressed by it. They expressed their regret that they were about to move far away, but they expressed their gratitude that they had been here at all. I was encouraged by their kind thanks, but felt anxious that a more conclusive work should be worked in them. So I asked them, "Have you believed in the Lord Jesus Christ? Are you saved?"

One of them replied, "I've been trying hard to believe."

"No," I said, "that won't do. Did you ever tell your father that you tried to believe him?" They admitted that such a response would have been an insult. Then I presented the gospel very plainly to them in as simple language as I could.

One of them said, "I can't believe it, I can't believe that I am saved."

Then I went on to say, "God bears testimony to his Son, that whoever trusts in his Son is saved. Will you make him a liar, or will you believe his Word?"

While I spoke, one of them startled us all as she cried, "Oh, sir, I see it all. I am saved! Bless Jesus for showing me this and saving me. I see it all."

The sister who had brought me these young friends knelt down with them while we praised and magnified the Lord with all our hearts. One of the two sisters, however, couldn't see the gospel as the other one had, but I feel sure she will. Doesn't it seem strange that even though both heard the same words, only one came out into clear light, while the other waits in the gloom? The change which comes over the heart when a person's understanding grasps the gospel is often reflected in the face and shines like the light of heaven. Newly enlightened souls often exclaim, "Why, sir, it's so plain. How is it I haven't seen it before now? I understand all I have read in the Bible now, even though I didn't care about it before. It has all come in a minute, and now I see what I never saw before."

I only share this one instance, but it's one among thousands which I've seen, in which the eyes have opened instantly. I can only compare the enlightened sinner to a person who has been shut up in a dark prison and has never seen the light. Then, suddenly, his liberator opens a window and the prisoner is staggered and amazed at what he sees when he looks across the hills and plains. To the believer, heaven-given sight is so magnificent a gift, and what is revealed to him so amazes him, that he barely knows where he is. Often, when Christ opens the eyes it's done in a moment and accomplished completely in that moment. However, in other instances it's a more gradual light. First, men are seen as trees walking. Then, by degrees, film after film is removed from the spiritual eye.

Now, you shouldn't be amazed if light appears so suddenly that it comes as a new sensation to the man and surprises him. Do you remember the first breath of spiritual life you ever drew? I still remember mine. For some of us, the first time we saw the sea and the first time we gazed upon the Alps is fixed in our memories, but these were nothing. They were still just pieces of this old world. We had only seen a little more of what we had seen before. But conversion opens up a whole new world. It teaches us to gaze into the invisible and see the things not seen by mortal eyes. When we receive new eyes, we see a thousand things which utterly astound and at the same time delight us. Are you surprised when young converts get excited? I'm not surprised. I wish we had a little more excitement in our gatherings for worship. Who hears the cry nowadays, "What must I do to be saved?" Or who hears a soul saying, "I've found him of whom Moses in the law and the prophets wrote"?

Let's give plenty of freedom to the work of the Spirit of God and believe that when he comes, men won't always act under the sober rules of proper etiquette, but will break through them, and even be suspected of being drunk, because they speak like men not in their ordinary minds. It's a strange and marvelous thing to men when the Spirit of God opens their eyes, and we must not be surprised if they barely know what they say and forget where they are.

One thing is certain: when the eyes are opened, it's a very clear thing to the man himself. Others may doubt whether his eyes are opened, but he knows they are. *One thing I know, that having been blind, now I see.* When the Lord in his infinite mercy visits a spirit that has been shut up in the dark for a long time, the change becomes so great that he doesn't need to ask if he's been changed or not, because he himself is assured of it by his own consciousness.

When the man is given eyes to see, he possesses a faculty that is capable of abundant use. The man who could see the Pharisees, could see Jesus for eternity. He who has his eyes opened can not only see the trees and fields around him, but he can also see the heavens and the glorious sun. Once a man is given spiritual light, he also immediately has the capacity to see divine mysteries. He will see the world to come and the glories yet to be revealed. Those newly created eyes are those which will see the King in his beauty and the land that is very far off. He has the ability to see everything that will be seen in the day of the revelation of our God and Savior Jesus Christ.

Oh, what a marvelous work is this! May every one of us know it personally. So do we know it? Have we had our eyes opened?

The Condition of the Healed Man

When this man's eyes were first opened, he had strong impressions in favor of the glorious One who had healed him. He didn't know who he was, but he knew he must be something very good. He thought he must be a prophet. When he came to know him better, he felt that he was God and fell down and worshipped him. No man has had his eyes opened without feeling intense love for Jesus, without believing in his deity, and without worshipping him as the Son of God. We don't want to be unloving, but we have a little common sense left. We can never see how a man can be a Christian who doesn't believe in Christ, or how a man can be said to believe in Christ who only believes in the smallest part of him, for example, if he only receives his humanity but rejects his Godhead. There must be a real faith in the Son of God. He is still blind and dark who doesn't fall down like the man in this story and worship the living God, beholding the glory of God in the face of Jesus Christ, and blessing God that he has found both a Prince and a Savior in the person of the Lord Jesus, who has laid down his life for his people. Oh, I'm sure if your eyes are opened, you love Jesus this morning, you feel your heart leap at the very thought of him, your whole soul goes after him, and you feel as if he has opened your eyes – those eyes belong to him – and your whole self too.

Therefore, this man became a confessor of Christ from that moment. They questioned him, and he did not speak bashfully and conceal his convictions, but he answered the questions at once. Stephen was the first martyr, but this man was clearly the first confessor, and he laid it out clearly before the Pharisees, straight to their faces, and in simple language. So, beloved, if the Lord has opened our eyes, we will not hesitate to say so. He has done it, blessed be his name! Our tongue might as well be stricken with eternal silence if we hesitate to declare what Jesus has done for us. I urge you who have received grace from Christ Jesus to become confessors of the faith, to acknowledge Christ, as you ought to do. Be baptized and united with his people. Then, in whatever company you are, however others may speak for him, or against him, take your stand and say, "He has opened my eyes, and I praise his name."

Then, this man becomes an advocate for Christ as well as a confessor, and an able advocate too, because the facts, which were his arguments, saved his adversaries. They said this and that, but he replied, "Whether that's true or not is not for me to say, but God has heard this man. Therefore, this man is not a sinner as you say he is. He has opened my eyes. So I know where he must have come from, he must have come from God." We have been arguing for a long time against faithlessness with arguments which have never achieved anything. I believe skeptics just pick up their blunted shafts and shoot them at the field of truth again and again. I also fear that the Christian pulpit has been a great instructor in faithlessness, because we've taught our people arguments which they never would have known if we had not repeated them under the intention of replying to them. But, beloved, you will never defeat a lack of faith except with facts. Share what God has done for you and prove it by your godly lives. Against the holy lives of Christians, unbelief has no power. Each man must stand ready with his sword of holy living, secure in the power of the Holy Spirit, and the attacks of your enemies, however intense their hostility, will utterly fail. God grant us, like this man, to learn the art of arguing for Christ by personal testimony.

So it came to pass that this man with his eyes opened was driven out of the synagogue. Speckled birds are always chased away by their fellow birds. One of the worst things that can happen to a man as far as this world is concerned is to know too much. If you barely keep up with the times, you may be tolerated. But if you get a little ahead of the age, you should expect to be treated badly. Be blind among blind men – it's the very demand of worldly wisdom if you want to save your skin. It's a very unsafe thing to have your eyes opened among blind men, because they won't believe what you say. You'll be very passionate, and, since they can't see, you have no common ground for argument, and you'll immediately fall to quarrelling.

So if the blind men are in the majority, it's probable that you'll have to escape out a door or window and meet people elsewhere.

When God opens a man's eyes to see spiritual things, immediately others say, "What's this fellow talking about? We don't see what he says he sees."

If the fellow is very simple, he turns around to these blind men and says, "I will explain to you now."

Dear friend, it's a waste of your time, because they can't see. If a man is born blind, you don't need to talk to him about scarlet, mauve, and magenta. He can't understand you, because he doesn't know anything at all about it. Move on, because it's no use reasoning with him. The only thing you can do with him is to take him where he can get his eyes opened. To argue with him is utterly useless, because he doesn't have the ability to see. If you knew a person to be devoid of taste, you wouldn't quarrel with him if he said sugar tasted like salt. He doesn't know what sweet means nor what salt means, but only uses the words without understanding them. In the same way, a man who is without grace in his heart doesn't and can't know anything about religion. He picks up the phrases, but he knows as much about the truth itself as a botanist knows about botany who has never seen a flower, or as a deaf man knows about music. Don't try to reason with such people. Just believe that they are incapable of learning from you by reasoning and go to God's Holy Spirit with this cry: "Lord, open their eyes! Lord, open their eyes!"

Be very patient with them, because you can't expect blind men to see, and you must not be very angry with them if they don't. Be very prayerful for them and bring the gospel to them in the power of the Holy Spirit. Then, who knows, their eyes may be opened. But don't be surprised if they say you are a fanatic, an enthusiast, a Methodist, a Presbyterian, or a hypocrite. Those are the kinds of words which the spiritually blind fling at those who can see. You say you have an ability which they don't. Therefore, they deny the ability, because they wouldn't like to admit that you have something they don't, and they put you out of the synagogue.

> The society of the world never was any benefit to us, and it never will be.

But notice, when this man was put out, Jesus Christ found him. So it was a blessed loss for him to lose the Pharisees and find his Savior. Brethren, what a mercy it is when the world casts us out! I remember a lady of title, who is now in heaven, who, when she was united to this church, was forsaken by all the people of position who had formerly associated with her. I said to her, and she joined in the sentiment, "What a mercy you are rid of them. They might have been a snare to you. Now you will have no further trouble from them."

"Yes," and she added, "for Christ's sake I could be content to be counted as the off-scouring of all things."

The society of the world never was any benefit to us, and it never will be. Trying to be very respectable and mingle in elevated society is a snare to many Christians. Value men for their real worth and not for their sparkle, and believe the greatest men are those who are holiest, and those who keep company with Christ to be the best company.

It is a great blessing to the church when it is persecuted. For that matter, we might be glad to have back the days of Diocletian again. The church is never purer, never more devout, and never increases more rapidly than when she enjoys the bad opinion of society. When we begin to be considered excellent people, and our church is honored and respected, corruption sets in. We get away from Christ and prove again that the friendship of this world is hatred toward God. *Ye adulterers and adulteresses, know ye not that the friendship of the world is enmity with God? Whosoever therefore that desires to be a friend of the world, makes himself the enemy of God* (James 4:4).

I pray that the Lord grant that we may have our eyes so opened that our testimony may bring upon us the charge of being strange. Then, if we remove ourselves from the company of those who cannot see the Lord, may we live even closer to Him, and this shall be a great gain to us.

The Lord bless you, beloved, for Jesus Christ's sake. Amen.

Chapter 13

The Question of Questions

Jesus heard that they had cast him out; and finding him, he said unto him, Dost thou believe in the Son of God? (John 9:35)

T he eye of the Lord Jesus is always on his chosen, and he knows every circumstance which happens to them. *Jesus heard that they had cast him out.* Our Lord had done too much for this man to forget him.

Where grace has performed a great work, its memory lingers. As it is written, *Thou wilt have a desire towards the work of thine hands* (Job 14:15). Let's take comfort in this: if anything has happened to hurt us, Jesus has heard of it and will act accordingly.

Our Lord sought out the outcast one. Unasked, he opened his eyes. Unsought, he looked after him in his hour of trouble. He was not easy to find, but our Lord is great at searching out his lost sheep, and he persevered until he found him. If we ever seem cast away from Christ or cast out by proud religionists, he will find us when we cannot find him. Blessed be his name!

Our Lord's objective was to present this man with something of real value. He had been cast out of the synagogue, so he needed comfort, but it would be a magnificent thing to comfort him in such a way as to lead him onward and upward in the divine life. Our Lord's way of comforting was to ask a question which would lead to heart searching and, ultimately, spiritual advance. It isn't the way you and I might take, but his ways are not our ways, neither are his thoughts our thoughts.

For my thoughts are not as your thoughts, neither are your ways as my ways, saith the LORD (Isaiah 55:8). Wisdom is justified in her methods.

It is the best thing, when a man is in soul trouble, to make him look at his own condition before God, and especially to his faith, because when he finds that he is right on the main point, this assurance will be a wellspring of comfort to him. We are sure that the Lord used the very best way to bring this man to well-grounded confidence when he said to him, *Dost thou believe in the Son of God?* He used this question to help him make a considerable advance in faith, because even though the poor man had believed in Jesus, up to the measure of his knowledge, his knowledge had been slender. Now he learned that the opener of his eyes was the Son of God. This is the type of faith the person of our Lord deserves, but many have never rendered it to him. Because of this, they miss the great power of his grace. The man was excommunicated. He was then placed under the ban of the Jewish church, but trust in the Son of God quickly removed any alarm he might have felt on that account. He who enjoys the favor of the Son of God will not tremble at the frown of the Sanhedrin.

Oh, I pray that the Lord would comfort many as I ask each one of you this one personal question: *Dost thou believe in the Son of God?* To young and old, to rich and poor, I will ask this serious question. It's not a confusing question on a difficult-to-understand point, but a simple and urgent question relating to every single person. It's not a profound and intricate problem – a question of free will or predestination, of postmillennial or premillennial advents. It's a practical question – pressing and present – and one that concerns every man in his everyday life, at this very moment. I ask you to picture me with my hand on your shoulder, looking you in the face, and saying, "Dost thou believe on the Son of God?"

This isn't a question out of which angry controversy should arise, because it has to do with yourself, and yourself only. Whatever discussion there may be will be confined within your own heart. It concerns you only, and it's even put in the singular: "Dost *thou* believe on the Son of God?" It was asked by Jesus himself to this man, so consider that. Jesus asks you the same question, apart even from your wife or friend.

The Question Needs to Be Raised

I'll begin pressing home the question, by the help of the Holy Spirit, by saying that the question needs to be raised. It must not be taken for granted that you believe on the Son of God. "Oh yes, I'm a Christian," says one. "I was born in a Christian country. I was taken to church while I was a baby, christened, and I now repeat the creed. Surely this is sufficient proof of my faith!"

Or maybe you say, "My mother took me to the meetinghouse before I could walk, and ever since, I have kept the ways of old-fashioned Nonconformity."

All this may be true, but it is not the point. "Dost thou believe on the Son of God?" This is a spiritual and vital question which cannot be set aside.

You reply, "My moral character has always been upright. In business, I have always paid my bills, and I've always been ready to help every charitable institution."

> Dost thou believe on the Son of God?

I am glad to hear all this, but it still does not touch the matter in hand. This question goes deeper than outward conduct. Hear it again: "Dost thou believe on the Son of God?"

Numbers of moral, friendly, generous, and even religious people have not believed on the Son of God. Please excuse me, but I can't let you slip through in the crowd. I must grab ahold of you with a holy intensity, that even forgets courtesy for the moment. I must ask even the best of you, "Dost thou believe on the Son of God?"

Even though this man had been scrupulously obedient, our Lord asked the question. It may be that I'm speaking to some who say, "I have been obedient to the duties of religion at all times. Whatever I've found to be commanded of God in his Word, I have carefully carried out." Wasn't it the same with this man born blind? The Savior put clay on his eyes and told him to go to the pool of Siloam and wash off the clay, and the man did exactly as he was told. He didn't go to another pool, but to the pool of Siloam. He didn't attempt to get the clay off his eyes by any other process than that of washing. He was very obedient to Christ. Yet, the Lord said to him, *Dost thou believe on the Son of God?* No outward observances, however carefully carried out, will make the question unnecessary. I'm afraid that some of you have *not* been very careful in fulfilling outward ordinances, and for this you are worthy of blame, but even if you had been scrupulously exact, no outward observances, however carefully followed out, can exempt you from the question, *Dost thou believe on the Son of God?*

This man had also passed through a very remarkable experience. He could honestly say, *One thing I know, that having been blind, now I see.* He could never forget the long night he experienced while a child, a youth, and a man. All those years, no ray of light had ever brought him joy. To him, night and day were much the same. He had sat in deep poverty all through that dreary darkness and learned no skill but that of a beggar. As the cooling water touched his eyes and washed away the clay, sunlight streamed in upon his lifelong midnight, and he saw. He had undergone all that change, and still the Savior asked him, *Dost thou believe on the Son of God?*

So, brother, you may be a very changed man and still not be a believer on the Son of God. You, my dear sister, may be a very different woman from what you used to be. When you tell your experience, it may be very unique and worthy of being recorded in a book, but this question must still be asked of you. Whatever your experience may be, do not forget self-examination. Don't say, "I never need to question myself. The type of experience as I have had settles my position without question. I'm not so childish as to look within, or have any doubt about my faith. Such a remarkable case as mine can't be suspected."

Don't talk in this way, because if our Lord, who knew the change this man had undergone, still said to him, *Dost thou believe on the Son of God?* I must press the question with even the most remarkable of people: *Dost thou believe on the Son of God?*

This man, in addition to receiving physical sight, had exercised a degree of faith in the Lord Jesus. If you follow the chapter through, you'll see that he had some sort of faith in Christ while he was blind, or he wouldn't have gone to Siloam to wash away the clay. And when he saw, he didn't doubt that Jesus had really made him whole, and he stated the fact publicly. He also said, *He is a prophet.* He went further still and said, *If this man were not of God, he could do nothing.* He had believed as far as his light helped him to believe, so that the seeds of faith were in him. Still our Lord Jesus Christ pressed him with the question, *Dost thou believe on the Son of God?* Beloved friends, you may never have been troubled with skepticism. It may be that you haven't even examined the grounds of your faith, because you've never been tempted to suspect them. You've embraced the gospel from your youth as true, so you've believed it without being confused. I am thankful that you have done so.

Still, do you believe in Jesus Christ as the Son of God? Is Jesus God to you? Do you trust him as able to do anything and everything for you? To you, is he *able also to save to the uttermost those that come unto God by him* (Hebrews 7:25)? If not, may the Lord help you to take this step, because, short of this, you have not received the true Christ of God. It is of very little use to say, "Oh yes, I believe in Christ. He was the noblest of examples. I believe in Christ. He was the most instructive of prophets."

Do you believe in him also as the Sacrifice, as the Priest, the Savior, and the Salvation? And, gathering all up into one, do you believe in him as the Son of God? Do you believe in the Son of God as revealed in Holy Scripture?

Furthermore, this man had spoken out bravely for Christ, as you saw in chapter 9 of the gospel of John. He was shrewd, sharp, and unanswerable. The learned doctors didn't even compare with the blind beggar whose eyes had been opened. He stood up for the man who had given him sight and allowed no charge to stand against him. His statements were short, but full, and his answers were themselves unanswerable. Who would have thought that a blind beggar could have crafted such a logical argument as he did? Yet to this bold confessor the Savior had to say, *Dost thou believe on the Son of God?*

My friend, as a preacher, you may be able to declare the gospel very clearly to others, and you may enforce it with powerful arguments, but *Dost thou believe on the Son of God?* Even in your case, the question must be asked. Some of you may remember that story which is told in one of Krummacher's books. I half forget it myself, but it goes something like this: The preacher had delivered a quite serious sermon. Then, on the following Monday, he was waited on by one of his hearers who said, "Sir, if what you said last Sunday was true, what will become *of us?*" Now, if he had said, "What will become of *me?*" the preacher would have explained still further to him the gospel in the usual way.

As it was, he stressed the word "us." His visitor, almost unconsciously, said, "Alas, dear sir! If these things are true, what shall we do?" The Lord used that plural pronoun to awaken the preacher who had not been converted even though he thought he had been.

I pray that we who speak for God may also hear the Lord speak to us! I know the good preacher, and love him very much, who, when he was preaching, as he had done for years, was saved through the personal application of his own sermon. He is a minister of the Church of England, but he did not know the Lord. While he was preaching, the Lord applied to his heart a gospel truth which so affected him that he spoke with the accent of conviction which is natural to a renewed man. At last a Methodist, who was in the church, shouted out, "The parson's converted! Hallelujah!" and all the people broke out with cries of praise. The preacher himself joined in the universal joy, and they sang together, "Praise God, from whom all blessings flow!"

Oh, what a mercy it is when the waiter at the Lord's feast is himself fed! Shouldn't those who are to bear the healing balm to the sick be themselves healed? I have not been ashamed to speak in my Lord's name, nor have I blushed to defend his cause before his enemies. Still, I must remember that I may have done all this, and still I may not know the King to whom I have been a herald. Friends, how terrible it would be to have cast out devils in his name, and still be unknown to him! Therefore, we press the question: *Dost thou believe on the Son of God?*

This man had gone further still, because he had suffered for Christ. He had been put out of the synagogue for bearing witness to the power of Jesus. But he still had to hear the question, *Dost thou believe?* Yes, you may have been laughed at by your relatives for your religiousness. You may have had to quit a good job because of your determination to be honest, self-controlled, and pure. You may even now stand under the ban of some cold-hearted church, because you displayed more passion than was desired. And even though I appreciate your faithfulness, you must excuse me if I buttonhole you in the Lord's name and say, as Christ did to this man, *Dost thou believe on the Son of God?* It's one thing to play the hero before our fellow men, and another to be true in the secret chamber of our own soul. You are bold in your confession, but do you really believe in the Lord Jesus? Can that bold confession be supported by your life? I hope you aren't a defender of the faith in the same manner as Henry VIII. He wore the title but was by no means worthy of it. Come, my eloquent friend, do you live according to how you talk? Do you feel yourself as you desire to make me feel? *Dost thou believe on the Son of God?*

You'll see, from my persistence, that I am not for letting anybody escape the personal question. My respected friend, who has been an officer of this church longer than anybody else, will not refuse to ask himself this question. My beloved sister in Christ, who has conducted a Bible class for years and has been so useful in the schools, will not refuse to answer this searching word. I must even dare to make this inquiry of a faraway minister. My father in Christ, whose shoe's buckle I'm not worthy to loosen, I must even ask you, just as I ask myself, *Dost thou believe on the Son of God?*

> This question must be asked, and asked of everybody, because many people nowadays do not believe on the Son of God.

This question must be asked, and asked of everybody, because many people nowadays do not believe on the Son of God. There are many who would be very offended if we denied their right to the name of *Christian*, who nevertheless do not know the Son of God. These folks admire a man who will concoct a sermon to show that they may be Christians, and not believe on Jesus as God. I will preach no such sermon until I lose my ability to reason, but I will press upon this unbelieving age this vital question: *Dost thou believe on the Son of God?* If you don't believe in this way, your faith falls short of that which Christ requires you to possess, and you had better be careful, or it will fall short of landing you in heaven. With a Savior less than divine, you have a religion less than saving. How is it with you? Will you believe on the Son of God alone, or run with the vain multitude who see nothing in him but a man?

I think every man here will say, "You don't need to apologize, dear sir, for asking the question, because it's one we have to ask ourselves." Indeed, I know it's true. Who is there that lives so purely that he never has to examine this issue? We've heard people cry out against the hymn:

> "'Tis a point I long to know,
>   Oft it causes anxious thought:
> Do I love the Lord or no?
>   Am I his, or am I not?"

But if a man never has an anxious thought about his position, I would have many anxious thoughts about him. One of our poets has well said:

> "He that never doubted of his state,
>   He may, perhaps, he may too late."

There are so many things about us, all of which we need to mourn over, and these cause us to ask the questions, "Is my faith the faith which works by love and purifies the soul? Do I truly believe on the Son of God?" At times, we rejoice in an absolute certainty as to our faith in Christ, and the Spirit himself bears witness with our spirit that we are the children of God. At other seasons, we are challenged with great searchings of heart, and no question causes us greater anguish than this: Do I believe on the Son of God? It will be tragedy to us if – after all our profession, and experience, and effort – we have no more than the name of faith, and the notion of faith, but are found devoid of the life of it in our souls. Yes, the inquiry of our text is a question which needs to be asked.

The Question Can Be Answered

Secondly, the question can be answered. I'm sure it can be answered, or our Lord wouldn't have asked it, because he was never so unpractical as to go around asking men questions about themselves which it was not possible to answer. It is a question to which you can give the answer, if you are willing, of "Yes" or "No." I beg you to take practical action to answer it.

It would be a most unhappy thing if this question couldn't be answered. Suppose we were condemned to live in a state of perpetual doubt in regards to our being believers in the Lord Jesus. This would produce an awakened man in a condition of constant anxiety. If I am not sure whether I am in the favor of God or not, I am in a sad condition. I remember hearing a Christian minister say to a group of people that no man could be sure that he was saved. Then I wondered what he had to preach that was worth preaching, because if we can't know that we are saved, then we can't be sure that we are at peace with God, and that would cause us to be in jeopardy every hour. There can be no peace to the mind of the awakened man if he doesn't know that he is saved. It's like one at sea who is half afraid that his ship is off course and may soon strike a rock, but isn't quite sure whether it is or not. The captain should not rest until he has taken his bearings and found out his position in reference to the dangers of the sea and the hope of reaching the desired haven. To leave his ship's position an unresolved point would be to continue in fear, and to invite danger. To leave your faith in question is to risk a vital point. He who can leave this hinge of the soul's condition unexamined must be sadly seared in conscience.

There is a possibility of knowing *with certainty* that you believe on the Son of God. Did I say there is a possibility of it? Thousands have attained this certainty. You can know that you believe on the Son of God as surely as you know that there is a queen of England, or as surely as you know that you exist, and you can know without falling into fanaticism or presumption.

Many among us are so immersed in the Lord Jesus that we could no more question the existence of faith in our own hearts, than we could dispute the fact that our hearts beat. Such assured people avoid no examination. For them, the more examination the better, because their hope has firm and deep foundations. They can give a reason for the hope that is in them. *But also if ye suffer anything for righteousness' sake, blessed are ye; therefore, be not afraid of their terror neither be troubled, but sanctify the Lord God in your hearts, and be ready always to respond to every man that asks you a reason of the hope that is in you with meekness and reverence, having a good conscience, so in that which they murmur against you as of evildoers, those that blaspheme your good conversation in the Christ may be confused* (1 Peter 3:14-16).

The confidence of the believer in the Lord Jesus is as sure as mathematical certainty, because we know whom we have believed, and we are persuaded that he is able to keep that which we have committed to him. *For which cause I also suffer these things; nevertheless, I am not ashamed, for I know whom I have believed and am persuaded that he is able to keep that which I have committed unto him against that day* (2 Timothy 1:12). There are believers in our Lord Jesus who have lived for thirty years without a doubt of their faith in him, because that faith has been in daily, happy exercise.

You can answer the question, "Dost thou believe?" because you are at this moment believing – distinctly and intensely believing. Those who dwell in the light of God's countenance and feel the Holy Spirit within them, bearing witness with their spirits, are in no doubt as to their possession of faith. If we feel a burning love toward God, a growing hatred of sin, a struggle against the evil which is in the world, and some of the likeness of Christ, we may safely conclude that these fruits of faith come from the root of faith. By the work of the Holy Spirit upon our life and heart we know and are sure that we have believed in Jesus as the Son of God. I hope I speak to many this morning who are enjoying assurance and know that they have passed from death into life.

This assurance requires some consciousness. How do I know that I live, breathe, stand, and walk? I can't explain to you the way I arrive at certainty on these things, but I'm quite sure that I do live, breathe, and so on. The very power to question the fact implies it. So a believer can be sure that he believes that Jesus is the Son of God. While he may not be able to give logical proof, he can still be conscious in his own soul that it is so, and he is correct in his assurance, because even the very ability to be anxious about grace is an evidence of grace. If there is any question about whether you've been a believer or not for the last twenty years, don't fight that question and drive it away, but begin now to believe, with the Lord's help. Turn your eyes to the cross, and trust yourself wholly to Christ from this very hour. Then you will believe, and the act itself will declare its own proof. Say from your heart:

> "Just as I am, without one plea,
>> But that thy blood was shed for me,
> And that thou bid'st me come to thee,
>> O Lamb of God, I come!"

By coming in this way, you will know that you have come, and by continuing to come, your assurance will grow that you have come. May the Holy Spirit cause the sacred fire to burn, and then you will feel the flame before long. To say, "I now believe on the Son of God," is the best way of answering the question about your condition.

If you want further help to answer the question, there are characteristics and evidences of true faith by which you can test yourself. Do you ask, Do I believe on the Son of God? Then answer this: Is Christ precious to you? For to you who believe, he is precious. If you love and prize him as the most precious thing in earth or heaven, you couldn't have this appreciation of him if you weren't a believer. Have you undergone the change called the new birth? Have you passed through a process which could be described

Do you love God?

as being brought out of darkness into marvelous light? If so, your new birth is a sure evidence of faith, because those things go together. Faith is a proof of regeneration, but regeneration is also a proof that you have faith in the Son of God.

Are you obedient to Christ? Obedience is evidence of faith, because faith works by love and purifies the soul. Has sin become bitter? Do you loathe it? Has holiness become sweet? Do you follow after it? I don't ask whether you are perfect, but is the whole current of your soul towards being perfect? Can you say that if you could live entirely without sin it would be the greatest delight you could have, or that absolute perfection would be heaven to you? That shows which way your mind goes. It shows that there is a change of nature, because no unrenewed heart yearns after perfect holiness. Your heart is bending towards Christ's perfect rule and sovereignty, and I'm sure that you have believed that he is the Son of God. You are resting upon him with a true and living faith if you take up his cross heartily and follow him. Again, do you love God? Do you love his people? *We know that we are passed from death unto life, in that we love the brethren* (1 John 3:14). Do you love his Word? Do you delight in his worship? Do you bow in patience before his rod, in such a way that you pick up the bitter cup and say, *Thy will be done* (Matthew 6:10)? These things prove that you have faith in Jesus. Pay attention to them.

But suppose, after using all these inquiries and tests, you still say, "Sir, this is a serious question and requires great care. I haven't settled it yet." Then follow this man in his method. He was asked, *Dost thou believe on the Son of God?* Then, he turned to the Lord and replied with another question to the Lord Jesus. We can resort to Jesus for aid. He who had once been blind eagerly asked, *Who is he, Lord, that I might believe in him?* So turn, in the moment of your distress, and cry, "Lord Jesus, I beg you to teach me to know you better, so that I can have more faith in you." Go to Jesus for faith in Jesus.

Also, there are certain great truths upon which faith feeds. To be sure that you have faith, you had better think about these truths. I pray that the Lord would be pleased to reveal himself to you, so you may know him and believe on him! You won't remain long in any doubt if you understand those glorious things which concern your Lord!

Know who he is, what he is, and what he has done. This will enable you to believe in him as the Son of God. In the same way as men who were pressed before the courts appealed to Caesar, you appeal to Christ himself. And you can be assured that you will find deliverance in him. Even if your faith is hidden from yourself, it isn't hidden from him. If you can't bring it to mind by thoughts of the work of grace within, turn your mind towards your Savior and Covenant Head in heaven, and faith will open itself, as the blooms of flowers open to the sun. The question can be answered.

The Question Should Be Answered at Once

Thirdly, the question should be answered, and it should be answered at once. If I could, I would concentrate all your thoughts on this one investigation which concerns each man so vitally: *Dost thou believe on the Son of God?* Answer this from your own soul. I am no father confessor. Be father confessors to your own selves. Let each man give his verdict at the bar of his conscience. Answer as if you're in the presence of Christ, because, like the man in the narrative, you are in his presence now. Answer for yourself before the heart-searching God.

Answer it to men also, because your Savior deserves this from you. Don't be ashamed to say outright, "I do believe on the Son of God." This fact must not be hidden away in a corner. Our Lord in Holy Scripture always puts open confession side by side with faith as a part of the plan of salvation. You will never find anywhere in the Word of God that he who believes and takes the Lord's Supper shall be saved. But you do find it written, *He that believes and is baptized shall be saved* (Mark 16:16). Why does baptism take such a prominent place? Partly because it is the ordained form of open confession of faith in the Lord Jesus Christ. The passage is parallel with that other passage, *if thou shalt confess with thy mouth the Lord Jesus and shalt believe in thine heart that God has raised him from the dead, thou shalt be saved* (Romans 10:9). What less can Christ expect than an outspoken faith, if there is any faith at all? Will you bring to him who redeemed you a cowardly faith, to him who intercedes for you a silent faith, or to him who opened your eyes a faith which doesn't dare to look your fellow men in the face? No. Speak out and let the world know that he who died on Calvary is the Son of God to you, even if he's not to anybody else. The question ought to be answered – answered before men and answered at once. Do not delay. Make haste to keep your Lord's command.

The question ought to be answered at once, because it is that important. If you don't believe on the Son of God, where are you? You are not alive unto God, *for the just shall live by faith* (Galatians 3:11). You can't stand, because it is written, *Thou by faith art standing* (Romans 11:20). You cannot work for God, because it is faith that works by love. Where is your justification if you have no faith? *A man is justified by faith* (Romans 3:28). Where is your sanctification? The Lord says, *that they may receive remission of sins and inheritance among those who are sanctified by the faith that is in me* (Acts 26:18). Where is your salvation without faith? *Believe on the Lord Jesus Christ, and thou shalt be saved* (Acts 16:31). You cannot be or do anything acceptable without faith, because *without faith it is impossible to please God* (Hebrews 11:6).

You are in an evil situation, and will soon be in a worse one unless you can say, "I believe that Jesus is the Son of God, and I trust him as my all in all." He who doesn't believe on the Lord Jesus Christ is under present condemnation, because *he that does not believe is condemned already* (John 3:18). Condemned already. Therefore, this question must be answered immediately, unless you are content to dwell under wrath and content to live unreconciled to God. While you sit in that position, you are in danger of the wrath to come. Can you be content?

You are losing time as long as you remain in ignorance as to your faith. If you aren't believing in Jesus, you are spending your days in death and alienation from God. If there's a question as to whether you have believed on the Son of God, it's no question that you are losing comfort and happiness. If you go up and down this troubled world without an assurance of your acceptance with God, you are losing power to honor the name of the Lord by a joyful conversation. You are in an inconsistent position, and an inconvenient one. If you really haven't believed in Jesus Christ, the Son of God, you are resting short of eternal life. Meanwhile, you come up to the Lord's house and take part in worshipping him while you deny him the first essential of true worship – your faith in him.

If you haven't believed that Jesus is the Son of God, the hope that you will ever do so grows fainter every day. The longer a man lingers in any state, the more likely it is that he will continue there. When men have grown accustomed to do evil, the prophet cries over them, *Can the Ethiopian change his skin or the leopard his spots?* (Jeremiah 13:23). It's an awful thing to have heard the gospel for a long time in vain. If even the appeals of Calvary are lost on you, what's left? Gospel-hardened sinners are hardened indeed. Some of you have been unbelievers in the Lord Jesus Christ for fifty years and, I fear, will die in unbelief. What then? The number of unbelievers is terrible. *If ye do not believe that I AM, ye shall die in your sins* (John 8:24). Tremendous words – *Die in your sins.* That is what will, in all probability, happen to many of you. No, it will surely happen unless you believe on the Son of God.

So, answer this question at once. Don't delay for an hour. If the answer is unsatisfactory, the situation can be changed if you attend to it at once. He that has not yet believed on the Son of God, may still do so. You still have time, but don't laugh in the face of mercy. The light of another Sabbath still shines upon you, and his patience is not yet exhausted. The gospel is still preached in your ears, so the day of hope is not over. The Bible is still open in front of you, and the gate of mercy is open for all who will enter by faith. So I pray that you would believe on the Son of God right now. You may not live to see another Lord's Day, so snatch the present opportunity. Soon, news will come to us about you, as it has so often come about others, "He is dead," or "She has gone." Since eternity can be molded by today, I pray that you would arouse yourselves. Examine your faith in Jesus, because if that's right, all is well. But if that is found insufficient, all is insufficient.

The Question May Be Very Important to Us if We Answer It

So my final point is this: the question may be very important to us if we answer it. *Dost thou believe on the Son of God?* Suppose you have to answer the question in the negative. If you are compelled to sigh and say, "No," then so be it and look the truth in the face. It will tend to wake you up from your carelessness if you know where you are. One came to join the Christian church the other day who said, "While I was at my work in the parlor, this thought suddenly came to me: 'You are an unsaved woman.' I couldn't shake it off. I went down to my cooking in the kitchen, but it followed me. From the fire and from the water, I seemed to hear the accusation, 'You are an unsaved woman.' When I went in to my meals, I could scarcely eat my bread because of this choking thought. It haunted me. 'You are an unsaved woman!'" It was not long before that unsaved woman desired the Lord, and became a saved woman by faith in Christ Jesus. Oh, I wish I could put this idea into some minds right now! You are an unsaved man. You don't believe on the Son of God, so you're full of bitterness and held captive by sin. I would like to make the seat you sit upon become hard and this building to grow uncomfortable to you, so that you would vow, "Please God, if I can only stagger home, I will seek my bedside and cry for mercy."

I wish you were even under greater urgency and would beg the Lord for mercy at once, on the spot. I think you would do so if you answered this question fairly and felt that the reply must be "No." But suppose you are able to say "Yes." This question will have done you great service, because it will have brought you great peace. As long as you leave this matter in doubt, you will be tossed back and forth. But when it's decided, you will enter into rest. Peace like a river will flow into your soul when you can say:

"I do believe, I will believe,
   That Jesus died for me;
That on the cross he shed his blood,
   From sin to set me free."

Know that he is yours, and you will rejoice in him. You can't obtain settled peace until you settle this question.

Once this is done, you will try to do something for Jesus to show your gratitude for his salvation. Until I know that I am saved, I will have no heart for holy work. A wise man stops at home and looks after his own concerns as long as he feels that they are in danger, but when they are all safe, he can look to the interests of his neighbors. When I know I'm saved and that there is nothing more for me to do in that matter, because Christ has finished it all, then I ask what I can do for him who has done so much for me. Where is the child or the man I can talk to about my Savior? I will go and look for lost ones and tell them of a present salvation. Perhaps I've never dared to speak to my wife or my children about eternal life, but now that I possess it, and know that I do, because I believe on the Son of God, I will begin to instruct others in this good doctrine. Yes, application grows out of assurance.

And what a help assurance will be in times of trouble! You may be facing trials, but if you can say, "I know that I believe in Jesus Christ the Son of God," you will have peace. Is it a surgical operation? You will lie still and yield yourself up to the surgeon's knife, come life or death, and you will do it easily. Is it cruel persecution which you have to face tomorrow? You will not be afraid, but, believing in Jesus, you will take up his cross. Are you growing old, and thinking of the time when you must die? It will not matter, because you know that you will only be going home since you believe on the Son of God. He never lets a soul believe on him in vain. He never casts away a poor heart that trusts him. What strength your faith will give you! You will be a hero, whereas you might have been a coward. Now that you know, and are sure, that you believe on the Son of God, you will fear no evil. This will fill you with holy enthusiasm and praise.

You've been saying, "I don't know how I can be so dull and stupid! I go to the house of God, and I don't feel the power of the Word. I'm afraid that I'm not a Christian." Well, as long as you have that crippling fear upon you, you will not be sensitive to the cheering truth. But when you know that you believe on the Son of God and are sure of your salvation, your heart will beat to another tune, and the music of the upper spheres will take possession of your bosom. I wouldn't be surprised if you sing, as Toplady does:

> "Yes, I to the end shall endure,
>   As sure as the earnest is given;
> More happy, but not more secure,
>   The glorified spirits in heaven."

You will begin to taste heavenly happiness when you have a sense of heavenly certainty. When you are moved with gratitude and filled with joy, the result will be a great concern for others who have not believed on the Son of God. You will look at unbelievers with sorrow and alarm. Perhaps they are very wealthy, but you will despise their gold, because it blinds their eyes. They might be very clever, but you will not worship their abilities, because the eternal light is hidden from their eyes. You will say to yourself, "They may have all their wealth and all their cleverness, but I have the Son of God."

In having Christ, you have more than Alexander possessed when he had won the world. He could conquer the earth, but he couldn't win heaven, because he knew nothing of believing on the Son of God. In this respect, you have done more than an angel could do, because an angel has no lost soul to trust to the Son of God and no sin to wash away in the Savior's blood. But you have trusted him, and you have been washed in his blood, and you are clean. Go home and sing, my brother. Go home and proclaim it to your friends that Jesus is the Son of God and abundantly able to save. Go home and weep some poor sinner to Jesus. Go home and refuse to rest until you can say to God, "Here I am, and the souls that you have given me. We are believing on the Son of God." Peace be with you! Amen.

Chapter 14

The Essence of Simplicity

Jesus heard that they had cast him out; and finding him,
he said unto him, Dost thou believe in the Son of God? He
answered and said, Who is he, Lord, that I might believe in
him? (John 9:35-36)

This text is from the story of the blind man to whom Jesus had given sight. His account of the cure provoked the anger of the Jews and their rulers. And since the man couldn't be convinced to agree with them that the one who had opened his eyes could also be a bad man, they cast him out of their assembly. That act signified to him that he would be, or already was, cast out of the Jewish church, set aside from the synagogue, and made the victim of excommunication. This was one of the most dreaded calamities that could happen to a Jew, and I don't doubt that this man considered it to be so.

It's not likely that any of you are feeling the same trouble, but you may be suffering from something similar. It may be that you have excommunicated yourselves. Within the court of your own bosom, your conscience has held a solemn court and pronounced upon you a sentence which continually rings in your ears. You barely dare to mingle with those who assemble in the house of God, because you feel yourselves unworthy to be among them. Up until lately, you were on the best of terms with yourselves and thought that all was right with God. You hoped that you stood on as good a foundation as other men, and even thought you were somewhat better than many around you. But now a process of enlightenment has come over your mind – you see practices to be seriously evil which before you regarded as amusement, and sin itself is seen differently than in former times. Are you such a person? Let me assure you that your state of mind is well known to me, because I knew it for many months. I too felt that I was cut off from the congregation of the hopeful and had no right to mercy from God. I didn't even dare to lift my eyes towards heaven. Instead, I complained to the Lord like Jonah did, "I am shut out of thy sight." For that reason, I speak with brotherly sympathy to any man who believes himself to be a castaway, shut out from the house of the Lord.

The man in the narrative, at the time when the sentence began to cast its gloom over him, was met by the Lord Jesus Christ who at once provided the necessary remedy. Christ came as the consolation of Israel. Where he found men burdened in spirit, he performed his gracious work. But he offered one remedy and prescribed only one way to obtain the cure. He spoke to the oppressed man concerning the Son of God and personal faith in him, because this is the ultimate consolation for broken hearts, this is the surest and best way to bring joy to souls which sit in the dungeons of despondency.

You will face the gospel, whether you reject it or accept it.

Our Lord began by saying to the outcast, *Dost thou believe on the Son of God?* Now, if any of you are in the state which I have just described – feeling guilty before God, lacking peace, with hearts alarmed at the coming and deserved judgment – I will come in Christ's name to you this morning with words of comfort, but they'll be no different than those which Jesus proclaimed. I have nothing to comfort you but the Son of God, and him only, by demanding that you believe on him, because only as you receive him by faith will he be a relief from sorrow to you. He who believes on the Lord Jesus will not be ashamed, but without faith you are without salvation.

We will labor to bring you all to the point at hand. For you who are not yet a believer, there will be a direct encounter between the doctrine of the gospel and your soul. You will face the gospel, whether you reject it or accept it. You will know, if you can understand plain words, that if you believe in Christ Jesus you will be saved. You will have the opportunity to decide whether you will do this or not and either believe on the Son of God or rekindle the sin of rejecting the only *name under heaven given among men in which we can be saved* (Acts 4:12). You will be brought to this point if words can bring you to it. Then I must leave the work of your decision in the hands of God the Holy Spirit. I beg you who love the Lord and are faithful in prayer to aid me with your petitions before the Lord, that the result of bringing the sinner face to face with the gospel may be that he decides to believe in Jesus, that faith be given to him, that the Son of God may become the object of his soul's confidence, and that in no case the hearer may be left to continue in unbelief and reject the Son of God.

You have seen at the mouth of the coal pits how as the full wagons run down the incline they pull the empty ones up to the pit's mouth, so they also may be filled. I pray to God that you who already have grace may exercise the power God has given you with himself, and through persistent prayer draw others to the Savior. While we are preaching, you be praying, and God will work by us both. Look at the unsaved ones around you with an eye of pity, then look to Christ, your exalted Savior, with the eye of faith and say to him, "Jesus, you who have redeemed countless numbers by your blood, work now by your eternal Spirit and redeem by power. Let the Spirit who rested on your own ministry – the Spirit who was with your servants at Pentecost, the Spirit who has also converted us to your truth – work mightily among the congregation this morning, so that all these may be led to obey you. When your cross is lifted high, let it bring life to the dead throughout the camp and be a lighthouse of safety to the awakened, and a pillar of hope to the despairing."

The Matter at Hand

In an attempt to be practical, we will, in the most direct way possible, lay down and define the matter at hand. With you, my anxious friend, the greatest and most important business that can concern you is that you find salvation. You don't possess it now, and your conscience tells you that. And even though you are well aware that you must obtain it, or be lost forever, you still only have a small chance of ever finding it. You have sinned, punishment awaits you, and you can't escape!

The most important thing is for you to be saved, and if you are really awakened, you will desire to be saved from sin as well as from its punishment. You would not only escape from the consequences of doing wrong, but also from the inclination to do wrong – from the constant power and defilement of past sin and from the tendency to sin again. You also desire to be forgiven, and by forgiveness to be set apart from the anger of a justly offended God and be made acceptable to the Most High. And if you are in your right mind, you will desire for all this to be done really and truly, not in appearance or fiction, but in deed and in truth. God forbid that you would ever be content with the name of being saved, with an external and professed salvation of outward rites and ceremonies, while your heart remains unpurified and your nature uncleansed. In some other areas of our lives, we can be deceived and not lose very much. But in matters of the soul, we must make sure, because if we are deceived there, it's all over for us. Let me be cheated with cheap metal instead of gold, if you must, but not with error in the place of saving truth, or deceptive ideas in the place of the works of grace. Let me be deceived about the food I eat, even if every morsel of it is adulterated, but don't let me be deceived about the Bread of Life which my soul craves after. Let me be true to my soul even if everything else is a lie!

Do you desire salvation from the power and guilt of sin, and do you desire it to be thorough and real? Don't you long for it *now*? If God has awakened you, you desire to be saved at once and tremble at the idea of delay. Sin is bitter to you now. It is a plague. The matter before us now is present salvation, personal salvation to be realized for your own self. If there is such a thing as looking up to the smiling face of a reconciled Father in heaven, you want to enjoy it *now*. If it's possible for the load of sin to be removed from a mortal's shoulders forever, you desire to be freed of that burden this instant. If there is a fountain in which a man can wash and every stain will disappear, you long to plunge beneath its cleansing flood immediately and be made whiter than the driven snow. If your soul is awakened, I praise God, because there is nothing beneath the sun that can rival in importance your soul's salvation.

Now the matter which I must press upon you is this: if you are ever to be saved, God has declared that salvation must come to you as a gift of his grace, an act of his free favor, and can only be received by you through your believing in his Son. As Christ consoled the man in the temple by saying to him, *Dost thou believe on the Son of God?* there is still no consolation, much less salvation for you, except through believing in God's own Son.

You've heard the story a hundred times of God's only begotten Son, who is the lover of men's souls, but we must tell it to you again. God won't save men because of their merits. If they have any merits, they don't require saving. If God owes you anything, produce the account and you will have it. If there are any obligations on God's part towards you, say what they are, and if they can be proved to exist, God will never give you less than you can justly claim. Unfortunately, my friend, if you are lodged where you deserve to be, where will it be but in the pit of hell? This being the case, you might as well be done with all claims and demands. God will only save you as a guilty person who deserves to be destroyed. He chooses to save you, because he chooses to display the abundance of his mercy in you. *By grace are ye saved* is the unchanging purpose of heaven (Ephesians 2:8).

It is further declared that this grace will be received by men through the channel of faith, and by that channel only. God will save only those who trust in his Son. Jesus Christ the Lord came into this world and took our nature upon himself, and being found in the likeness of man, he took the transgressor's place. The transgressions of his people were laid upon him, charged to his account, and he suffered for them as if they had been his own sins. He was scourged, tormented, crucified, and slain. The stripes he bore were the punishment due to human sin, and the death he endured was the death threatened to transgressors. Now, whoever trusts in Jesus will participate in the result of all the Redeemer's substitutionary agonies, and the sufferings of Christ will take the place of the believer's suffering, and the rewards of Christ will be instead of the obedience which man should have rendered.

Faith in Jesus makes us righteous through the righteousness of another. It causes us to be accepted in the Beloved, perfect in Christ Jesus. As by the first Adam we fell, so by the second Adam we rise again.

The way to take part in the benefits of the death of the Lord Jesus is simply by believing in him. Believing in Jesus is not a mysterious and complex action. It doesn't require a week to explain what faith is. Faith believes what God has revealed concerning Christ, and it trusts in Christ as the divinely appointed Savior. I believe that Jesus was God's Son, that God sent him into the world to save sinners, that to do so, he became a substitute to justice for all those who trust him, and, since I trust him, I know that he was my substitute, and I am clear before God. Since Jesus died for me, God's justice cannot put me to eternal death, because Jesus my substitute has died for me.

To believe in the Son of God is the point, and nothing else. God's truth cannot demand a second payment for a debt which has already been fully paid on my behalf. The rationale of the whole thing is as plain as possible. Whoever in this world – old or young, Jew or Gentile, literate or illiterate, rich or poor, immoral or moral – trusts in Jesus will be saved. No, he *is* saved the moment he does so, but *he that does not believe is condemned already because he has not believed in the name of the only begotten Son of God* (John 3:18). Let a man's character be what it may, but if in that character there is no faith, he is a lost soul. On the other hand, let that character be what it may, but if he comes to the cross and believes in Jesus, he begins a new life from that moment. God will give to him all the grace and excellence of character to adorn his faith, and his faith will save him.

Trusting in Jesus, believing in Jesus, that is the matter at hand. I want to bring my hammer down upon this anvil with every stroke, and if the Lord is pleased to place before me some heart that he has melted in the furnace of conviction, if any soul is brought to faith in Jesus, the work is done. To believe in the Son of God is the point, and nothing else.

A Question Which Involves the Whole Basis of Faith

Now, we notice that there is a question in our text which involves the whole basis of faith. The man said to Jesus, *Who is he, Lord, that I might believe in him?* All through the narrative, this man proves himself to be a very clever fellow. I don't know that Holy Scripture gives us an instance of a more common-sense man than this man whose eyes were opened. So when he is told that he must believe in the Son of God, he gets right to the point and says, *Who is he, Lord, that I might believe in him?* It's as if that was all he wanted to know, and then the faith would surely come. When a soul is seeking faith, this question is the main point, and the hinge of the whole matter lies there. This man didn't say, "Lord, who am I that I should believe?" Not at all. That would have missed the point. If I read a story in the newspapers with questionable credibility, I don't begin asking what my own character is, but I ask who the authority for the story is. I don't look within, but I look to the person claiming belief. The story is true or not, it doesn't matter what I may be. My character doesn't concern the truth or falsehood of the statement. I must inquire into the statement itself. So this man didn't make any remarks about what he might have been or might still be, but he hung the issue on this nail: *Who is he, Lord, that I might believe in him?*

So all the arguments for your faith are encompassed in that question. You don't need to say, "Who do I think I am, that I could believe? I've lived a life that has been defiled with sin. I have gone from one transgression to another. I have resisted my own conscience, and I have stood against the gospel." It doesn't matter. There you stand with all your defilement, and God says to you, "Whoever believes on the Lord Jesus Christ has everlasting life." That is the saving matter, nothing more and nothing less. Will you believe in the Lord Jesus, or not? You are nothing at this point. If God's witness is true, it is true whether you are a big sinner or a little sinner. If it's false, it won't be any truer if you are good or bad, worthy or unworthy. If Jesus is able to save, he should be trusted. And if he is not able, no one should rely upon him. The whole question rests on that.

Nor should you raise any objections as to your present condition. You say, "But at this moment I feel so hard of heart. I can't weep as some can. Repentance is hidden from me. Prayer is heavy, groaning work for me. Even when I'm listening to the gospel, my attention isn't riveted to the truth as it should be. I am lacking in everything good. I am void of everything that can recommend me to mercy."

I answer, "What of it?"

Suppose I tell a man that the sum of ten thousand pounds has been left to him in a will. Is there any point in him showing me his rags, his empty cupboard, and his wretched bed? Does his poverty make me a liar? Why does the man introduce such irrelevant information into the good news? Either it is true or it is not. His condition has nothing to do with the truth or falsehood of my declaration. If the man were wrapped in scarlet and fine linen, it wouldn't make my statement any truer. Even if the dogs lick him as they did Lazarus, that doesn't give him a right to deny my truthfulness when I tell him a fact.

So, sinner, your condition has nothing to do with the question of whether Jesus is to be trusted or not. *For God so loved the world that he gave his only begotten Son, that whosoever believes in him should not perish but have eternal life* (John 3:16). Will you believe in him? Will you trust the Lord Jesus? If you desire to trust him, the question becomes, Is he worth trusting? But you've missed the point if you say, "I am this," or "I am that." Isn't that true? I appeal to your own common sense.

"But I might go back to my old sins," one says. "I can't trust myself. I've made some changes before, and they haven't lasted. My ship set out to sea and went down in the first gale. With the temptations that will come, I can't expect that I will bear up and enter heaven."

Now, what does the question of believing in Jesus have to do with your good resolutions, or your miserable failures? Whoever trusts Christ will be saved. If you trust him and are lost in the future, God's Word will not be true. The question is, can you trust Christ? And that turns around and makes the other moot. Is he worthy to be trusted? There is no other question. The case is something like that of a man in a far-away sea. His ship is wrecked and breaking to pieces. He barely keeps his hold on a piece of floating debris. Then the lifeboat comes up close to his side and is ready to take him on board. Now, if there's any question in that man's mind about getting into that lifeboat in order to be saved, the only rational one that I can conceive is, "Will the boat carry me to shore? Is she seaworthy? Will she outlive the breakers? Can she reach the land safely?" You can't imagine the poor fellow saying, "I'm shaking too much with a fever to be rescued by that boat," or "The sea has washed the last rag from off my back," or "The boat won't suit me," or "Another time I may be wrecked on the coast of Africa, and there may be a lifeboat." No, no. Man alive, there's the boat! Is she seaworthy? That is the question. If so, get into her. If Christ isn't worthy of your trust, don't trust him. And if he *is* worthy of all confidence, then be done with your idle questions and cast yourself upon him. *If we receive the witness of men, the witness of God is greater: for this is the witness of God which he has testified of his Son. He that believes in the Son of God has the witness of God in himself; he that does not believe God has made God a liar; because he does not believe the witness that God has testified of his Son. And this is the witness, that God has given eternal life to us, and this life is in his Son. He that has the Son has life; and he that does not have the Son of God does not have life* (1 John 5:9-12).

Still, we will keep to this point: Jesus is worth trusting and worthy of the sinner's unwavering faith. He is worth trusting, because *he* whom you are commanded to rely on by the command of the gospel *is God himself.* You have offended God, and it is God who came into the world to save sinners. Your sins were launched against Christ like arrows from a bow, but he, against whom those bolts were shot, has come in the fullness of his power and the infinity of his mercy to save them that believe. Can't you trust yourself in almighty hands? Is anything impossible with God? An angel couldn't save you, but surely God himself can? How can you limit the Holy one of Israel? How can you set constraints on boundless love, or place limits on limitless grace? If Jesus were man and not God, unbelief would have a good excuse. But if the Savior is divine, there is no place for distrust.

I feel as if I couldn't help but believe in Christ now that I know him to be divine. Faith has grown to be a necessary act of my mind. Save me! Who will persuade me that he can't? Come forward, you demons with your arguments, and plead with me. You can't inject a doubt into my soul while I know him to be God. He can shake the heavens when he pleases and make the earth tremble. He holds up the universe on his shoulders. Can't he save my poor soul? Yes, he can. *Who is he that I might believe in him?* He is divine, and therefore I believe.

Next, the Lord Jesus Christ, in whom the sinner is commanded to trust, is *commissioned by God to save.* He came into the world as a Savior, not alone on his own account, but as Messiah sent of God. He has the full agreement of the sacred Trinity. It is the will of the Father, the will of the Holy Spirit, and the will of the Son, that *whosoever believes* in Jesus should be saved. He was anointed by the Lord for his peculiar work. I feel as if this is special grounds for trust in him. If

Christ were an amateur Savior, who had taken up the trade of saving on his own account, there might be a question. But if God has divinely commissioned him to save, why can you doubt anymore? He has been authorized by the Eternal, rest in him.

Then there's the fact that the Lord Jesus Christ *has actually done all that is necessary* for him to do for the salvation of all who trust him. Years ago, before Jesus Christ came into the world, if I had been sent to preach the gospel, I would have had to proclaim, "Jesus will take upon himself the sins of believers and lay down his life for his church." But now I have a more encouraging message: Jesus has carried his people's sins away forever, and he has suffered on their behalf all that was required to end their transgressions. He has paid whatever was demanded by the justice of God as a payment for the injured honor of the law. Christ has suffered the equivalent of all the sufferings of all the elect in hell forever. He has endured everything that was necessary so God might be just and still the justifier of him that believes. The cup of vengeance is not full and needing to be drained. It is empty and turned bottom upwards. Jesus drank it dry. The works necessary for our redemption, much greater than the efforts of Hercules, have all been accomplished. Christ has gone into the grave, has gone out of the grave, and has gone up to his glory. He has entered heaven, because his work is done. Now he sits down at the right hand of the Father in the position of rest and honor, because he has perfected forever all those who put their trust in him. Now, how can you refuse to believe in Jesus? To me the argument seems impossible to resist. Since it's true that Christ has died, the just for the unjust, and that all who trust him will be saved, I will also trust him and find peace through his blood.

The point we trust God's grace is bringing you to is this: Jesus deserves to be trusted. And trust him we will, because *he is full of power to save.* He is now upon the throne, and all power has been given to him in heaven and in earth. We know he is full of power to save, because he is saving souls every day. Some of us are the living witnesses that he can forgive sin, because we are pardoned, accepted, and renewed in heart. The only way we obtained those gifts was that we trusted him – we did nothing else but trust him. If any soul that believes in Jesus would perish, I would perish with him. I sail in that boat, and if it sinks, I have no other to switch to. I vow before you all that I have no other hope. I don't have even a shred of reliance in any sacrament I have undergone or enjoyed, in any sermon I have ever preached, in any prayer I have ever prayed, in any communion with God I have ever known. My hope lies in the blood and righteousness of Jesus Christ. I shake off – as though it were a viper into the fire, as a deadly thing only fit to be burned – all pretense of relying on anything I may be, or can be, or ever will be, or do.

> You don't ever have to drag mercy out of Christ like money from a miser.

None but Jesus. This is the settled pillar which we must build on. It will hold us up, but nothing else can. Since by the authority of infallible Scripture we know that Jesus has this power, why is it that souls seeking rest don't obey the command and rest themselves freely upon him? This is the climax of human depravity, that it rejects the witness of God himself, and chooses to perish in unbelief.

Jesus Christ is by no means unwilling to save sinners. On the contrary, he delights to do it. You don't ever have to drag mercy out of Christ like money from a miser. It flows freely from him like the stream from the fountain or the sunlight from the sun. If he can be happier, he is made happier by giving his mercy to the undeserving. When a poor wretch who only deserves hell comes to him, and he says, "I have blotted out your sins," it is joy to Christ's heart to do it.

When a poor blasphemer bows his knee and says, "Lord, be merciful to me a sinner," it makes Christ's heart glad to say, "Your blasphemies are forgiven. I suffered for them on the tree."

When a poor little child, by her bedside, cries, "Gentle Jesus, teach a little child to pray and forgive the sins which I have done," the Savior loves to say, "Allow these little children to come to me, because this also is a part of my payment for the wounds I endured in my hands, my feet, and my side."

When any of you come to him and confess your transgressions and trust yourselves in his hands, it will be a new heaven to him. It will put new stars into his ever-bright and lustrous crown. It will make him see the fruit of the anguish of his soul and give him satisfaction. Don't we also have arguments to prove that Jesus is worthy to be trusted?

Every Sinner Is Bound to Faith or Unbelief

Every sinner is bound to either faith or unbelief. You are bound either to trust in Christ, in whom God commands you to trust, or to refuse to trust him. I'm not sent to preach to some of you, but only to everyone who has ears to hear. I have never learned to preach a restricted gospel to part of a congregation. The commission received by every true minister of Christ is: *Go ye into all the world and preach the gospel to every creature. He that believes and is baptized shall be saved, but he that believeth not shall be damned.* Since you are all creatures, the gospel is preached to all of you – sensible or insensible, spiritually dead or spiritually alive. As long as you are able to hear the gospel, one message comes to you all out of the excellent glory. Whoever will, let him come and take of the water of life freely. *Believe on the Lord Jesus Christ, and thou shalt be saved.*

But I know what your course of action will be unless the Spirit of God prevents it. Many of you will try to avoid the decision between believing and not believing, which I have put so nakedly before you. You won't like to say, "I will not trust Christ." Yet you won't trust in him. So what will you do? Why, you will yet again fall back on your old excuses: "But I am such a sinner. I am so unworthy!"

I've already shown how that plea is not relevant and shouldn't be thrust into the business. The question is one and only one: Will you believe on the Son of God? So why do you raise another question about yourself which has nothing to do with it. Yet I will meet you on your own ground and answer you. For argument's sake, let's agree that you are a special and horrific sinner. If this is true, then of all men in the world you are the man who should trust Christ, because it is written: *This is a faithful saying and worthy of acceptation by all, that Christ Jesus came into the world to save sinners* (1 Timothy 1:15). You've been a drunkard, a fornicator, an adulterer, a thief, in fact, a devil of a man. Well then, you've been a sinner. That's all it comes down to, and Jesus Christ came into the world to save sinners. Therefore, instead of being shut out by your character, you are shut in by it. You are the sort of man that Christ came to save. You can't run away and say, "He didn't come to save me, because I am not a sinner." You don't dare do that.

It's very likely that you will turn around on me and say, "My reason for unbelief is that I don't feel like I should." This objection should never be voiced. Because I feel a pain in my foot this morning, is that a reason why I shouldn't trust in an honest man, or believe a statement which comes to me on good authority?

I will, however, disprove this argument on your own ground. You are so sinful that you are, in all respects, undeserving. Well, Jesus came to save his people from their sins. Clearly, you are one of the very sort of people he came to save, because you are full of sins. His salvation is all by grace, and since you have no good thing about you whatsoever, you are a perfect fit for mercy, free mercy, great mercy! Salvation, all by grace, exactly suits you. Since you are an empty vessel, then it's clear you want to be filled. Since you are a filthy vessel, you need washing. And Jesus proposes to both cleanse and fill. His proposal is exactly adapted to your circumstances. You are the very man for grace to bless.

"Ah, but," says another, "I feel myself lost, utterly lost." What? Do we have to first do battle with some of you because you feel too little? And then with others, because they feel too much? We must come back to our one fixed point, and remind you again that both excuses miss the mark. That one point is: Will you, or will you not, believe in the Lord Jesus, whom God has set forth to be the Savior of men? But even if you are crushed with sorrowful feelings, there are special reasons for your attention to the gospel call, since some invitations are especially directed to you, such as: *Ho, every one that thirsts, come ye to the waters,* and *If any man thirsts, let him come unto me and drink.* If there are special messages of grace for you who are somewhat awakened to a sense of need, then I beg you to be quick to accept the testimony of God so that your souls may live.

The one question for every unconverted sinner is: Will you believe on Jesus Christ? But I hear you saying, "Well, I might do better in the future. I think I might, by some exertions of my own, get into a better condition." How can you hope so? Haven't you made a pretty mess of it up until now? You had better give up the vain attempt. If you have done so badly in the past, there remains little encouragement for you to try in the future. Let despair drive you to faith.

The worst of your conduct is that you are going exactly contrary to God's plan. God says, "I will not save you on the basis of merit, because you have none." That's really a gracious declaration of his, because it only shuts out false hopes since *by the works of the law shall no flesh be justified.* So if you say, "I will seek salvation on the basis of works," you are flying in God's face. Is this wise? I would much rather recommend that you accept at once what he so freely gives. Follow the example of a person the other day in dealing with another. He wanted to purchase something from his brother.

His brother had asked him a certain amount for it, and he said, "I will give you half."

"No," said the brother, "before I'll take so small a price, I would rather just give it to you."

"Thank you. I'll take it," was the immediate reply.

That is what I would prefer you do. Don't offer your petty price to God, when he is ready to give the blessing without money and without price! I've never known such fools as men are about the things of God. If they can get a good thing for nothing all the world over, they'll take it in an instant, and yet they rebel against free grace. Years ago, we paid twenty million to set free the slaves in Jamaica, but before the bill was paid, there was no end of objections raised in the House of Commons and elsewhere. Many people voiced their objections, but I never heard of a Negro appearing before the House to voice objections on behalf of the slaves. No black man came forward to say that the blacks were unworthy and undeserving. Neither did the slaves propose that part of the money should be paid by themselves. No, it's not in human nature to request others to put conditions on their free gifts in that way. Yet, we reject all that is reasonable and want to encumber sovereign grace. When God says, "I will blot out your transgressions now and save you once for all, only trust my dear Son," it's strange, it's madness that men should invent objections and plead for a gospel with conditions and hard terms.

> Don't offer your petty price to God, when he is ready to give the blessing without money and without price!

So what will men do if driven out of this? I have often seen a sinner turn to downright falsehood and say, "It is too late," even though he knows very well that it can never be too late. The gospel says, *He that believes and is baptized shall be saved.* It does not say, if he believes when he is twenty-five years of age, or thirty-five, or fifty-five, or one hundred and five, but it stands the same for all ages. It's never too late to believe the truth, and that's the point.

Dost thou believe in the Son of God? Then the sinner will say that he feels within himself that there is no hope. So, because he happens to believe a lie, he will think that God's truth is also a lie and refuse to believe that which God solemnly declares – that there is salvation in Jesus Christ! I don't have time to mention all these falsehoods or to address all the schemes of men who seek to escape from their own mercies. In Pompeii, I saw this motto on a shop door: *Erne et Habe bis.* It means "Buy and you shall have." I could only think that if I were walking the streets of the New Jerusalem, I would have seen a very different statement – *he that has no money; come ye, buy, and eat; come, buy wine and milk without money and without price.* Now if a shop opened in London in which all the goods were to be had without money and without price, would you quarrel with the shopkeeper and petition for an act of Parliament to shut his shop up and say it was wicked, because you would rather go on the old terms and pay for all you have? Not at all. So why is it that you stand against free grace's golden motto: Trust in Christ and you shall have. Here's an instantaneous pardon, perfect pardon, everlasting pardon, sonship through Christ, safety on earth, glory in heaven, and all for nothing. It's the free gift of a gracious God to undeserving sinners who trust in Jesus! Never has an angel had a more gracious, more godlike message of mercy than I have. How I wish I could glow with a seraph's zeal and cry with a cherub's voice while proclaiming it. I pray to God that men would leave their foolish reasonings and believe in Jesus Christ.

Everlasting Things

I remember well, when I was placed in a similar condition to many of you, when I knew myself to be ruined and undone, and heard for the first time and truly understood it, the words "Look unto me and be saved, all ye ends of the earth." I know how it stood that morning. I was like Naaman by the Jordan's shore. There flowed the flood. The old nature said, *Are not Abana and Pharpar, rivers of Damascus, better than all the waters of Israel? May I not wash in them and be clean?* (2 Kings 5:12). Human nature said, "I want to feel something. I want to have John Bunyan's experience. I want to have my mother's experience. I want to feel a broken heart. I want to groan more bitterly. I want to be kept awake so many more nights, and all that sort of thing."

Suppose I had still resisted. If God's grace had not come in and made all that wicked pride of mine break free, I don't know where I would be right now, or if I would even still be living among men. I might be in hell, gnawing my tongue, because I thought it was a good idea, after hearing a plain gospel sermon, to reject the gospel when it was proclaimed. And all because I wouldn't believe what is indisputably true and wouldn't trust in him whom no one ever trusted in vain.

I know there are some in my condition, in whom the good Spirit will say, "Wash and be clean."

And the soul will sigh and say, "It seems too good to be true."

But the good Spirit will reply, "Are not *my ways higher than your ways, and my thoughts more than your thoughts* (Isaiah 55:9)?"

Unbelief will say, "Your sins are many."

But the good Spirit will answer, "*If your sins were as scarlet, they shall be made as white as snow; if they were red like crimson, they shall become as wool* (Isaiah 1:18)."

Then the heart will suggest, "But I have rebelled against you, O God, for so long."

And the sweet Spirit of God will whisper, "I have blotted out your sins like a cloud, and like a thick cloud your iniquities. Return unto me, for I am married to you, says the Lord."

And I trust that, at this very moment, many hearts will say, "Then I will simply rest my soul's salvation upon Christ, the Son of God, who is the only Savior of the lost. From this day on, I will never hope to be a self-saved man or look to anything but him who on the bloody tree endured the wrath of God on behalf of as many as believe on him."

If you trust Jesus in this way, as surely as you live, you are saved! Go in peace. It is not I who speak these words from these poor lips of clay, but he who was nailed on the tree, whom all heaven adores, speaks this morning through me. He says to one, "Daughter, be of good cheer, your sins are forgiven." To another he says, "Son, your sins are forgiven. Take up your bed and walk." Forgiven one, I urge you to do it, and as you leave this house this morning, saved and full of joy, tell others about it. Never stop telling others about it and live to love him who has saved you!

The other day, I saw a picture by Rubens in which he had painted Mary Magdalene kissing the feet of Christ while they still gushed with founts of blood on the cross. It was a strange picture, but I felt like, if I had been there, I would have kissed them too, even though they had been crimson with his gore. Oh, blessed feet! Oh, blessed Savior! Oh, blessed Father who gave his Son to be so blessed a Savior! Oh, blessed Spirit of the blessed God that led our wicked, proud hearts into obedience and trust in Jesus. Blessed be the God and Father of our Lord Jesus Christ who has transferred us unto a lively hope by the resurrection of Jesus Christ from the dead. The Lord bless you. Amen.

Chapter 15

Sight for Those Who See Not

*And Jesus said, For judgment I have come into this world,
that those who do not see might see and that those who see
might be blinded.* (John 9:39)

The great day of judgment is still to come. God in infinite patience
waits to be gracious, giving men time to repent and to be reconciled to him. Jesus came into the world for judgment, but not for that
last and eternally unchangeable judgment which awaits us all. That hour
will still arrive – we have the declaration of God's Word for it. *When the
Son of man shall come in his glory and all the holy angels with him, then
he shall sit upon the throne of his glory, and before him shall be gathered
all nations; and he shall separate them one from another as a shepherd
divides his sheep from the goats* (Matthew 25:31-32). There is no question as to this sure fact, even if many more centuries should pass away,
the dreaded judgement will be held in due time. *The Lord is not late
concerning his promise, as some count lateness, but is patient with us,
not willing that any should perish, but that all should come to repentance*
(2 Peter 3:9). He is full of tenderness and patience, so he waits. But the
vision will come – it will not tarry. Settle this in your minds and live
as in the presence of that sobering court of justice.

Even though the day of judgment is not right now, our Lord Jesus is
still carrying on a form of judgment in the world. His fan is in his hand,
and he will thoroughly purge his floor. He sits as a refiner, separating

his silver from the dross. His cross has revealed the thoughts of many hearts, and everywhere his gospel is acting as a discoverer, as a separator, and as a test by which men may judge themselves, if they are willing. It is a very happy situation when a man is willing to accept the Lord's judgment day by day and permits the law itself to judge him, before the lawgiver has to come before the court. Paul says of those who gladly receive a present judgment: *But being judged, we are chastened of the Lord, that we should not be condemned with the world* (1 Corinthians 11:32). Saints are judged now by a fatherly discipline, so that they won't be judged later by judicial condemnation.

Our Lord's great design in coming into the world is the salvation of men. *For God did not send his Son into the world to condemn the world, but that the world through him might be saved* (John 3:17). But in order to receive that salvation, it's necessary for men to know the truth about themselves and to take up a truthful position before God, because God will not endure a lie, neither will he save men based on lies. He will deal with all his creatures according to truth. If he condemns them, it will be because righteousness requires it. If he saves them, it will be because he has found a way where mercy and truth have joined together.

So then, everywhere throughout the world, wherever Christ comes – by his gospel and the consequences of it – a judgment is going on. Men are set before the judgment seat of their Savior. They are tested, tried, exposed, and declared. As soon as light comes into the world, it begins to judge the darkness. It wouldn't even be known to be darkness if the light had not revealed the contrast. Where the gospel comes, some hearts receive it at once and are judged to be honest and good ground – men who are willing to accept the gospel and come to the light so that their deeds may be seen clearly that they are performed in God. Other hearts immediately hate the truth, because they are the children of darkness. Therefore, *men loved darkness more than the light because their deeds were evil* (John 3:19). So you see how, without it being the main intention of Christ's coming into the world, it still becomes a secondary effect. It's related to the purpose of his coming, that his very appearance among the sons of men should judge them.

In this mirror they see their own appearance and discover their spots. By this guideline they test their own uprightness and see how far they lean towards evil. Under the sign of the gospel, the Lord has set up a public weighhouse. Can you picture the great scales? They are correct to a hair. Come forward and test yourselves. Even in this banqueting house of love, truth marks her own and sets her brand on counterfeits. God has a fire of trial in Zion and a furnace of test in Jerusalem.

I pray that the gospel may have a dividing effect in this house. Wherever Jesus Christ comes, the most evident effects follow. *I have come into this world, that those who do not see might see and that those who see might be blinded.* Christ isn't indifferent to those in the right or to those in the wrong. Whoever you may be, if you hear the gospel, it will have some effect upon you. It will either be to your soul *the savour of life unto life*, or else *the savour of death unto death* (2 Corinthians 2:16). It will be antidote or poison, curing or killing, softening the conscience or searing it. It will either make you see, or, because you imagine that you see, its very brightness will make you blind like Saul of Tarsus who cried,

> You cannot be indifferent to the gospel if you hear it.

I could not see for the clarity of that light (Acts 22:11). You cannot be indifferent to the gospel if you hear it. None of you can escape the fact that Christ said, *For judgment I have come.* And that judgment must take place in your mind and conscience whether you are willing or not. This coming and judgment have a wonderfully clear and visible effect. We're not talking about a little improvement or a slight alteration. It is the turning of things upside down, so *that those who do not see might see and that those who see might be blinded.* It is a very violent change from light to darkness, or from darkness to light. In either case, it's an absolute reversal of a condition. The gospel will do just that for you. If you live without it, it will make you die. If you believe that you are dead without it, it will make you live. *He has put down the mighty from their thrones and exalted the humble. He has filled the hungry with good things, and the rich he has sent empty away* (Luke 1:52-53).

There will always be some effect upon the human mind wherever Christ comes, and this effect will be a very evident one by changing all the conditions as much as if the laws of nature were reversed. The Lord's approach to a soul will lift it into the light more and more gloriously, or it will plunge it into deeper darkness, deeper responsibility, deeper guilt, and consequently deeper misery.

We can free from guilt that faithful preacher of the Word who, in the middle of his sermon, suddenly stopped, and cried, "Woe is me! What am I doing? I am preaching Christ to you, and while I hope some of you are receiving him, and that I am leading you toward heaven, many others of you are rejecting him, and in this way I am increasing your responsibility and your guilt. So I am doing evil instead of good to you. Woe is me!"

God help his poor servant. I have often felt the sweet preaching of the gospel to be bitter work. I'm not surprised that dark thoughts come over the diligent preacher. I wish those who hear him would join with him in his anxieties. May we unite in deep concern. I will pray for God's blessing upon every one of you, and you pray that no word of mine would be unprofitable to you. When preacher and hearer work together the same way the chariot wheels move to music, that music is salvation. Come, Spirit of the living God, and make it so.

That Those Who See Not, May See

Christ has come so that those who see not, may see. It is a very wonderful thing about the gospel that it's meant for people who think themselves most unsuited for it, and most undeserving of it. It is sight for those who see not. The other day, an anxious friend gave me a description of himself which was enough to make a man horrified to hear it. With many sighs and tears, he described to me the condition of a man lost by nature and by practice, and unable to help himself in any way. When he had completed his story – I let him finish it and touch it up with a few extra strokes of black – I took him by the hand and said, "I'm sure that you are one of those whom Christ came into the world to save. You have given me the most accurate description possible of one of God's elect when aroused to see his natural state before the Most Holy God. You are one of those for whom the gospel was intended." I spoke boldly, because I knew that I was only stating the truth.

I know Jesus Christ came into the world to open men's eyes since he's opened the eyes of some of those around me, because they have bright eyes which smile on me as I speak and seem to say, "No optometrist is needed here!" I look all around, and I see nothing for the great Opener-of-eyes to do until I pause at the pew over there, and there sits a blind man.

There are one or two here whose natural eyes have been sealed in darkness for many years. I say to them, "If Jesus Christ has come to open anybody's eyes, he has come to open the eyes of the blind." It must be so. Infirmity and disability are necessary to prepare for the receipt of the blessing of sight.

Suppose I heard that Jesus had come to make lame men leap like a deer. Well, I would look around and say that he didn't come for that young girl, because she can skip like a gazelle and run like a fawn. He didn't come for that young man, because I just saw him on his bicycle flying over the ground as swiftly as a swallow skims the stream. Neither did the healer of the lame come for that strong brother over there who enjoys a quick, long walk. But just now, a lame man limped down the aisle on his crutch. Didn't you hear his heavy movement? Well, if Jesus Christ came to heal lameness, that's the kind of person that he had his eye upon.

When I hear about a charity breakfast being distributed, I never imagine that the gathered assembly will consist of members of the Houses of Lords and Commons, or of the royal family. I don't suppose that even one of those honorable elites will be present at a festival with beggars unless they desire to observe. If I went to a charity breakfast and saw some of their kind with bowls and spoons, I would say, "Get out. You aren't the people that ought to be here. You have no right to be here. The richer and the more respectable you are, the less right you have to be sitting at a meal that was meant for the poorest of the poor."

Now turn the parable around. If you are blinded in your spiritual sight, Christ came to open your eyes. If you are lame, so that you can't run to him, Christ came to restore you. If you are as poor as spiritual poverty can make you, as poor as sin can make you, and if you are as unable to help yourselves as the dead in the graves, then remember this great truth: *For the Christ, when we were yet weak, in his time died for the ungodly* (Romans 5:6). It sounds strange, doesn't it? But it's true. Christ died for our sins, not for our virtues. It's not your completeness, but your incompleteness which entitles you to the Lord Jesus. It's not your wealth, but your poverty. It's not what you have, but what you don't have. It's not what you can boast of, but what you mourn over that qualifies you to receive the gospel of the Lord Jesus Christ. He came with the intention that those who can't see might see. Blind eyes, I have good news for you. Souls that sit in darkness and in the valley of the shadow of death, my feet are beautiful to you, because I bring you glad tidings of exceeding joy – light for the blind, joy for those in despair, and grace for the guilty.

I want you to consider the blind man of whom we were reading in the narrative just now as a sort of model blind man – the kind of blind man that Jesus Christ delights to look upon, and to whom he rejoices to give sight. This blind man *knew* he was blind. He never had any doubt about that. He had never seen a ray of light, and yet he believed that he was blind. It's not as easy a matter as some of you may think, because I've met with thousands of blind men who laugh at the idea of sight, because they've had no experience of it. They refuse to believe more than they can understand or feel. This sightless beggar had to be told that there was such a thing as sight, but once he was told, he believed it. All his experience after that point confirmed the unhappy fact.

Once he was fully persuaded that it was true, he had taken up the proper position for a poor, blind man. He sat by the wayside and asked for alms. The man whom Christ delights to bless is the man who knows his right place and is willing to occupy it. He does not conceal his blindness, and talk as if he carried a telescope around with him and gazed all night at the stars. Many of you unconverted people think a good deal too much of yourselves. You will have to come down a good many notches before you'll be in your true places. You are so excellent, and so intelligent, and so humble, and so well-meaning, and so everything that you ought to be, are you not?

Salvation will never come to you. The spirit of peace will never dwell in a nest which reeks of pride. In your own false judgment, you are within an inch of being perfect, whereas the Lord knows that you are not even half that distance from hell if his justice would be let loose upon you. You dream fine dreams in your conceit – believing that you have kept the law from your youth up, and that you are abundantly religious, and excellent, and admirable, and all that you ought to be. As long as you think of yourselves in this way, the blessing is hindered and kept away. You self-exalting ones are not the kind Jesus came to bless. He said himself, *I came not to call the righteous, but sinners to repentance* (Luke 5:32).

Perhaps someone here is saying, "I don't understand it. I can't seem to grasp this gospel. I barely know my own condition. I know that I'm unhappy. I know that I'm not right, but I can't describe myself or see myself correctly. As to this faith of which I hear so much, and this atoning blood which seems so mighty to cleanse, I seem as if I can't understand it or grasp it. Unfortunately, I am so blind!"

You speak the truth, my dear friend, and in that way you are like the blind man in the gospel. I pray that in the same way Jesus healed *him*, he will also heal you. I pray with strong confidence, too, because my Lord has certain established ways. When he comes in contact with certain situations, he acts in the same method with them. Jesus is not arbitrary. He has a way of procedure from which he doesn't deviate, so when he comes in contact with a situation such as yours, he does the same with each instance of it, to the praise and glory of his name. Take up the position of a blind beggar and sit down and cry for light and healing, and you will certainly have them.

> You self-exalting ones are not the kind Jesus came to bless.

This blind man not only believed that he was blind and knew it, but he also had a sincere desire to be enlightened. It wasn't grief to him that Jesus had come so that he might see. It brought him an intense joy to hear that Jesus had opened the eyes of other blind men. And even though he may have feared that his case was one too out of the ordinary – for since the world began it was not heard that any man had opened the eyes of one who was born blind – yet he was pleased to find that Jesus Christ had stopped, looked upon him, and was placing clay upon his eyes. He felt a gladness and an enthusiasm in his heart when he was commanded to go to Siloam and wash. His whole manhood accepted the Savior's act and deed. He surrendered to the surgery of the Christ with the full consent of his being.

Are you hungering after Christ? Oh, soul, if you know your need for him and have a strong desire after him, the heavenly work has begun! If there is within your spirit a burning longing to be reconciled to God by the death of his Son, your cure is already half accomplished. Some of you have written me letters lately which show the actions of your hearts. These are still blind movements, but they all grope for the light. Poor souls, what hope I have for you! Especially for him who with a broken heart has begged for our prayers these many months and still hasn't come out to light and liberty. I am so glad to see the strength, intensity, and agony of your desires. Your unbelief grieves me, but your eagerness encourages me. I pray to God that you would trust my Lord Jesus Christ and rest in him! Still, I am glad to think that you can't rest without him. I am glad that you can't be quiet until he quiets you. No pillow will ever ease your head but my Lord's bosom. No hand but his can ever heal your bleeding wounds. I'm glad that this is true, because the type of sinner you are is well described by Hart:

> "A sinner is a sacred thing:
> The Holy Ghost hath made him so."

The Spirit of God has set apart the blind soul to be a monument of the illuminator's skill. He has made the lost soul to be the place where Christ can set his foot and display all the splendor of his love.

This man is also a model to every other blind man, because he was very obedient. As soon as the Lord said to him, *Go, wash*, he went. There was no question with him about Siloam. He had no Abana or Pharpar[1] which he preferred to that pool. He was fully submissive. He stood still and let the Master put the clay on his eyes. It didn't look like an operation that could do him any good, but he believed that Jesus was a prophet, so he waited and let him do whatever he pleased with him. I am so glad when I see a poor soul offering a full surrender to Jesus. Some of you heard last time about the sweetness of yielding yourselves up to Jesus. How I wish you could feel it now. You will be a great deal more passive than active in your conversion. He will give you quickness of foot *after* he has given you life. But, at the beginning of the new life, the first thing is to own your death and to be willing to receive life completely from him in his own way. The Scriptures illustrate this: *But now, O LORD, thou art our father; we are the clay, and thou our potter;*

---

[1] *Are not Abana and Pharpar, rivers of Damascus, better than all the waters of Israel? May I not wash in them and be clean? So he turned and went away in a rage.* (2 Kings 5:12)

such that we all are the work of thy hands (Isaiah 64:8). What can the clay do to help the potter? Nothing, except that it must be pliable and yield to his hand. The clay must not be stiff, and hard, and unwilling to be molded, or it will be set aside. Be submissive to the saving hand!

When you are brought into such a state of heart that you are willing to be anything or nothing so that you may be saved, dear soul, you are near to the kingdom. If you can say, "I would give my life to be saved," or, "If the Lord refuses anything at my hands, I will gladly consent to be nothing if he will only save me," then you are on the doorstep of grace. I would so completely yield myself up to Christ so that I only feel what he would have me feel and nothing more – to be what he would have me be, to do what he would have me do, and nothing beyond. If you are submissive in this way, I will tell you to take heart and have hope. The Spirit of God is at work in you. You are very near to Christ. Believe on him, trust in him, and live, for he has come with the intention that those who cannot see, may see. Stop at that sacred purpose of amazing grace, and let your despair fly away.

This is our first point: this blind man becomes our model.

Next, we notice that this kind of man owns that he does see. He has been so thoroughly convinced of his blindness that when he gets his sight, he owns it with glad surprise. To him the newly given light is such a blessing that he is overjoyed with it and gladly cries, "Now I see!"

Some people don't know whether they are converted or not. I hope that they are saved, but such people are not generally of very much use. We have to spend our time and strength in taking care of them, and comforting them, and enabling them to rise above sheer despair. But the man who has been totally blind, and has known it, when he gets sight is equally sure that he sees. You can't make such a man doubt the greatness and truthfulness of the change. He comes out and says, *One thing I know, that having been blind, now I see.* I delight in clear, sharp-cut conversions. I don't condemn those dear friends who come into light by slow degrees. Far, far, far from it! I delight in them, but still – for a useful testimony and for a change of character – there is nothing like a conversion which is like life from the dead, and like turning from darkness to light, and from the power of Satan unto God. The old-fashioned convert is the man for me. He knows something and holds fast by what he knows. His is experiential knowledge, and you can't beat it out of him.

I like to think of some of you utterly blind people who can't help yourselves at all, because when you receive the light, you will know it, and you won't hesitate to come out and say so. In your case, the poor preacher won't be robbed of his wages as he often is when he saves a soul by God's grace but never hears of it. The gospel will not be deprived of its witnesses. The church will not be left without her helpers, and the Lord will not be robbed of the reward of glory which is his due. We expect grand testimonies for Jesus from you blind men when the Lord causes you to see.

When the blind man's eyes were opened, he began to defend the man who opened his eyes. He did it well, too. He said, *Indeed this is a marvellous thing that ye do not know where he is from, and yet he has opened my eyes.* On he went with arguments which confounded both the scribes and the Pharisees. When the Lord takes a big blind sinner, and washes him, and opens his eyes, then the man will not allow Christ to be spoken against. He will speak up for his Lord and Master, because he can't help it. You won't find him mute, as some professors are. Some of your cultured Christians don't speak for Christ more than once in six months, and then it would be better for them to have held their tongues, because they speak so halfheartedly. Here is a man with an open mouth, and he speaks right from his heart under the guidance of the Spirit of God. He is not ashamed to own what the Lord has done for him. We want many recruits of this sort.

> When the blind man's eyes were opened, he began to defend the man who opened his eyes.

The present-day church wants men and women who are so thoroughly and certainly converted that when they speak about Christ they speak positively and with a power which none can deny or resist. I think I hear you poor, darkened, desolate one crying out, "Oh, sir, if the Lord were to save me, I wouldn't be ashamed to own it. If he ever brings me in among his people, I will tell them all about it. I will tell the very devils in hell what sovereign grace has done for me." Oh, my poor brother, you are Christ's man! You are the kind of man he delights to bless. You poor, devil-dragged sinners who are almost at your wits' end, and would even take away your own lives if it weren't a most horrible sin, you are the very ones the Lord looks upon with mercy. He said himself, *The Spirit of the Lord is upon me because he has anointed me to preach the gospel to the poor; he has sent me to heal the brokenhearted, to proclaim liberty to the captives and recovery of sight to the blind, to set at liberty those that are broken, to proclaim the acceptable year of the Lord* (Luke 4:18-19). Only trust yourselves in his dear hands, and believe that he can, and that he will save you, and you shall be saved. Then I know that you will own his name, defend his truth, glory in his cross, and live to his praise. Those who are blind will be made to see, and then the Lord Jesus shall be the Lord of their hearts, the Master of their lives, and the Beloved of their souls.

The best thing about this man was that when his eyes were opened he desired to know more. When Jesus Christ spoke to him, saying, *Dost thou believe in the Son of God?* he asked, *Who is he, Lord, that I might believe in him?* When he found that the Son of God was the same, divine One who had opened his eyes, we read that at once he worshipped him. Notice that at the end of John 9:38 we read, *And he worshipped him.* He was no Unitarian. He saw the Son of God in the man who spoke with him, and he reverently adored him.

If our Lord Jesus had not been God, he would have told the man to rise, and he would have torn his garments in horror at the very idea of receiving divine worship. Instead, our Lord used this example as a proof that the man's eyes were opened, and immediately said that he had come for that very purpose – that those who were blind might see. Friends, if you have not seen Jesus of Nazareth to be God, you have seen nothing. You can't be right in the rest unless you think rightly of him. Until you get to know that Jesus is both Lord and Christ, exalted on high to give repentance and forgiveness of sin, you still need the scales to fall from your eyes, because the eternal light has not come to you. Once someone receives the true light from God, he will know the Lord Jesus not as a delegated God or a glorified man, but as God over all, blessed forever. He will have a God to save him, and nobody else, because who could save us but the Almighty? I wouldn't trust a tenth of my soul with ten thousand Gabriels. I couldn't be at peace with it anywhere but in him that is able to save completely – even that same God who made everything that was made.

So I have shown you how this model blind man is the very man to whom the Lord Jesus will give sight, because the results that follow are glorifying to Christ. Are you such a person? Then be comforted.

But how is it that such blind men come to see clearly? The main reason is sovereign grace, but still there are other reasons. First, there is no conceit in them to hinder Christ. It's not our littleness that hinders Christ, but our bigness. It's not our weakness that hinders Christ; it is our strength. It's not our darkness that hinders Christ; it is our supposed light that holds back his hand. It is easier to save us from our sins than from our righteousness. Our self-righteousness is that hideous boa constrictor which seems to coil itself around and around our spirit, and to crush all the life out of us that would receive the gospel of the grace of God. He who thinks that he knows, will never learn. He who is blind and thinks that he sees, will remain content in the darkness all his life. Dear friends, if you know that you are in the dark – a darkness that can be felt – if it seems to horribly cling to you so that you can't get rid of it, if you seem unable to even obtain a ray of light, then you are in just the right state to receive the eternal light from the Lord Jesus Christ.

The next reason is that people such as this always refuse to speculate. They want certainties. When a man feels his own blindness and spiritual death, if you discuss with him the fine new nothings of modern theology, he says, "I don't want them. They don't matter to me. There is no comfort in them for a lost soul."

A poor thief was converted some time ago, and he was taken to hear a certain preacher who is exceedingly broad in his views. When the thief came out, he said to the friend who took him, "If what that man said was true, it would be a fine thing for me, because I could do whatever I want and still get off easy. But I know that it is a lie. Therefore, I don't want to have anything more to do with him or his doctrine. A sinner like me deserves to be damned forever, and it is no use for anybody to tell me the contrary. Therefore, I want a Christ that can save me from eternal damnation. If this man's Christ only saves men from the little bit of damnation that he has preached, he is no good to me."

That was a very sensible observation. We all need a Savior from eternal damnation, and we don't care about those little saviors from a little hell which are so often proclaimed today. We have a lot of sham sinners around, and we have a number of ministers who preach a sham savior and a sham salvation. And the sham sinners like it this way. But if Christ really deals with you – pulls you down to the last course and digs your foundations up – then you will want a Christ who will begin with you on no terms but those of free grace. You will want a power that will work the whole miracle of salvation for you from beginning to end. If you are utterly without strength, that makes you reachable by the strength of grace. When a man gives up his pretty speculations and just sticks to the old teaching from the divine Word, he wants a great Savior to save him from a great hell, because he understands that he has been a great sinner and greatly deserves the infinite wrath of God. If your salvation is too big for you, that will be a great deal better than getting one that is too small for you. However, if you think that the salvation of Jesus is too great for you, it shows that you are not the man for whom it is meant. Our fear is that you are one of those who see, but will be made blind. If you feel your blindness and cry out to God about it, you are the man for whom the sight-giving Savior died.

Again, people who are thoroughly blind are the kind of people who are glad to lean on God. A man who can see a little doesn't want guidance from someplace else or someone else. He says, "No, I don't want it." Take an illustration from myself: I used to be very resistant to wearing glasses for some time, because I could almost see without them, and I didn't wish to be an old man too soon. But now that I can't read my notes at all without wearing glasses, I put them on without a moment's hesitation, and I don't care whether you think me old or not. So when a man comes to feel thoroughly guilty, he doesn't mind depending on God. If you sinners think that you can do a little without God or only need just a little help from God, then you will keep away from the Lord Jesus. But when you come to this – I must perish if Christ is not everything to me – then you *will* have him, because he never refused a soul that came to him in that style.

You may have heard the story of the slave and his master who were both under conviction of sin at the same time. Almost the next evening the slave found joy and peace through believing, but his master was under conviction for months. So he said to his slave one day, "Sam, you know we were both pricked to the heart at that meeting, and here you are rejoicing in Christ, and I'm still doubting and despairing. What can be the reason for this?" The slave said, "You see, master, Jesus Christ come along and brought a fine robe of glorious righteousness. He said to Sam, 'Here is a robe for you!' I looked at myself, and saw all rags from head to foot. So I took the robe and put it on directly. I was so glad to have it. Jesus said the same thing to you, master, but you said, 'My coat is very respectable. I think I can make it last a little longer.' You patched up the hole in the elbow and mended the skirt a little and continued to wear it. Your coat is too good. If your coat was all in rags, like Sam's, you wouldn't wait. You would, this very day, take the glorious robe of righteousness." That is the whole truth of the matter. Some of you are not poor enough to be made rich by Christ.

A man said to me the other day, "Sir, I've lost hope in myself."

"Give me your hand," I said. "You are on the right road, but I want you to go a little further. I want you to feel that you are too great a fool even to lose hope in yourself. When you cry, 'I cannot feel my own foolishness like I should,' then I think your folly will be ended."

I like to hear a man cry, "I feel unhappy, because I can't feel. I am grieved to think that I can't grieve. I am in an agony, because I can't get into agony." You are getting right, my brother. You are the sort of man that God will bless. Now, look away from yourself, agony and all, and just trust in Jesus Christ who is able to save completely those who come to God by him. Own your blindness, and you will find the light streaming into your eyes. Since you are content and willing to lean wholly on God, the Lord will guide you into peace and joy. What a mercy it is when we are brought to our last resort and are compelled to hide in Jesus because we have no other shelter!

> "'Tis perfect poverty alone
>   That sets the soul at large;
> While we can call one mite our own,
>   We get no full discharge.

But let our debts be what they may,
However great or small,
As soon as we have naught to pay
Our Lord forgives us all."

Once more, our Lord Jesus Christ delights to work in those who are thoroughly blind, in order to give them sight. It is his pleasure, his royal recreation. I know that a true man is never as glad as when he has helped those who want help. The plague and worry of this London life to some of us is that so many ask us for help who should never be helped at all, except by the policeman and the jailer. They cringe, and fawn, and make up lying stories. Then when we say, "We will visit you to see if it's true," they ask in mighty indignation, "Do you think I am a liar? Don't you believe what I say?"

I have had to answer, "No, I don't believe a word of it, or you would gladly give your address so that we could look into your statements." They don't want to be looked into. That is their horror, because it spoils their game. They want to get money without work, and they thirst for an opportunity to get drunk at other people's expense. A true man doesn't like to work among liars and cheats of this kind. It makes him sick and angry, but many men have still been willing to go down to the worst place in "horrible London" and to do good to those who are really poor and helpless. One doesn't like giving to impostors, but where there is real need, the generous heart is happy to offer aid. Now, you poor soul, you are no impostor. Your need is real. You can say, "A poor beggar? Ah, that I am! Does the Lord want to ask about me? I beg him to ask. Search me, O Lord. Test me and know my heart. I know that you will see no righteousness in me. There is nothing in me which I can depend on. I am a helpless, miserable wretch, unless your infinite mercy comes to me."

> Our Lord Jesus Christ delights to work in those who are thoroughly blind, in order to give them sight.

My Lord Jesus Christ rejoices to work among those such as you. He likes blessing those truly in need. What a joy there is in that great heart of his when he can save souls from the borders of hell – when he can stretch out his hand and snatch them like brands from the fire.

He knows that you will love him as much as that woman did who had much forgiven and therefore stood and washed his feet with her tears and wiped them with the hairs of her head. He takes delight in you who can't take any delight in yourselves. To you who are dried up and barren, he will bring living water. He will open rivers in high places for the thirsty ones and fountains in the midst of the desert for those who faint.

I have felt a wonderful satisfaction in feeding a poor half-starved dog that had no master, and nothing to eat. How he looked up with pleasure on my face when he had been fed to the full! Depend on it – the Lord Jesus Christ will take delight in feeding a poor hungry sinner. You feel like a poor dog, don't you? Then Jesus cares for you. He doesn't care about kings and princes and those great people whose grandeur dazzles those who look upon them, but he cares about poor sinners. If you are nothing, Christ loves you, and he will be everything to you. If you will only come to him just as you are, with no conditions of any kind except your urgent need and dread of the wrath of God, you may come and be sure of a welcome.

Someone said to me this week, "I'm afraid to come to God, because I believe that I'm only driven to him by the motive of fear."

"Ah," I replied, "it was the devil who told you that, because in Hebrews 11, among the first of the great heroes of faith we read that *By faith Noah, having received revelation of things not seen as yet, with great care prepared an ark to the saving of his house* (Hebrews 11:7)." Fear is not a selfish motive. It's a very proper motive for a guilty man to feel. Where else can such poor sinners like us begin, except with selfish fear? Don't judge yourself about that. The prodigal went home because he was hungry, and his father did not refuse him admittance. As to its being selfish to fear, it would be more selfish to defy your God. You shouldn't say, "It's too selfish of a motive." Why, what but a selfish motive can be expected from such a selfish wretch as you are?

A boy has been rebelling against his father and left his home in a rage, swearing that he will never go back. His father sends him a letter which says, "Return, everything is forgiven. Only confess your fault, and I will restore you to the family and treat you as lovingly as ever."

The boy reads this letter and says, "It's very kind of my father. I think I will go home."

But a wicked companion says, "Then you are going to eat humble pie. It will be very selfish of you after everything you've said about not backing down. Are you going to knuckle under to your father?"

It's the very devil tempting the boy, isn't it? And so, it was the devil who whispered to my friend that it would be wrong to turn to the Lord through fear. Fear is a blessed thing: *The fear of the LORD is the beginning of wisdom* (Proverbs 9:10). Even slavish fear of God is a great deal better thing than assumption.

Oh, you poor blind one, look to Christ and live! I was about to say, "You dead ones, come." And I do say it, because God says it: *Awake thou that sleepest and arise from the dead, and the Christ shall shine upon thee* (Ephesians 5:14). Someone says, "What's the use of talking in this way to dead people?" My dear friends, I don't suppose that it would be of any use for you to do so, unless you are sent by God on such an errand. But I'm as much sent to preach to the dry bones as Ezekiel was when he stood in the valley and said, *O ye dry bones hear the word of the LORD* (Ezekiel 37:4). In the name of the eternal God, I say, "You guilty sinners, fly to Christ and live." Come along, you who are the very worst in your own opinion – you who are on the brink of hell. The Lord said, *Look unto me, and be ye saved, all the ends of the earth; for I am God, and there is no one else* (Isaiah 45:22). He will not cast you away, but he will receive you now. May God grant that you come for Jesus's sake. Amen.

About the Author

Charles Haddon (C. H.) Spurgeon (1834-1892) was a British Baptist preacher. He started preaching at age 17, and quickly became famous. He is still known as the "Prince of Preachers," and frequently had more than 10,000 people present to hear him preach at the Metropolitan Tabernacle in London. His sermons were printed in newspapers, translated into many languages, and published in many books.

Other Similar Titles

The Soul Winner, by Charles H. Spurgeon

As an individual, you may ask, How can I, an average person, do anything to reach the lost? Or if a pastor, you may be discouraged and feel ineffective with your congregation, much less the world. Or perhaps you don't yet have a heart for the lost. Whatever your excuse, it's time to change. Overcome yourself and learn to make a difference in your church and the world around you. It's time to become an effective soul winner for Christ.

As Christians, our main business is to win souls. But, in Spurgeon's own words, "like shoeing-smiths, we need to know a great many things. Just as the smith must know about horses and how to make shoes for them, so we must know about souls and how to win them for Christ." Learn about souls, and how to win them, from one of the most acclaimed soul winners of all time.

Available where books are sold.

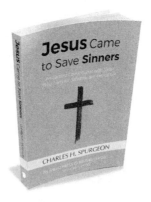

Jesus Came to Save Sinners, by Charles H. Spurgeon

This is a heart-level conversation with you, the reader. Every excuse, reason, and roadblock for not coming to Christ is examined and duly dealt with. If you think you may be too bad, or if perhaps you really are bad and you sin either openly or behind closed doors, you will discover that life in Christ is for you, too. You can reject the message of salvation by faith, or you can choose to live a life of sin after professing faith in Christ, but you cannot change the truth as it is, either for yourself or for others. As such, it behooves you and your family to embrace truth, claim it for your own, and be genuinely set free for now and eternity. Come and embrace this free gift of God, and live a victorious life for Him.

Available where books are sold.

Faith's Checkbook, by Charles H. Spurgeon

Faith's Checkbook is a one-year devotional meant to encourage you to take God at His Word – to take hold of God's promises by faith. Each day you will be presented with a specific promise from the Bible, along with accompanying exhortation by Charles Spurgeon.

This is your "spiritual checkbook," if you will. God's bank account of provision is ample, and it cannot be overdrawn. Every situation you might face is equally met with a promise that, if accepted, will sufficiently see you through.

"God has given no promise that He will not redeem. He does not offer hope that He will not fulfill. To help my brethren believe this, I have prepared this little volume."

– Charles H. Spurgeon

Available where books are sold.

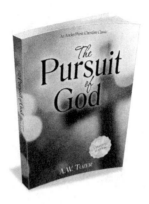

The Pursuit of God, by A.W. Tozer

To have found God and still to pursue Him is a paradox of love, scorned indeed by the too-easily-satisfied religious person, but justified in happy experience by the children of the burning heart. Saint Bernard of Clairvaux stated this holy paradox in a musical four-line poem that will be instantly understood by every worshipping soul:

> We taste Thee, O Thou Living Bread,
>   And long to feast upon Thee still:
> We drink of Thee, the Fountainhead
>   And thirst our souls from Thee to fill.

Come near to the holy men and women of the past and you will soon feel the heat of their desire after God. Let A. W. Tozer's pursuit of God spur you also into a genuine hunger and thirst to truly know God.

Available where books are sold.

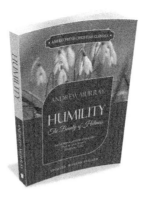

Absolute Surrender, by Andrew Murray

Is humility a Christlike attribute that should be pursued? And even if it should be, can genuine humility actually be attained? Often so practical in application that it is overlooked, the answer is found by studying the life and words of Christ (*whosoever will be chief among you, let him be your slave*). This little book is a loud call to all committed Christians to prove that meekness and lowliness of heart is the evidence by which those who follow the meek and lowly Lamb of God are to be known. Never mind that your initial efforts will be misunderstood, taken advantage of, or even resisted. Instead, learn from the One who *came not to be ministered unto, but to serve*. For a Christian to be alive, for the life of Christ to reign in and through us, we must be empty of ourselves, exchanging our life for His life, our pride for true, Christlike humility.

Available where books are sold.

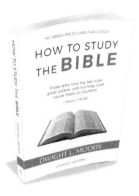

How to Study the Bible, by Dwight L. Moody

There is no situation in life for which you cannot find some word of consolation in Scripture. If you are in affliction, if you are in adversity and trial, there is a promise for you. In joy and sorrow, in health and in sickness, in poverty and in riches, in every condition of life, God has a promise stored up in His Word for you.

This classic book by Dwight L. Moody brings to light the necessity of studying the Scriptures, presents methods which help stimulate excitement for the Scriptures, and offers tools to help you comprehend the difficult passages in the Scriptures. To live a victorious Christian life, you must read and understand what God is saying to you. Moody is a master of using stories to illustrate what he is saying, and you will be both inspired and convicted to pursue truth from the pages of God's Word.

Available where books are sold.

***Pilgrim's Progress,* by John Bunyan**

Often disguised as something that would help him, evil accompanies Christian on his journey to the Celestial City. As you walk with him, you'll begin to identify today's many religious pitfalls. These are presented by men such as Pliable, who turns back at the Slough of Despond; and Ignorance, who believes he's a true follower of Christ when he's really only trusting in himself. Each character represented in this allegory is intentionally and profoundly accurate in its depiction of what we see all around us, and unfortunately, what we too often see in ourselves. But while Christian is injured and nearly killed, he eventually prevails to the end. So can you.

The best part of this book is the Bible verses added to the text. The original Pilgrim's Progress listed the Bible verse references, but the verses themselves are so impactful when tied to the scenes in this allegory, that they are now included within the text of this book. The text is tweaked just enough to make it readable today, for the young and the old. Youngsters in particular will be drawn to the original illustrations included in this wonderful classic

Available where books are sold.

Printed in Great Britain
by Amazon

36792878R00155